GANDHIAN THOUGHT
AND COMMUNICATION

GANDHIAN THOUGHT AND **COMMUNICATION**

Rethinking the
Mahatma in
the Media Age

Edited by
Biswajit Das

Los Angeles | London | New Delhi
Singapore | Washington DC | Melbourne

First published in 2020 by

SAGE Publications India Pvt Ltd
B1/I-1 Mohan Cooperative Industrial Area
Mathura Road, New Delhi 110 044, India
www.sagepub.in

SAGE Publications Inc
2455 Teller Road
Thousand Oaks, California 91320, USA

SAGE Publications Ltd
1 Oliver's Yard, 55 City Road
London EC1Y 1SP, United Kingdom

SAGE Publications Asia-Pacific Pte Ltd
18 Cross Street #10-10/11/12
China Square Central
Singapore 048423

Published by Vivek Mehra for SAGE Publications India Pvt Ltd. Typeset in 10.5/13 pt Sabon by Zaza Eunice, Hosur, Tamil Nadu, India.

Library of Congress Control Number: 2019951354

ISBN: 978-93-5328-668-2 (HB)

SAGE Team: Rajesh Dey, Vandana Gupta, Anand Singh and Rajinder Kaur

To
Professor Yogendra Singh (Babuji)
for being my inspiration and mentor in life.

Thank you for choosing a SAGE product!
If you have any comment, observation or feedback,
I would like to personally hear from you.

Please write to me at **contactceo@sagepub.in**

Vivek Mehra, Managing Director and CEO, SAGE India.

Bulk Sales

SAGE India offers special discounts
for purchase of books in bulk.
We also make available special imprints
and excerpts from our books on demand.

For orders and enquiries, write to us at

Marketing Department
SAGE Publications India Pvt Ltd
B1/I-1, Mohan Cooperative Industrial Area
Mathura Road, Post Bag 7
New Delhi 110044, India

E-mail us at **marketing@sagepub.in**

Subscribe to our mailing list
Write to **marketing@sagepub.in**

This book is also available as an e-book.

Contents

Section C: Revisiting the Mahatma in the Media Age

Foreword

Mahatma Gandhi:
A Life So Keenly Observed*

When one learns that Gandhi was the *fourth* and *last* child of his father's *fourth* and *last* marriage, one wonders if his birth— exactly 150 years ago in a coastal town in western India—was not ordained by a sacred celestial decree.

Few historic figures intrigue, fascinate and excite the intellect as Mohandas Karamchand Gandhi. While the world called him *mahatma* (great soul) and his fellow Indians *rashtrapita* (father of the nation), to the common man he was simply *bapu* (father)—a diminutive, bare-bodied and saintly man in whose presence the subjugated and the colonized felt inspired to believe that the cloak of human indignity could be cast aside and humanity reclaimed.

So boundless and timeless is the relevance of Gandhi's lifework that in felicitating him in 1939 on his 70th birthday, Albert Einstein said, 'Generations to come … will scarce believe that such a man as this one ever in flesh and blood walked upon this earth.'[1] And, so relevant is he for the youth of today that in 2009 when Lilly, a 9th grader at Wakefield High School in Arlington, Virginia, asked President Barack Obama, 'If he could have dinner with anyone, dead or alive, who would it be,' Obama, without

---

* Inspired by: A. Singhal, 'Mahatma Is the Message: Gandhi's Life as Consummate Communicator,' *International Journal of Communication and Social Research* 2, no. 1(2014): 1–16; A. Singhal, 'The Mahatma's Message: Gandhi's Contributions to the Art and Science of Communication,' *China Media Research* 6, no. 3 (2010): 103–106.

[1] See https://www.goodreads.com/quotes/131951-generations-to-come-will-scarce-believe-that-such-a-one (accessed on 26 September 2019).

hesitation, picked Gandhi, noting that he brought change 'Not through violence, not through money, but through the force of his personality, and his ethical and moral stance.'[2] Whether Einstein or Obama, or mere mortals like us or a 9th grader like Lilly, Gandhi inspires our spirit, churns our mind and rouses our humanity.

That is why 150 years after his birth and 71 years after his death, comes this finely edited and thoughtfully compiled anthology. In between its covers, through events and anecdotes, texts and utterances, thesis and antithesis, analysis and reflection, the editor—Professor Biswajit Das—and a diverse set of carefully chosen authors allow us to rediscover and reclaim the historic Gandhi for contemporary times. With a deft and critical eye, the authors offer a diverse set of interpretations of Gandhian thought and philosophy, bringing attention to his communicative practices—whether rhetorical, metaphoric or symbolic—as in the adoption of *charkha* (spinning wheel); his belief in the transformation of others through *satyagraha* (insistence on truth) and *ahimsa* (non-violence); his subjecting of all aspects of his life—private and public—to full and open scrutiny; and his embodiment of *aparigraha* (non-possession)—to manifest poverty, chastity and self-denial. So steeped was Gandhi in this ethos of *aparigraha* that when he was asked why he travelled in train in third class, he said, 'Because there is no fourth class.'

For this and other reasons, Gandhi continues to fascinate. Eknath Easwaran tells the story of a woman who came to Gandhi's Sevagram Ashram in Wardha and asked the Mahatma to persuade her little boy to stop eating too much sugar.[3] 'Sister, come back after a week', Gandhi said. Puzzled, the woman left and returned a week later. 'Try to not eat too much sugar, it is

---

[2] See https://timesofindia.indiatimes.com/world/us/Obama-says-he-would-like-to-have-dinner-with-Mahatma-Gandhi/articleshow/4988799.cms

[3] E. Easwaran, *Gandhi the Man: The Story of His Transformation* (Tomales, CA: Nilgiri Press, 1997).

not good for you', Gandhi told the little boy. The boy's mother asked: 'Bapu, why didn't you say this to him last week?' Gandhi responded: 'Sister, last week, I too was eating sugar. First, I had to try to see if it was possible.'

In the ultimate analysis, such 'small' communicative actions are Gandhi's intellectual gift to us. That is why the editor and authors have assembled this anthology. Their prose is rich and their analysis rigorous as they revisit Gandhi's journeys in colonial England, in fragmented South Africa, and in a colonized and, finally, an independent India. They look backward and forward while honouring the present.

I invite you to read this book. In so doing, you will understand the debt we owe to a life so keenly observed.

Arvind Singhal, PhD
Samuel S. and Edna H. Marston Endowed Professor of
Communication, The University of Texas, USA;
Professor, School of Business and Social Sciences, Inland
Norway University of Applied Sciences

Acknowledgements

It is a pleasure to acknowledge people and institutions who made the volume possible and see the light of the day. First and foremost, I would like to thank my students opting a paper on Intellectual history of communication and doctoral students whose young and curious minds compelled me to look at Indian intellectuals and their contributions in engaging with communications. Teaching in the class was extremely challenging as most of the communication theories and perspectives are alien. The students were neither much excited nor baffled with these constructions, rather posed sensible questions about how to indigenise and ground communication with locale moorings. Gandhi was unanimously considered as an alternative. Gandhi was not mere a journalist, as some would refer, he was indeed an intellectual. Treating Gandhi as mere a journalist would probably be an attempt to undermine his contributions. He wrote in various formats be it in newspapers, magazines and books like any public intellectual during his time. But his selective use of rhetorics and skilful craft of using symbols, myth, metaphor and strategy to express his thought was phenomenal and had a wider reach across the globe. His writings haunt generations of people, even present-day media, both online and offline, have not escaped the spectre of Gandhi.

I owe a deep sense of gratitude to NCRI (National Council of Rural Institutes), Hyderabad, for a generous grant to host a national seminar of which this volume forms a part, and for entrusting to me the editorial work. Mr Sandeep Bhusan was kind to go through the editorial draft. If there are inadequacies, the responsibility would be entirely mine. I am grateful to Prof. Jeet Uberoi, Prof. Suresh Sharma, Prof. Bishnu Mohapatra, Prof. Rita Kothari, Prof. Salil Mishra, Late Prof. A.D. Rodrigues, Prof.

Daniel Drache, Prof. Shri Prakash, and Prof. Asha Sarangi for their valuable insights and rich contributions. My thanks to the project staff of CPEPA, CCMG and entire administrate staff, particularly Mr Sonvir Singh, of the Centre for Culture, Media & Governance (CCMG), Jamia Millia islamia, New Delhi. I may particularly mention Shri Shambhu Das Sahu who has helped me with his most efficient and constant support during the finalization of the volume.

Prof. Arvind Singhal, Prof. Lisa Trivedi, Prof. Hira Singh, Prof. Brian Martin and Prof. Wendy Varney expressed their keen concern and the need for such a volume. I express my sincere gratitude and thanks to them. I would like to thank the contributors of this volume for their sheer tenacity and trust on me. I particularly thank Dr Dev Nath Pathak who helped me with the initial coordination and primary editorial work on this volume. Apart from professional colleagues, I must also acknowledge the support I have received from my family members: my wife Archana and son Aniket bear the brunt of my work pressure and deadlines. I would like to sincerely thank them for all their care and patience during the preparation of the manuscript.

I would like to express my gratitude to Mr Vivek Mehra, CEO and MD, and Mr Rajesh Dey, Managing Editor, Commissioning, SAGE Publications, for bringing out this volume for the benefit of the readers in India and abroad.

Introduction

Biswajit Das

Writing and editing a volume on Gandhi is an extremely challenging task as much has been said, contested and critiqued in scholarly contributions in India and abroad. What is important for us is not to excavate the new but to imagine ways of saying that might help in exploring the unexplored terrain in order to provide insights to understand Gandhi from a communication perspective. An engagement with Gandhi's style of communication has to be an engagement with Gandhi as a communicator. Gandhi as a communicator was extremely transparent and straightforward. He spoke through multiple platforms. Gandhi was earnest enough to admit that 'what I say now is what applies, what I said earlier is not true anymore because I have done some thinking since then.' This statement clearly reveals Gandhi as a thinking mind with a deeper purpose behind every act of communication. However, a communication perspective needs to embrace several facets, even instances where Gandhi did not succeed as a communicator. There are also occasions where Gandhi's communication was successful because others around him made it possible.

What is equally important is the perception. This perception refers to a kind of aesthetic dimension that Gandhi was continuously referring to behind each of his communicative actions. This is especially true for the manner in which Gandhi selectively appropriated elements from Hindu mythology in a bid to communicate with the larger public sphere. Besides Gandhi's own act of communication, people organized *Gandhi Katha*, stories narrated about Gandhi in groups and gatherings, that were part real and part derived from his body of work. Gandhi's communication is not only what he said, but also the reception, its interpretation, its reinterpretation, its creative interpretation and its wrong interpretation. They together constitute a Gandhian perspective of communication.

In Gandhian thought, the power of a symbol is not independent of the truth of the message. Further, for Gandhi, the medium as the message works diametrically opposite to the manner in which it was enunciated by Marshall McLuhan. In the Gandhian point of view, the message is not independent and not every medium can carry every message. Thus, the medium is not neutral in the sense of truth and truthfulness.

This brings us back to the aim of this anthology. The aim is indeed to take the Gandhian mode of communication and reflect through his contributions issues that will illustrate the role of communication in the constitution of society. The proposed anthology is an attempt to provide a pathway to the field of intellectual history of communication. Currently, the field remains in a state of uncertainty and fuzziness in Indian communication studies. The flow and impact of knowledge in communication in Indian academia clearly reflects a bias of North American and European scholarships. Although they have made a definite impact, rarely has there been an attempt to engage with Indian intellectuals, thinkers and scholars whose ideas could potentially inform communication studies in Indian society.

Gandhi's life and experiences provide an interesting insight in this regard. Gandhi's activities during the freedom movement have been presented as having been primarily concerned with the winning of political freedom for India and against British imperialism. However, the manner in which he did it, and the philosophy and the tactics together, taking the literal and the metaphorical as one truth, not two truths, is a matter that is of scholarly interest. Where does one locate his contributions in terms of theory and method? Gandhi was not a theoretician. He did not consciously construct a blueprint, either of his theory or of an ideal social order. He often said that his *life* was his message. This implies that Gandhi's ideas and ideals were not codified at one place in the form of a doctrine but were diffused in the form of his activities. People had to extrapolate his ideas and ideology from an assemblage of his actions. Gandhi was no Marx, and he did not leave behind an explicitly worked-out theory codified in a manifesto. There is certainly no Gandhian manifesto that we can use today to identify his theory and vision. Gandhi did leave behind many decades of political and social activities. Gandhi himself said that anyone wishing to follow him, after he was dead and gone, should simply look at what he did and how he did it, rather than look for any well-codified doctrine.

Conventional Social Sciences are premised on Western enlightenment and rationality. Critiques contextualized Gandhian writings within a narrow confine of modernity's celebration of scientific and technological progress in society. These assumptions were unacceptable for Gandhi. Gandhi, through his writings, made a trenchant critique of enlightenment premised on the philosophy of progress through instrumental modernity. Gandhi felt such a progress undermined and displaced cultural values and faith from its technologies of enquiry and constructed a new social order around market relations overseen by secular state. When we read Gandhi, we are moved by his text, not just by his iconic texts such as *Hind Swaraj* or his autobiography but by his numerous writings, correspondences and short letters. Gandhi was metaphorical; he knew how to use the language. He was an experimenter with idiomatic vernacular expressions of language. Gandhi used language not in a very formal instrumentalist sense, but as a linguistic being to capture human agency.

Critiques have not delved into the imagination, metaphor and the use of symbolic and cultural resources that Gandhian writings and practice carry within. Culture, for Gandhi, is an activity, a productive activity: something similar to labour, in Marx's own words, which produces and reproduces, if not commodities in that sense, but a way of life, a mode of life, which enables to critique, to create, recreate, realize and therefore transform.

Culture, for Gandhi, is a set of symbols, experiences, signs, grounded in the real world. That is to say, culture for him rests on the materialities of life.

Gandhi engaged intensively with the language question throughout his life—not only with respect to English language versus Indian languages but with respect to what should be the language of a country like India. Language, for him, was a vehicle of culture, of civilization. Civilization, for him, was not simply in terms of West and East civilizations but also a question of modernity. What Gandhi brings to bear in this very unusual little booklet, *Hind Swaraj*, is to say that the very basis of value which modernity proposes sits on a hollow ground.

In Gandhi's *Hind Swaraj*, the word 'Western civilisation' is used not in an ethnic sense, but to explain the modern West. It is a marker of what happened to Europe in its transformation to modernity, a transformation of a phenomenal and remarkable order. In fact, the success, the reach and the depth of the transformation are such that not just the small continent called Europe sacked the world in terms of power, but the very modes of thinking, formulation of ideas and the language used to exercise power.

The fundamental argument of *Hind Swaraj* is that the locus of value in modernity is shifted out of the human locus into the world of things. And, therefore, the modern quest which began as a quest to make 'man as the measure of things' has become 'things as the measure of man'. It has been reversed, and that is the paradox that Gandhi was addressing. In order to bail out from this dilemma, he used the word 'swaraj', which is a most interesting word, expression and concept. The term 'Swaraj' begins with 'Swa' that refers to the individual self, the little life that is given to all of us, but with a profound sense of completeness. Also, the *swa* of the collective, social, political auteur, but this little *swa* in its littleness rests on the infinity of an interior life that never be without transcending cosmic reference. In fact, there is a rise of both the sense of loneliness and the quest to transcend, and the power to question our own principles, markers of identity, even in the moment of most critical measure.

Gandhian ideas cannot be grasped by applying fixed categories and traditional philosophical assumptions. Second, categories plucked out of literary theory do not convey an overall sense of what Gandhi actually stood for. Finally, his entire weltanschauung has to be located in the proper historic context.

Gandhi was a prolific writer, wrote and spoke always with a context and according to the demands of the situation as he perceived them. Gandhi did not use the word 'modernity' to address the realities of contemporary modern life. He was a great political strategist, and his dialectic is also strategic. He preferred the notions of modern civilization to analyse the harsh facts that colonial people were facing in India. It is important to note that while talking about a civilization, he focused on the negative aspects of modern civilization, and he often made it synonymous with Western civilization. Gandhi had been convinced while writing *Hind Swaraj* that the chief driving force of Western societies is imperialistic and its principal agenda for the colonized is to exploit the wealth and other resources from colonial lands for the benefit of the West.

Gandhi's emphasis on the negative features of modern civilization has another concrete context. He was aware of the fact that many Indian expatriates, in modern language, were in the hypnotic grip of all-pervading Westernized wisdom that was not good for the welfare of humanity in general and India in particular. Most of the expatriates were patriots in spirit, but their patriotism was limited and constrained due to their wrong political understanding. Expatriate Indians were ideologues of individual heroic action that had the potential of inflicting violence. He found this ironically similar to the violent nature of the colonial state apparatus when it came to dealing with the lot of the subjugated people.

There was yet another irony that bedevilled the modernist world view of the expatriate Indians—They hated British officials but loved the system designed by them. They also did not understand the real nature of colonialism. Gandhi, during the South African period, had realized and personally experienced many cases of imperialistic excesses. He also saw the real face of the proponents of modernity. Gandhi, through *Hind Swaraj*, tried to interrogate the hegemonic power of the colonial state over the minds of intellectuals and subjugated masses.

While explaining the issues of nationalism, Gandhi understood the necessity of ground political work and lauded the thoughtful intervention of early nationalists. He called Dadabhai Naoroji the father of Indian nationalism. He profoundly expressed in *Hind Swaraj* that religion is a personal matter, and in fact there are as many religions as human minds in this world. Religion cannot be the basis of nationalism of any kind. One should not try to mix the cultural notions of communalism or some other identity with nationalism just to undermine its very positive historical value. Gandhi was of the view that Indians should contribute to the overall knowledge of world civilization and the problems faced by the world in a manner that reflected their wisdom.

At various points in time, he reaffirmed his faith in *Hind Swaraj*. There are three possible reasons behind it. First, Gandhi, during the course of the national movement, did develop an instrumentalist relationship with modern technology. He used it, but without really becoming a slave of it. He did see the total capacity of modern civilization to capture the minds and hearts of the people. Gandhi did not want to deprive himself and the movement and the people around him of the advantages of modern technology.

Second, Gandhi's political life was actually a series of many failures and disappointments and frustrations. Chauri Chaura was one disappointment. Rowlatt satyagraha (lit. holding firm to truth) was not very successful. Bardoli education was not very successful—the peasants paid a huge price for it. He wanted the Congress to do some spinning. He wanted to make spinning a compulsory part of Congress activities. Finding that there were not many takers, he eventually gave it up in 1922. Therefore, *Hind Swaraj* provided a kind of psychological cushion for him in the face of failures and setbacks. The third reason is related to the nature of modernity itself. Although the economic, political and social superiority of modernity is not in doubt, it was seen as morally vacuous. The sources of morality tend to dry up. A hectically mobile, egalitarian, instrumentalist society finds it generally hard to generate moral resources. In Gandhi's search for morality, *Hind Swaraj* became a mental signpost. For him, tradition was a huge reservoir of morality. *Hind Swaraj* served exactly that purpose. Gandhi made a selective appropriation of modern technology. In his debate with Nehru in 1945, when Nehru argued that villages were a backward place and a villager is insular and obscurantist, Gandhi retorted, 'The ideal village lives in my mind. I am allowed to imagine. And my village will consist of intelligent men and women who would practice hygiene, cleanliness, etc..' What Gandhi talked of was not the existential village. Gandhi, here, is perhaps marking a distinction between historical fact and the immense possibilities that lie hidden.

Gandhi's usage of symbolic resources is phenomenal. He termed worker struggle as 'Dharmayudha' (*Dharma* in Indian philosophical tradition refers to righteousness without any particular religious context, and Yudh refers to a war. So, *Dharmayudh* means a war for righteousness). One may call it a religious struggle, but it was not a religious struggle in that sense because dharma, for Gandhi, again, was a very polysemic word, where language was employed in a non-traditionalist sense. Gandhi advised workers to remain firm in their commitment to strike. For him, satyagraha is a struggle where wresting the best wages possible is not the issue. It is important to hold one's honour and dignity. Gandhi told workers not to rely on finances from outside to survive during the course of the strike. They have to work, and work is very important. A few lessons to learn from this experience: Gandhi interpreted the strike as a moral struggle against injustice. He placed it in the context of a broader struggle, not only in India but the world over, including in South Africa, where Gandhi had a first-hand experience of a successful 'Dharma Yudh'.

Gandhi wanted the striking workers to act as satyagrahis who would be prepared to suffer for the achievement of justice; there should be no ill will against the mill owners. He told workers to earn their livelihood by working in the period of the strike and not to depend on contributions from sympathizers. This, according to him, amounted to dole and would end up degrading workers in the eyes of the employers and others. Gandhi sought to maintain a balance between the interests of both the parties so that none would claim victory, which would obviate lasting bitterness between them. His retrospective assessment of the strike was positive, because it ultimately restored faith among the workers and taught them to remain steadfast in the face of adversity.

However, there was a partial failure of communication as the ideas which Gandhi wished to convey to the workers as well as to the mill owners were not fully carried through. Certain methods of communication employed by Gandhi were quite new, and, although these newer channels widened his reach, they also created newer forms of misunderstanding. Moreover, the messages which he tried to convey also had certain novelty so far as the conduct of the labour strike was concerned. The vivid mythological as well as secular imagery he invoked was not easy to grasp in the mundane and conflict-ridden world of labour relations. Finally, his conception of the satyagrahis was quite new and idiosyncratic, and, in a way, it remained so until the end, at least for the majority of the people. Thus, certain communication failure was in-built in the polysemic nature of Gandhi's various concepts. It does not mean, however, that it was a total failure.

Given the challenges he faced in his political career, Gandhi was constantly looking for better and more effective methods of communication all the time. The open letter and the pamphlet were used by the early Congress leaders in their agitations. The pamphlet, for instance, was a very effective means of communication in those days, and could really be dated back to Tom Paine's Rights of Man in the 1790s. The pamphlet worked at several levels. It shorter and was easier to read than a book or even perhaps a newspaper. In addition, it could be easily disseminated as it was cheap.

In times of repression, a pamphlet and the very act of its possession itself become a symbol of defiance. This, for instance, is to be found in the case of something called the Green Pamphlet, which Gandhiji brought with him from South Africa in 1896, and which listed the grievances faced by Indians in South Africa. Owing to its green colour, it came to be known as the Green Pamphlet. This pamphlet was sold out at his first meeting in India, and thereafter several editions of it were brought out. And the more the government tried to repress it, the more popular it became.

Similarly, the open letter addressed to the authorities, which would begin by informing people about their latest problems and grievances, served two purposes. First, it addressed the authorities; second, it educated people about various issues. Gandhi's swadeshi exhibition in 1923 after the withdrawal of the non-cooperation movement illustrates the power of spinning and weaving.

It also provided a unique platform to people from across the country to compete at plying charkha. The phenomenal success of the swadeshi exhibition in 1923 was visited by almost a lakh people. And thereafter it became a great crowd-puller in the following years. As Lisa Trivedi[1] says, this became a visual means of communication which transcended language; it also explains the centrality of charkha to the concept of swadeshi itself. Gandhi

---

[1] Lisa N. Trivedi. Visually Mapping the 'Nation': Swadeshi Politics in Nationalist India, 1920–1930. *The Journal of Asian Studies* 62, no. 1 (February 2003): 11–41.

used several such visual symbols to communicate and convey this philosophy. Even the burning of foreign cloth can be seen as yet another visual symbol. The Gandhian khadi movement responded to the colonial challenge not merely at the level of economics and culture but also by providing alternatives to the colonial science and knowledge system at each and every level.

One of the primary objectives of the khadi movement was to revive household spinning by challenging the notion of inferiority of Indian cotton production. For this, the khadi movement had to look at the alternative indigenous crops. The response of the khadi movement was, thus, not one of culture only, but very much a technological one too. Talking about the essence of the scientific method, Gandhi once remarked: 'No science has dropped from the skies in the perfect form. All sciences develop and are built through experience.' The spinning wheel was very soon appropriated as a symbol of loyalty and an image to reflect true nationalist spirit by Gandhian leaders. It was a symbol of identification for Congress leaders. Regional leaders often circulated their photographs depicting quite prominently the charkha, Gandhian cap and khadi dress.

The khadi campaign sought to divide Indians into two classes: those who believed in it and wore khadi, and those who did not. However, Gandhi's class division was enforced non-violently, though it was not entirely free of coercion. It provided a mobility of passage from one class to another. His emphasis on non-violence was intended to provide a possibility for the transformation of an individual's political alignment. Wearing khadi in that sense was a transformative experience. One could change one's class affiliation through personal conviction and a change of the heart.

Khadi became an ideological symbol on which one's political and personal beliefs could be vindicated. One's clothing became an index of one's political affiliations. A formal recognition of the choice regarding clothes did not arise as an actual outcome of khadi. The dilemma of choosing khadi or other clothes was enforced through a sustained campaign. Khadi's core semiotics lay in it being presented as a commodity of colonial resistance. In refurbishing charkha, there was the use of tradition. But the new reinvented charkha was put in the service as modern carrier of import substitution. Khadi gradually transformed itself into political fabric. A wearer of khadi became, in the eyes of authority, a rebel. Khadi's transformation from clothing to a political uniform gave the cloth a character. It became a commodity of conscious choice. The ideological investment in khadi enhanced the character of the cloth.

The present anthology engages with some of the core issues of communication that may be discerned from Gandhian writings and contributions so as to develop a starting point for any creative engagement with Indian communication. This anthology is divided into three sections that engage with the questions of knowledge, practice and strategies of communications and, finally, relevance of Gandhian communication in the present era. Any discussion on the knowledge of communication in Indian society needs to address these key attributes that contributes to the formation of communication and the constitution of Indian society. The first section squarely addresses these seminal issues and Gandhi's take on these issues. This section engages and brings back communication to the centre stage by addressing the question of modernity in an Indian way through the prism of Gandhi. This section outlines the reasons for disenchantment with a Western notion of modernity and creates avenue for re-enchantment from the Gandhian perspective.

Prafulla C. Kar's chapter on 'Nationalism, Religion and the Critique of Modernity' is an interesting account of engaging with the questions of modernity based on a re-reading of Gandhi's seminal text *Hind Swaraj*. Kar reads *Hind Swaraj* as a radical departure from the Western perspective of nationalism. Kar mentions that Gandhi was quite conversant with the spirit and trajectories of Western nationalism based on violence. Gandhi was very clear that neither violence nor adaptation of Western modernity provides a pathway for India. Gandhi's *Hind Swaraj* provides an alternative critiquing the ideology of enlightenment that premises itself on the philosophy of progress through instrumental modernity. The Western 'instrumental modernity' is not free from 'value'. Gandhi demolished the myth of the Western civilization and its various agencies. Gandhi interrogated the word 'civilization' opposed to 'savagery' and deployed as a mode of self-valorization. Kar highlights that Gandhi's critique of modernity is a critique of 'body-politic' which is infected by a disease. This disease is caused by the industrial culture's obsessive celebration of bodily pleasure directly or through its metonymic or metaphoric substitutions. Any nation engendered on the principles of industrialism reposes its faith in progressive ideology, which potentially transforms the artefacts of the past into obsolescence. This historical rupture devoid of continuity is unacceptable to Gandhi.

Gandhi opines that religion should be the basis outlining the core principle of nationalism. However, it should not be based on any doctrinaire conception of religion. Gandhi's notion about 'home rule' clearly suggests that freedom should be an essential attribute of nationalism. Kar highlights that Gandhi's notion of freedom provides a corrective to the enlightenment notion predicated on the thesis that freedom is always from something, and not towards something. The enlightenment notion takes an escape route, and is thus a retreat from a condition; Gandhi's notion, on the other hand, is based upon a proactive move, a return to the past, to a condition of its subliminal presence. Therefore, Gandhi anchors his nationalism more on the strength of inner freedom than on the external need.

Gandhi's experiments with 'truth' in a way show that truth is not a matter of theoretical speculation but a liveable force that enables one to live a life of peace and harmony in the company of others, despite their different religious persuasions. Religion is one such idea that still persists in our time, despite the skewed epistemological assertion of some scholars that it belongs to a bygone era. Gandhi brings religion back to the centre stage of his philosophical thought and accords it a new dimension. Gandhi views religion for its entrenched ethical values and practical lessons for living through good conduct. Thus, Gandhi's concept of nationalism is based neither upon religion in the fundamentalist sense nor on secularism in the modernist sense. The kind of secularism which Western modernity promotes views a religious way of life as detrimental to the spirit of the nation. Gandhi is opposed to a sanitized version of secularism bereft of any traces of quintessential religiosity. Alok Bajpai, too, adds in his chapter on *Hind Swaraj*: A Critique of 'Modernity' and an Argument for Indian Modern Consciousness by highlighting that *Hind Swaraj* should not be read as 'Programmatic Statement' or 'Political Action Plan Chart' of Gandhi. Bajpai cautions that 'any generalization about Gandhi on the basis of literal interpretation of *Hind Swaraj* is not a fair way to claim an understanding of Gandhi'. In fact, Gandhi was fed up with those hard-core Gandhians who lacked the skill of 'discriminatory knowledge' to discern the essence of his philosophy. Bajpai suggests that *Hind Swaraj* has to be understood as the argumentative and dialogic side of Gandhi. Gandhi argued on various issues pertaining to societal implications and the necessity for intervention. Gandhian dialectic is simple, but the ideas it imbues are not always so. His ideas are highly contextual, complex and often subtle. Gandhi was aware of it. For instance, for the language of *Hind Swaraj*, which was originally written in Gujarati, he acknowledged to its English readers constraints of language to convey the exact meanings and aspirations. Gandhi himself was a historic product of modern times and he had acquired his knowledge of contemporary society and its peculiarities within the parameters of modern political consciousness. Gandhi's criticism of modern civilization is synonymous with Westernized notions in a colonial context.

Bajpai comments that *Hind Swaraj* is also a strong case of argument for 'mass-empowerment through democratic means'. Gandhi's concrete understanding of mass consciousness is intricately related with this objective of social change because without it any attempt to mass empowerment might be derailed. Gandhi, in *Hind Swaraj* and in other writings also, treats mass consciousness as tantamount to soul force or truth force. Thus, *Hind Swaraj* is a strong argument in favour of complete decolonization of Indian society and culture. Despite criticism, Gandhi's commitment to *Hind Swaraj* was on account of its pro-poor, anti-imperialist and anti-colonial orientation together with democratic politics and secularism. Ratnakar Tripathy interrogates some of the basic assumptions of Gandhi and its implications on the contemporary events in his chapter Confession as Public Communication: Reflections on Gandhi's *The Story of My Experiments with Truth*. Tripathy questions the very idea of experiment instead of experience and intrigued by Gandhi's selection from the stock of experiences and the urgency to share and communicate publicly. Tripathy suggests that the word 'experiment' may seem to carry a warning, an appeal not to react with total empathy and instead listen to the man with a sense of scientific or simply objective detachment, and in the process perhaps learn to distance oneself from one's own experiences. Second, the experimental language would also seem to convey a strong sense of selection which turns his autobiography into a series of carefully and closely focused life accounts underlined in red. Free communication here does not mean idle babble or a general or indiscriminate exposure of one's life events, the reason being there is a sense of great urgency attached to Gandhi's autobiographical outpourings. All his experiments are part of experience but not all experiences may be called experiments. Why Gandhi chose those life events that are to be brought into relief as the outstanding experiences he wished to share with great urgency? Gandhi, in his autobiography, addresses matters that are of utmost importance and urgency to him, even more so than his political work. Gandhi's near dismissal of his political work should not be taken literally, though. What he probably means is that the values at the core of his political thought and work did not come from politics, and instead originated in the several other spheres of his life. Having thus stated and underlined the above premise and the urgency to communicate, Gandhi goes on to talk about his own bewilderments, confusions, traumas and even dead ends like closure of intimate relationships with utmost candour.

The great autonomy attributed to the realm and the category of 'politics' in the era of democracy would thus begin to seem baseless in a Gandhian universe. It would seem, instead, that politics, like many other realms of life, must seek its fundamental values from other aspects of life even as it grows and develops into a somewhat autonomous realm. Tripathy comments that Gandhi's contribution lay in clearing up the public spaces for a wider and freer public discourse—and he made a start with himself rather than offering to bare others or going barging rebelliously through the countless social walls and laments that the democracy of procedures through its endless series of rules tries to re-train us over and over again in the basic and almost congenital skill, instead of creating more opportunities and occasions for free communication. Public discourse when undemocratic or anti-democratic thus creates a topography of communication where the highs and the lows, the significant and the trivial get decided by the authorities, even when the citizen is empowered to vote and effect changes in regimes. In Gandhi' autobiography, the earth-shaking matters and the trivia weave together in a much better semblance of daily life than the abstract hierarchies determined by our greatest of democratic institutions.

Tripathy justifies the need to focus on the representative–represented relationship in the age of democracy and its ever-changing equations. There is indeed a good basis to claim that despite the abstractness and the unquantifiability of such changes, it may just be the most basic measure for the maturation process of democracy. Even though the modern idea of the state carries within it vestiges of autocratic forms, being based as it is on the state–subject relation, the democratic representative or the government is in no position to look at the citizen as their own subject and must invoke the state in all its haloed symbolism in order to reduce the citizen-voter into subject hood. Admittedly, this conceptual play is not just a sleight of hand on the part of the political representative, since it forms the very basis of the nation state. Ironically, as long as a state lasts, it must be seen as both immortal and the embodiment of the collective will, a myth essential to the idea of the state. The idea of political representation, on the other hand, has no such mythical burdens to carry. Tripathy suggests that rather than visualize a linear scheme for democratic evolution and maturity, it suffices to keep in focus the representative–represented relationship and its dynamics in its various aspects. One may posit two essential but mutually contradictory traits of this contested relation—first, the desire to retain full control over the actions and decisions of the representative on the citizen's part, and second, the expectation that the citizen would spend the least possible time to ensure such control. The classical phrase 'eternal vigilance' would thus seem an impossible ideal to attain and may be modified into the requirement 'best possible result for diminishing vigilance' or control over politics and governance through least effort. In this 'efficiency' model of democratic politics, the electorate hopes to achieve the maximum possible political effectiveness through minimum possible intervention. Tripathy concludes with his three differential readings of *My Experiments...* from different stages of life. I am struck by the unceasing and obsessive sense of subversion of illegitimate power that Gandhi's autobiography seems to convey. The subversive force of the Gandhian enquiry seems particularly effective when applied to politico-juridical abstractions and concepts. While other subversive ideologies such as Marxism dream sweetly of elimination of the state, even as they erect an enormous megalith as a supposedly interim state, the Gandhian impulse is to keep sifting away all the chaff of false pretences to power. This is why Gandhi keeps coming back to politics in the shape of an intervention rather than a permanently dwelling 'ism' before vanishing again into the thin apolitical skies.

In the second section, Gandhi's craft of myth, metaphor and strategies are discussed. It starts with Shashi Bhushan Upadhyay's chapter on An Unfinished Communication: Gandhi and the Ahmedabad Labour Strike, 1918. Upadhyay highlights the varied forms of communication employed in the course of the resistance movements against mill owners. However, certain forms of communication used by Gandhi were quite unique. Use of press, pamphlets, petitions, open letters and public speeches were adopted in the earlier phase of the nationalist movement. Most of these forms relied on the modern British forms of communication. Although during the swadeshi movement some new forms such as *Prabhat Pheris* and street singing were used, they remained confined within certain regions, and their momentum petered out once the movement declined.

During the Gandhian movements, earlier forms of communication continued and people's participation in them rose massively. However, some novel forms of communication were devised by Gandhi. Upadhyay comments that the novelty consisted not in their being modern, but in the fact that the earlier nationalist movement had not used them. In fact, they were mostly, at least in Gandhi's interpretation, derived from traditional Indian forms, which struck a chord with the masses. Satyagraha was one such polysemic agitational and communicational strategy which captured the imagination of the people. It encompassed such things as agitation, demonstration, strikes, picketing, sit-in, protest, negotiation, economic boycott, emigration to escape oppression and non-cooperation.

Other symbols in the network of Gandhian communication included spinning wheel, fasting, prayer meetings and *padyatra* (foot march). Upadhyay extends these channels of communication with the help of studying Gandhi's earliest public engagements in India and how far they were successful in transmitting his views to the public, particularly the mill workers in Ahmedabad. The struggle was termed as 'Ek Dharmayudha', the meanings of which unfolded as the struggle proceeded. In one of the meetings addressed to the workers, Gandhi said, 'we must remain firm... and must not resume work even if we have to die'. It was true that the workers were poor, but 'they possess a wealth superior to money'. It was 'their courage and their fear of God'. He also assured them that they would not be allowed to die of starvation. He, therefore, drew a parallel between various types of struggles going on in the country in which the satyagraha was being applied. This signified that he was placing this particular struggle in the broader context of the nationalist quest. He wanted the workers to be real satyagrahis who would struggle to achieve their aims regardless of consequences through particular means, which would be moral, ethical and spiritual. On the same day, in a meeting with the striking workers, he cautioned them not to heed the advice of those who tell them to accept whatever the mill owners had agreed to pay. Gandhi advised them to rely on the strength of their hands and feet, which would get them work anywhere. Only then could they assert their dignity and standing before the employers who should not take them for granted. Gandhi also tried to persuade the industrialists to be reasonable and sympathetic to the workers' cause. Gandhi's fast created quite a stir, and the mill owners were forced to meet him and offered to do whatever he wanted. Gandhi was not very happy with this situation because he felt that the employers had given in due to his fast and not either in appreciation of the workers' condition or due to workers' struggle. Upadhyay equally highlights the partial failure of communication as the ideas which Gandhi wished to convey to the workers as well as to the mill owners were not fully carried through. Certain methods of communication employed by Gandhi, such as leaflets, public meetings and dissemination through newspapers were derived from the earlier and contemporary forms. However, certain other methods such as prayer meetings, intense personal communication and, finally, fasting, were quite new. Although these newer channels widened his reach, they also created newer forms of misunderstanding. Moreover, the messages which he tried to convey also had certain novelty so far as the conduct of labour strikes was concerned.

Upadhyay concludes by saying that the vivid mythological and secular imagery Gandhi invoked were not easy to grasp in the mundane and conflict-ridden world of capital–labour relations. Gandhi's conception of the satyagrahis was quite new and idiosyncratic and, in a way, it remained so till the end, at least for the majority of people. Thus, certain communication failure was in-built in the polysemic nature of Gandhi's various concepts. It does not mean, however, that it was a total failure. The Ahmedabad labour union remained different from the rest of unions in the country, and the influence of Gandhi's ideas was responsible for this unique struggle.

Sadan Jha, in his chapter Multi-verse of Gandhi's Charkha: Spinning Experiences and the Question of Information, refers to Gandhi's use of 'believing eye'. Gandhi used this phrase in the context of his reply to a Gujarati correspondent regarding the decline in national education. Jha comments that the believing eye is an embedded eye and quite different from an observer's eye. The embedded qualities in the former case come from its inseparable attachment with the experiences of both seeing an object and having inner belief/faith in the object. For Jha, Gandhi's believing eyes also take us to the cusp between information and experiences and reflects that the spinning wheel is one of the most popular and sacred among Gandhian symbols. 'For me', Mahatma Gandhi once wrote, 'nothing in the political world is more important than the spinning wheel'.[2] The spinning wheel (charkha), for Mahatma Gandhi, was not just a tool of political emancipation but it was a metaphor of 'ancient work ethics' and a symbol of economic and social reaction to the British rule. This 'ancient work ethics' and the goal of the 'swaraj' (self-rule) in Gandhian framework had to be mediated in and through the 'daily life'. For him, 'it is in the daily life where dharma and practicality come together' and the spinning wheel was the realization of this possibility. Thus, any study of Gandhism needs to bring into focus this metaphor of 'ancient work ethics', this site of 'daily life' and this symbol of social and economic reaction. In Gandhian discourse, the spinning wheel signifies 'decentralization against centralized production' system. Jha comments that Gandhi had no exposure to the spinning wheel nor had any understanding of the difference between the loom and the spinning wheel. However, his deep conviction about the sacred nature of weaving and looms was written prefixed with 'ancient' and 'scared' in the *Hind Swaraj*.[3] In India, weaving and spinning were much more than simply an indigenous way of producing textile goods. Spinning was very much a part of everyday lives and activities of

---

[2] Mahatma Gandhi. *Collected Works of Mahatma Gandhi*, Vol. 19 (Delhi: Publication Division, 1976), 454–56.

[3] Anthony J. Pareled. *Hind Swaraj and Other Writings* (Delhi: Cambridge University Press, 1997), 109.

women of almost all sections of society. Jha observes that Gandhi hardly invented any idea or any symbols. All what he did was a careful selection and reworking of old symbols. This process transformed the nature of even ordinary everyday objects. Objects and metaphors that were closely related to a wide cross-section of Indian people and were part of day-to-day life of the nation very soon acquired different connotations. Gandhi invested new meanings and gave them new vitality and life.

In Gandhi's language, the past remained open; it was a realm of experience and hence it was open to very many usages. It is always difficult to control and contain production of meanings in these open realms of the past experience. Hence, *charkha* as an emblem of common men's suffering and their past always carried the very many meanings, and one of them was a symbol of resistance. A symbol of freedom had to be devoid of its experience of resistance. In Gandhi's scheme of things, *charkha* was never a tool for statecraft. In his doctrine, state and society were not separated from each other. In other words, *Swaraj* was premised not in the language of Western science and modernity. Modernity needed precision in its language to define and segregate the whole in parts.[4] Modern statecraft needed categories and constituencies

---

[4] Zygmunt Bauman writes, 'The typically modern practice, the substance of modern politics, of modern intellect, of modern life is the effort to exterminate ambivalence: an effort to define precisely—and to suppress or eliminate everything that could not or would not be precisely defined.' He further writes that 'the sovereignty of the modern state is the power to define and to make the definitions stick—everything that self-defines or eludes the power assisted definition is subversive'. He quite insightfully refers to Paul Ricoeur's formulation of close ties between science and state power and writes,

the practice of science is in its innermost structure no different from that of state politics; both aim at a monopoly over a dominated territory, and both reach their aims through the device of inclusion/exclusion (of science Ricoeur writes that it is 'constituted by the decision to suspend all affective, utilitarian, political aesthetic, and religious considerations and to hold as true only that which answers to the criteria of the scientific method'.

that should not overlap. In *Swaraj*, categories of life cannot be disentangled from each other; hence, from the perspective of modernity, it was a language disorder, an ambivalence that had to be erased or at least reworked. Hence, the wheel was cleaned from its strings and spindle, history from the past, freedom from resistance and singularly identifiable figure of Ashoka from common men with a potential of plural identifications.

Keval J. Kumar's chapter, titled 'Gandhi: Journalist, Communicator and Satyagrahi', reflects on the voluminous writings, speeches and interviews of Gandhi. Kumar reflects on his humility: 'I am not made for academic writings; action is my domain,'[5] he famously remarked. Gandhi had prior experience of rejuvenating the Natal Indian Congress in South Africa. He recognized the imperative need for a strong mass-based organization for effective communication with the masses. One of the secrets of Gandhi's remarkable success in communicating with the vast majority of the rural masses was that he used—and helped develop—the communication facilities of the Congress Party. Without the party, Gandhi's message would not have been transmitted so successfully.[6] He set about transforming an elite and passive debating body which met once a year into a mass political organization, manned by full-time political workers and capable of mobilizing public opinion and bringing it to bear on governmental policy and administration.[7] He also made its structure and procedure more rational, professional and dramatic,[8] through his revision of its constitution in 1920. Because of Gandhi's prior experience in the reorganization of the Natal Congress in South Africa, the

---

Zygmunt Bauman. *Modernity and Ambivalence* (Cambridge: Polity Press, 1993), 7–8.

[5] Quoted in B. R. Nanda. *In Search of Gandhi: Essays and Reflections* (New Delhi: Oxford University Press, 2002), 254.

[6] Kusum J. Singh and Bertram M. Gross. 'The Village Communicator', *Seminar*, 235, 12–13.

[7] Lloyd I. Rudolph and Susanne H. Rudolph. *The Modernity of Tradition* (Chicago, IL: University of Chicago, 1967), 232. The Rudolphs' essay on Gandhi has been reissued under the title *Gandhi: The Traditional Roots of Charisma* (Chicago, IL: University of Chicago, 1983).

[8] Ibid.

Gujarat Sabha and of service societies, he had come to recognize the power of a common language, especially the mother tongue, to weld a people together, to raise their self-esteem and to ensure dynamic participation. The same power he imbued the Congress with. It was the deft stroke of a mass communicator at work. He saw language as a powerful means of achieving national unity,[9] not the suppression of regional languages by Hindi but the addition of Hindi to the former so as to enable provinces to establish a living contact with one another.[10] The Hindustani he advocated as the national language was neither the Sanskritized Hindi nor the Persianized Urdu but a happy combination of both. It would also freely admit words, wherever necessary, from the different regional languages, as also assimilate words from foreign languages, provided they can mix well and easily with our national language. Thus, our national language must develop into a rich and powerful instrument capable of expressing the whole gamut of human thoughts and feelings.[11]

Gandhi insisted on the use of the mother tongue (and not Hindi) in education, especially at the primary and secondary stages, for that is the language one is nourished on and sustained by. 'I must cling to my mother tongue as to my mother's milk', said Gandhi, 'in spite of its shortcomings. It alone can give me the life-giving milk'.[12]

As a mass communicator, Gandhi understood the intimate attachment of people to their own languages and dialects, and the most effective appeal was one couched in the listener's own dialect. Gandhi's mastery over the nuances of spoken and written English provided him easy access to the educated elite in India and Britain, and indeed to an international audience. Gandhi's communication was both people based and two-way process.

---

[9] Ibid.

[10] Ibid., 239.

[11] M. K. Gandhi. *Thoughts on National Language* (Ahmedabad: Navjivan, 1956), 55.

[12] Ibid., 30.

This technique of communication not only broke the barriers between elite and various strata but allowed messages to work effectively. Gandhi's padayatras suited the Indian tradition and the primitive development of modern communication systems in the country. Gandhi made it a point to speak in traditional terms familiar to his audience. Yet he often invested these terms with new meanings. 'I use the old words, giving them a new meaning', he wrote.[13] His continuous circulation of terms and meaning was context specific. He wrote 'When I visit the Frontier Province or address predominantly Muslim audiences I would express my meaning to them by calling it *Khuda Raj*, while to a Christian audience I would describe it as the 'kingdom of God on earth.'[14] He also lent this religious term a secular interpretation. 'What is Ramraj?', he asked, 'It can be religiously translated,' he stated,

> as 'the kingdom of God on earth; politically translated, it is perfect democracy in which inequalities based on possession and non-possession, colour, race or creed or sex vanish. In it land and state belong to the people, justice is prompt, perfect and cheap, and therefore, there is freedom of worship, speech and the press – all this because of the reign of the self-imposed law of moral restraint. Such a state must be based on Truth and Non-Violence, and must consist of prosperous, happy and self-contained villages and village communities.'[15]

The most powerful means of communication to Gandhi was, however, one's life lived according to the principles of truth and non-violence. 'Those who believe in the simple truths I have laid down', said Gandhi, 'can propagate them only by living them.'[16] Indeed, ideally speaking, satyagraha or soul force transcends all media, for it is self-propagated. Truth and non-violence, the language of the soul, can best be represented by life itself, not by

---

[13] *Harijan*, 16 September 1939.
[14] *Harijan*, 18 August 1946.
[15] *Harijan*, 1 June 1947.
[16] *Harijan*, 28 March 1936.

mere words, spoken or written, or even symbols. As he reminded Christian missionaries once:

> The moment there is a spiritual expression in life, the surroundings will readily respond. There is no desire to speak when one lives the truth. There is thus no truer or other evangelism than life.[17]

But this life must be lived in the spirit of direct personal service to the people, and of suffering, for service involves suffering. In the words of Gandhi, 'the silent and undemonstrative action of truth and love produces far more permanent and abiding results than speeches or such other showy performances'.[18] And again, 'non-violent action does mean much silent work and little speech or writing.'[19]

The 'silent work' he had in mind was what he termed 'constructive service'. It refers to direct personal service of the masses, suffering for them, organizing them, educating them in the ways of non-violence and thus bringing about a peaceful atmosphere of solemn determination.

The third section of the anthology revisits Gandhi in the media age. Gandhi and Gandhian practices have been used and abused in contemporary times. The question arises why Gandhi captures contemporary imaginations and how that imagination is experienced in current social practices and reality? Arunabha Ghosh and Partha Ray's chapter on Munna and Gandhi: Rethinking Gandhi, 'Gandhigiri' and Popular Hindi Cinema reflects on the consumerist culture and revisit of Gandhi. The authors reveal that Lage Raho Munnabhai, a film made in 2006, cashing in on Gandhi and his ideas, created a wave in the cultural life of the nation that generated a flurry of commentaries on the subject. This is a simple yet tricky question. Why Gandhi should be brought back to the public consciousness through popular cinema in the new millennium where consumerism and the concomitant violence have become the norm. The causes may be immense as

---

[17] *Harijan*, 12 December 1936.
[18] *Young India*, 8 August 1929.
[19] *Harijan*, 10 June 1939.

the collapse of the value system and the material prosperities lead to different sets of anxieties and social tension in society. The film represents Gandhi as common man with an uncommon commitment to truth and *ahimsa*, the two most important values that are part of the national myth but lost in translation by today's politically and economically dominant class. It is a paradox that Gandhi is a figure whom all pay lip service to but seldom follow. The authors highlight that 'Gandhi as a subject is fit to be "reinvented" and the process has been going on long after his political relevance has been lost not only on the contemporary world but also on the nation of which he is the undisputed spiritual "father"'. It is ironical that

> Gandhi erected no monument to himself, except the masterwork of ambiguity which is the *Autobiography*. He was not carried on the shoulders of any definite ideology, not even nationalism. He can therefore be continuously reinvented according to the needs and fashions of the times, and this reinvention has been going on incessantly.... The future certainly holds other Gandhis in store.[20]

As Ashis Nandy rightly points out in his essay 'Gandhi after Gandhi' distinguished between four Gandhis.[21] While the first Gandhi is the Gandhi of the Indian state and Indian nationalism, the second Gandhi is that of the Gandhian, who, according to Nandy, 'does not touch politics'. The third Gandhi is the Gandhi of the 'ragamuffins, eccentrics and the unpredictable' and 'is more hostile to Coca-Cola than to Scotch whisky and considers the local versions of Coca-Cola more dangerous than imported ones'. Finally, the fourth Gandhi walks the mean streets of the world, threatening the status quo and pompous bullies in every area of life. In some sense, perhaps all these Gandhis are alive today, each with his own eccentricities. The authors pose a question 'Does *LRMB* make Gandhi contemporary?' and comment that what is

---

[20] Claude Markovits. *The Un-Gandhian Gandhi: The Life and Afterlife of the Mahatma* (New Delhi: Permanent Black, 2003).

[21] A. Nandy. 'Mahatma Gandhi – Gandhi after Gandhi'. *The Little Magazine*, 2005. Available at http://www.littlemag.com.

unique, though, of the Gandhian ethical scheme is the uprooting of fear. '*Abhay*', or fearlessness, comes from the courage to face truth. Since the real adversary resides within, it is a constant and continuous battle with the self.

Dev Nath Pathak's chapter on *Reading Gandhi* with/in Popular Cinema: A Pedagogue's Perspective provides a much closer look at the way Gandhi is construed in a classroom setting in a school. The pedagogy is constructed in a for-and-against framework while discussing historical personalities like Gandhi. Teaching, thereby, amounts to propaganda and rabble-rousing. The prerequisite anarchy, meaningfully cultivated for engaging with the ideas and characters of historical significance, does not reflect in either curriculum or pedagogic practices. No wonder, then, Gandhi is not discussed beyond, the mystique halo of a Mahatma, of postcard value utilized for textbook presentations. Or, on the other extreme, Gandhi is yet another character that evokes both hatred and wonder. As a corollary, engagement with Gandhi, in schools and colleges, is merely for serving the official requirement, as it were. This leads to usage of Gandhian ideas, signs and symbols, for mouthing politically correct platitudes. Else, who cares what Gandhi was and what were his ideas, unless it is packaged with business efficiency to make it palatable for the new middle class.[22] What does the above instance indicate: a

---

[22] This is the broad outline of the general view students in schools (XIth and XIIth standards) and colleges would offer. I am using this as a point of departure for this paper. By the repackaging of Gandhi, to make it palatable for the new middle class, I mean the acceptance of *Lage Raho Munna Bhai* (Rajkumar Hirani, year 2006), which did fairly good business and offered a new perspective on engaging with Gandhian ideas in cinematic narrative. In a recent feature, an expert on Indian cinema, Dwyer regrets an abysmal cinematic representation of Gandhi. Speaking of *LRMB*, she says,

It is not the historical Gandhi, a challenging and difficult figure who urges us to abandon consumerism, but a Gandhi of India's new middle classes. This is not a political Gandhi but a Gandhi who is an inner conscience and moral guide, as well as a Fairy Godmother who will help us to realise today's dreams.

pedagogic inertia, a syllabic problem, a skewed relation between syllabus and pedagogy, an institutional error in designing and teaching and so on?

It is not impossible to note the plethora of cinematic representations of Gandhi and his ideas in the kaleidoscope of Hindi cinema. These representations, overt as well as covert, suggest of socio-cinematic common sense on/about Gandhi. Unlike the academic discourse on the theory and actions of Gandhi, the socio-cinematic common sense entails a fluidity and spontaneity. By virtue of being a kind of common sense, it also reflects the ontological character through the mix of locality, context, agency and emotion. Pathak highlights two levels of irony. First, Gandhi was agnostic about the usage of modern media. Khwaja Ahmad Abbas,[23] the filmmaker, engaged with Gandhi in a bid to convince him of the validity of cinema as a medium.[24] To this, Gandhi remained sceptical till the end. However, Gandhi never shied away from posing in front of camera, which generated visuals for circulation in print media. Peter Ruhe,[25] in a visually stunning work *Gandhi: A Photo Biography*, uses images from the photo works of Gandhi's foremost biographer Vithalbhai Jhaveri and Mahatma Gandhi's great nephew Kanu Gandhi. As Ruhe mentions, M. K. Gandhi consented to be photographed by Kanu on three conditions: that the freedom movement will not fund the photography, that Kanu will not use flash while photographing, and that Gandhi will never pose for the photographs. Similarly, despite Gandhi's agnosticism towards cinema as a medium, he remained an intriguing object of communication through popular cinema. This level of irony reveals a significant meaning for the present discourse. For, it is at this level of irony,

---

[23] Khwaja Ahmad Abbas is a filmmaker, who is popularly known for his films like *Saat Hindustani* (*Seven Indians*, 1969) and *Do Boond Paani* (*Two Drops of Water*, 1972). Both the films won national awards.

[24] Akhil Gupta. 'Attenborough's Truth: The Politics of Gandhi'. *The Threepenny Review* 15 (1983): 22–23.

[25] Peter Ruhe. *Gandhi: A Photo Biography* (London: Phaidon Press, 2004).

Gandhi is available as a fluid object susceptible for all kinds of cinematic (mediated) casting. The availability of Gandhi as a fluid object, owed to the ambivalent relation between Gandhi and visual media, adds to the complexity of socio-cinematic common sense. The post-independent India is, furthermore, rife with a variety of visual representations on Gandhi, such as postal stamp, currency, signposts, statues and, of course, the presence of the economic enterprise of the Khadi Bhandar (business of homespun).[26] On the second level of irony, Gandhi appears as a source of lesson in the prescribed literatures in various courses offered to undergraduate students. These prescribed literatures present Gandhi and his values/ideals in an arguably absolute manner. Each piece of literature would propose the validity claim of indubitable understanding of Gandhi, leaving little room for the critical-intellectual engagement of learners and teachers. This occasions a second level of irony. For, Gandhi himself was not in favour of indubitable claim of absolute understanding.[27] The second level of irony leads us to comprehend the phenomenal scholarship on Gandhi, dubbing one man and his ideas in diverse ways. Ironically enough, each way of presentation of Gandhi appears indubitably absolute. For example, it is a postmodern Gandhi for Ruloph and Rudolph (2006),[28] while for T. N. Madan it is a Gandhi with 'altruistic individualism'.[29] The list of casting Gandhi in one or other category would be nearly inexorable. The purpose is not to recount the list. It is much rather to comprehend the significance of the multiplicity of perception, which

---

[26] See the work of Trivedi on the symbolism of Gandhi in historical context vis-à-vis discourse on the cultural history of Khadi: Lisa N. Trivedi. *Clothing Gandhi's Nation: Homespun and Modern India* (Bloomington: Indiana University Press, 2007).

[27] Akeel Bilgrami. 'Gandhi, The Philosopher'. *Economic and Political Weekly* 38, no. 39 (2003): 4159–69; Akeel Bilgrami. 'Gandhi, Newton and the Enlightenment'. *Social Scientist* 34, nos 5 and 6 (2006): 17–35.

[28] Lloyd I. Rudolph and Susanne Hoeber Rudolph. *Postmodern Gandhi and Other essays: Gandhi in the World and at Home* (Chicago, IL: Chicago University Press, 2006).

[29] T. N. Madan. 'Gandhi's Altruistic Individualism'. *The Hindu*, 2002. Available at http://www.hindu.com/thehindu/2002/10/02/stories/2002100200031000.htm.

goes into the construction of social common sense. At this level, the present discourse gears to ask whether the multiple analytical imagination of Gandhi in academic writings could afford to have the contribution from an oral context in which teachers and students operate. Pathak's insights are interesting, specially his three levels of analysis of Gandhi in Hindi cinema: as a personality in historical and biographical contexts, as an absolute inspiration in the background of diverse cinematic narratives, and as an idea at a mundane level of everyday life. While Gandhi in biographical and historical contexts has been dominant attraction in cinema, the other two levels of cinematic engagement with Gandhi are relatively humble. It was about almost five decades before the Attenborough's *Gandhi* (1982) dazzled the audience all over the world, that Gandhian inspiration defined the cinematic engagement with the concern for social reforms in India. It is obvious that Hindi popular cinema graduated from putting Gandhi as an absolute source of inspiration to historicizing him. Many facets of Gandhi emerged in this cinematic tryst with Gandhi. He is a poser, a communicator, a debater, an ideologue, a propagandist, a conscience-keeper and a historical culprit. Much of it could also be attributed to the cinematic construction and reconstruction. However, the significance of the constructed imageries is undeniable. In the ontological framework, while Gandhi could inspire guilt as well as ethical strength, there is also a possibility that the complexity of the Gandhi as a persona is revealed. Notion of history, historiography, biography, nation and its tryst with modernity, possible negotiations between contradictory ideals in the present context and so on surface in the cinematic panorama that reveals Gandhi in diverse ways. In the light of the forgone discourse on cinema and Gandhi, it is not difficult to figure out the complexity of socio-cinematic common sense about/on Gandhi that emerges as a consequence of cinematic engagement with Gandhi. The above discourse establishes that in the preceding five decades, on the one hand, Hindi cinema has generated complex common sense and, on the other, it has rendered Mohan Das Gandhi as a fluid matter to be recast in all possible contexts rather than only as a historical icon.

Pathak concludes by saying that there happens to be an uncreative discrepancy between socio-cinematic understanding and the academic proposition on Gandhi, which could be detrimental to the basic objective of a course like Reading Gandhi. There is little chance for teachers and students to realize themselves in the lectures on Gandhi, which could be in principle about self-realization. The two domains of production of common sense, popular cinema and (undergraduate) academics, yield two sets of images and ideas about/on a historical icon like Gandhi. In larger analysis, cinematic attempts seem to be more versatile and engaging than the academic attempts. Both domains have evident commercial consequences. But, then, the ideas from the cinematic mills are more layered than those from the academic mills. In ideal sense, the domain of academic production and circulation of knowledge ought to be critically engaging with the same of the non-academic such as cinema. However, as it were, academic is predisposed to dismiss the common sense altogether with the prejudices that cinematic is illogical. A youthful engagement with the ideas of M. K. Gandhi, is, indeed, a casualty. These are interesting insights by Dev Pathak and the casualty therein in any engagement on Gandhi for the present-day youth.

However, Gandhi's images are floating everywhere like a simulacrum in Baudrillard's conception. Gopalan Ravindran's chapter on the Rhizomatic Constructions of Gandhi on Web 2.0 has highlighted controversial encounters of Gandhi, in his virtual and rhizomatic self, on what is emerging as the most participatory, discursive and user-generated plane of the Internet, the Web 2.0. Among the prominent ones was a hate group, 'I Hate Gandhi' on *Facebook,* which was eventually shut down, due to protests and legal action under the IT Act 2000.[30] As Gopalan observes, those who hate Gandhi are otherwise alive and kicking in other parts of Web 2.0, such as YouTube and blogs. On the other hand, there is equally strong likes for Gandhi on Web 2.0. Gopalan comments that *Gandhitopia* (www.gandhitopia.org) is

---

[30] 'Facebook Bans Online Hate Group on Mahatma Gandhi', *DNA,* 2011.

one of the several sites on Web 2.0 which strives for the promotion of Gandhi's name in a concerted manner. The question of presence and absence is not important, but what is striking about the presence of Gandhi on Web 2.0 as a rhizomatic site where not only the binary notions of Gandhi, but also the most discursive notions of Gandhi, come into play. Gandhi as a rhizomatic subject on Web 2.0 warrants a closer scrutiny. Interestingly, a good number of videos on Mahatma Gandhi have an Italian connection in terms of their origin, language and so on. These videos seek to play the role of enchantment, whereas the videos with the African connection seek to play the role of disenchantment with Mahatma Gandhi.

Gopalan highlights that Gandhi is juxtaposed with Hitler to bring out the aspects of material subjectivity between their ideologies and personalities. Gopalan makes a differentiation in his analysis of (a) Web 2.0 as the super umbrella assemblage, (b) YouTube as the umbrella assemblage, (c) the growing groups of Mahatma Gandhi videos on YouTube as assemblages and (d) the individual videos as sub-assemblages. Gopalan highlights that it requires a large time-frame study to understand the umbrella assemblages; hence, the present chapter attempts an examination of two of the groups of videos on YouTube which focus on the themes (a) 'One World' and (b) 'The Power of One'. Among the YouTube videos on Mahatma Gandhi, these two groups of videos have large viewership and variants. Variants are the mutating categories of the original upload. Viewership is indicated by the number of views indicated at the right-hand bottom corner of the video player in YouTube. Gopalan analyses various videos uploaded and concludes that there appears to be an abiding faith in the 'One World' notion of Mahatma Gandhi, if not as an explicit form of content, but as an explicit form of expression, thereby pointing to the molecular line of the assemblage. The variant of this video is also instructive to understand the nature of Mahatma Gandhi videos as an assemblage where the possibilities of connections, heterogeneity, multiplicities and ruptures are real. Gopalan concludes by saying that 'to read the constructions of Mahatma Gandhi on Web 2.0 through the rhizomatic prism of Deleuze and Guattari is as instructive as it is interesting. The manner in which the words and ideals of Mahatma Gandhi are connected, contested and ruptured in multiplicitous and hetero-geneous ways by Indians, Italians, Africans, Asians and others in the planes of Web 2.0 show that Gandhi remains a crowd-puller in its virtual *avatars* as well. This chapter also attests to the need to rethink Gandhi in antithetical locations and coloca-tions where Gandhi coexists with the likes of Hitler, encounters hate campaigns and yet conveys his message of love and truth to Italians and Indians alike through the plane of immanence that is Web 2.0.'

The final chapter by Shuaib Mohamed Haneef, titled Digital Civil Disobedience Movement: Revisiting Gandhian Thoughts in an International Commune, extends the Gandhian notion of civil disobedience to understand the confrontation over land. Haneef highlights that in spite of Auroville's control over media resources such as Internet television, Internet radio, Auronet, and the Intranet, members of the community launched a prolonged pro-test resembling Gandhi's civil disobedience. Much of this protest, a sort of digital activism, occurred through blogs and discussion forums of Auroville Intranet. The protest called into question the difference between unified civic identity and the multicultural identity of Auroville based on transcending religion, geography, colour, creed and caste. The reports centring on the land issue that appeared in the *News and Notes*, a newsletter brought out by Auroville's governing body, were reportedly filtered and did not address the concerns of those who opposed the governing body's decisions. However, the democratic deficit created by the newsletter was offset by the space and freedom given to the mem-bers in the virtual space. The intranet with access privileges given exclusively to the members of Auroville encouraged collective participation, and sharing of views created an anti-hierarchical networked platform for the users. Haneef, with the help of the underlying strategy of civil disobedience, seeks to understand the electronic civil disobedience movement at the Ashram centred on dialogue, discussion, open access and grassroots protests. The Internet, a site for communication and action, deterritorializes boundaries and facilitates networked interaction across multiple languages and cultures. Taking cue from the Civil Disobedience Movement of Gandhi, the protest in the Auroville-run Intranet was characterized by civil dissent. The intranet posts bring out trenchant criticism of the Working Council alleging that 'they are not gods'. While analysing the findings, Haneef comments that the Intranet reveals the deliberative communication the members engage in and their strong open opposition to the Entry Service who posted a message condemning the action of an individual involved in the Udumbu land issue.

It is quite evident from the following comment posted by the Auronet representative who after seeing the comments and seven members flagging a post (that of the Entry Service in the beginning) highlighted the rules of flagging a post to which erupts a slew of messages defending why the members flagged the post again undergirding the principle of disobedience or civil disobedience in a multicultural community through the Internet Infrastructure. Despite the Auronet representative defending the nature of comments a lot of dissent was registered by the Auroville netizens. A few gave diegetic replies instructing the Auronet to change the rules implicitly reproving the bias in the decision taken by the governing council and other bodies with regard to the Udumbu land issue.

Haneef concludes that the efforts of Auroville to function as a multicultural entity in realizing the goals of the Mother are no less intense and the various institutions contributing to health, education and village development are in consonance with what Gandhi encapsulated in his ideology of rural development. A democratic space will have conflicts and resolving them through participation and enfranchising every member of the community to express views is what Gandhi solely believed in. The political power of a community emerges from the freedom enjoyed by the members of a community in sharing their views and participating in a deliberative communication. A few members express the absence of democratic currency and the Internet emerges as a popular space for the people to express and rise against the Working Council and question its decisions. On the other hand, the idea of cultural imperialism may not be undermined. Thus, Auroville creates fissures within and creates communities within community.

Together, 10 chapters are included in this anthology, representing diverse works, understanding and interpretation and finally extending Gandhian concepts to understand present milieu. This anthology does not only testify Gandhian thought and communication, but also contributes a tangible resource and reference book to assist in further opening up the critical-intellectual space for communication in India.

SECTION A

Communication and Re-enchantment of Modernity

1

Nationalism, Religion and the Critique of Modernity
Gandhi's Hind Swaraj

Prafulla C. Kar

In this chapter, I have chosen to focus primarily on national-ism, which figures as a key concept in *Hind Swaraj*,[1] which I think is the most profound text Gandhi wrote at a moment in Indian history when the country needed a proper direction for its onward journey. This text in a way has tried to provide that direction. Is nationalism a Western construct or an idea that is also relevant to a non-Western, non-nation-state context? Many scholars have written about its genesis and development and have connected it with the emergence of industrial culture in Europe in the 18th century. In his book *Nations and Nationalism*, for example, Ernest Gellner[2] has stated that nationalism developed as a distinctively European idea after Europe made a conscious decision to reject its agrarianism and religious orientation in favour of industrialism and a secular ideology. These epistemic

---

[1] Gandhi, M. K. 1997. *Hind Swaraj and Other Writings*. Edited by Anthony J. Parel. New Delhi: Foundation Books.

[2] Ernest, Gellner. 1983. *Nations and Nationalism*. Ithaca, NY: Cornell University Press.

developments within European culture led to the emergence of modernity as Europe's identity marker. Gandhi's rethinking of the entire *topos* of nationalism needs to be placed against this European context. *Hind Swaraj* seems to be proposing a radical theory of the nation to counter the conventional theories disseminated by the Western scholars. He was evidently disturbed in 1909 by the way the spirit of nationalism was being expressed by some of the Indian freedom fighters, mostly operating from foreign soil, whose proposed modes of action were unacceptable to him. Therefore, he felt that it was his duty to his country to speak out against the dangers of these modes of action for the long-term durability of the emergent nation. It was as if he was driven by an 'inner voice' to take such a step, which he did in a forceful manner by using the method of a dialogue to vindicate in a step-by-step logical way the efficacy of his argument. He did not substantially retract from his views expressed in *Hind Swaraj* despite criticism of some of his ideas from many of his friends and followers. This is also a point to keep in mind. Why did he continue to maintain his so-called recalcitrance so far as his idea of nationalism is concerned? I would like to address some of the issues in this chapter.

As we know, Gandhi's immediate intentions were to challenge and thwart the methods adopted by some Indian revolutionaries to make India free from the British rule. One group was tempted to use violence for achieving the result; another group, which was influenced by Western modernity, was in favour of retaining some of the institutions established by the colonial regime even after the overthrow of that regime. Gandhi was opposed to both the groups. He was clear in his view that neither a turn to violence nor an adaptation of Western modernity would be beneficial to India. India, he suggests, needs to follow a different route, a route which India had taken for a long time but that route was temporarily suspended during the period of its colonial subjugation. That route needs to be revived and made ready for use in the changed context. In other words, in order to build a new nation on a ground which is already saturated by a rich sedimentation of its past, one must utilize the material that is already available on the soil itself, rather than going after imported material. Both revolutionary violence and modernity of the Western type are imported methods and hence not suitable to Indian culture; they will not strike root naturally on its soil. Care and caution, he felt, are needed in formulating ideals for a new nation. He tries to re-define nationalism in an astonishingly fresh way by taking into account the rich legacy of Indian culture. His concept of nationalism, as outlined in *Hind Swaraj*, is carefully orchestrated to counter the encroachment of certain European ideologies on the Indian consciousness meant to perpetuate in India their legacies. *Hind Swaraj* is meant to provide, first of all, a direction to the Indian freedom fighters at the beginning of the 20th century to facilitate the success of their journey to arrive at its destination, and second, to theorize in a new way the concept of a nation, which would be the benchmark for the future. In a subtle way, he is also critiquing the whole notion of theory as an abstract speculative idea having little bearing on everyday life. He takes advantage of a specific political ferment of the time, which is also the dawn of the 20th century, to formulate a new vision, which is forged symbolically as an inevitable destiny that results from a creative transformation of a historical contingency. Benedict Anderson's eloquent words in his *Imagined Communities*, 'It is the magic of nationalism to turn chance into destiny',[3] through their somewhat analeptical re-figuration corroborate what Gandhi was trying to achieve way back in 1909. The force of this radical re-formulation is as valid in 2009 as it was in 1909.

The chance that Gandhi envisaged was the impending freedom of India to achieve which all freedom fighters, irrespective of their modes of action, were unanimous in their view, but if that magical moment of struggle is not transformed into the efficacy of a destiny (a proper destination), India would miss a unique opportunity for realizing its goals. How would one then

---

[3] Anderson, Benedict. 1991. *Imagined Communities: Reflections on the Origin and Spread of Nationalism*. Revised Edition. London and New York: Verso, 12.

characterize the new nation that is to be forged out of the exit of colonial power? What would be the guiding spirit of nationalism that would keep the country intact? Gandhi is concerned with these and many other related questions, and tries to build a context for turning a chance into destiny. That chance was not merely to fight for political independence, but more importantly to assert India's unique identity in the world and to account for its prevalence, while Greek and Roman civilizations, which gave modern Europe its guiding principles, have perished on the way. Gandhi felt that the time had come at the dawn of the 20th century to carefully reflect upon these questions and to build a new India on the solid foundation laid by its ancestors and to look ahead of its time by reclaiming its rich legacy and facilitating its smooth passage to the present time so that a chasm between its past and future is not created. Colonial powers have always tried to create such a chasm so that the subjugated country develops a dependency syndrome and loses its ability to stand on its own. Gandhi felt that a nation must transcend itself in order to justify itself as a nation. This is not a paradox; its meaning lies in the implication that as long as a nation continues to remain fixated on its narrow contingencies alone without moving beyond its manifest insularity, it will not endure as a nation. This vision of transcendence derives from the strength of its foundation, its received wisdom from the past. *Hind Swaraj* is an attempt to conceptualize such a nation for India.

I would like to return to this conceptualization after an engagement with Ernest Renan's 1882 classic essay 'What Is a Nation?'[4] Renan's essay is an attempt to define what a nation is by identifying first what it is not. With the decline of religion as a prime force in life in Europe around the 18th century, the idea of a nation became a new factor for defining the contours of European identity. Thus, the concept of the 'nation' replaced that of religion. The French Revolution seems to have inaugurated such a shift in attitude. The Enlightenment thought accelerated

---

[4] Renan, Ernest, ed. 1992. 'What Is a Nation?' In *Qu'est-ce qu'une nation?* Paris: Presses-Pocket.

that shift, and it was Immanuel Kant who brought together such filiative notions as liberalism, democracy and cosmopolitanism under the rubric of the nation. Renan had this context in mind in his definition. First, let us mention what the nation is not, according to Renan. The nation, to him, is not a geographical concept, which means that it is not defined by a territorial enclosure or any other geographical conditions. However, a nation has to be distinguished from a nation-state, which is defined in terms of its territorial integrity. However, it does not mean that geography does not have anything to do with the development of a national spirit; what it means is that a nation always transcends its geography. The nation is also not a biological or a racial concept. A group of people, who are biologically and racially similar, do not constitute a nation, whatever other affinities they might have with each other. The nation is also not a linguistic concept. People speaking the same language may share their experience together in many interesting ways, but cannot build a nation only through linguistic affinities. Renan seems to suggest by highlighting what the nation is not that there is something uncanny and inscrutable in the idea of a nation that cannot be captured in tangible terms but can only be felt and experienced in spiritual terms. Renan calls it a 'spiritual principle', which is the 'outcome of profound complications of history'.[5] He also says that the nation is a 'soul'. Two things, Renan says, constitute this 'spiritual principle': 'One is the possession in common of a rich legacy of memories; the other is present-day consent, the desire to live together, the will to perpetuate the value of the heritage that one has received in an undivided form.'[6] The 'profound complications of history' provide the condition for conceptualizing the idea of a nation. The 'spiritual principle' seems to antedate a nation, in the sense that it is in the spirit of the nation that a nation is engendered, not vice versa. Wherefrom does that sprit come? Renan seems to think that such spirit gets reawakened by memories and epiphanies through which heritage is preserved and taken forward.

---

[5] Ibid., 18.
[6] Ibid., 19.

Benedict Anderson has a more evocative way of articulating this notion. By borrowing the concept of 'simultaneity' from Erich Auerbach's *Mimesis* and 'homogeneous empty time' from Walter Benjamin, he says that a nation is created from a 'homogeneous empty time' 'in which simultaneity is, as it were, transverse, cross-time, marked not by prefiguring and fulfillment, but by temporal coincidence, and marked by clock and calendar'.[7] He says again, a nation is 'always loom[s] out of an immemorial past, and still more important, glide[s] into a limitless future'.[8] Stathis Gourgouris says even more eloquently in his work[9]: '[Any nation] *cannot* be reduced to or contained in its history. It is something more, something else. Or, simultaneously with its being *there* (*in* history, *in* geography—*in* a narrative, it *is* elsewhere'. Gourgouris's notion that a nation is present simultaneously 'here' and 'elsewhere' evokes Moby Dick's omnipresence, as it is reported in Melville's novel, that the white whale is seen in many places at 'the same instant of time'. Gourgouris also employs the term *mythistory* to endorse Anderson's notion of nation as an 'imagined community' which blurs the boundary between history and myth. This definition implies that nation is an allegory which is always energized by the combined pull of memory and prophecy. Renan's view of the spiritual constitution of nation, which is corroborated by both Anderson and Gourgouris, is close what Gandhi had in mind.

At a crucial time in India's history when attempts were being made by some misdirected revolutionaries to bring Indians together under the urgency of leading an agitation against the British, Gandhi came on the scene as if to direct the course of events. During his stay in England, he had met several such revolutionary leaders and discussed ideas with them, and read many books, both Indian and Western, and had already made up his

---

[7] Anderson, *Imagined Communities*, 24.

[8] Ibid., 11.

[9] Gourgouris, Stathis. 1996. *Dream Nation: Enlightenment, Colonization, and the Institution of Modern Greece.* Stanford, CA: Stanford University Press, 31.

mind about what role he had to play to turn that chance into a destiny. By rejecting both the extremists and moderates from the Indian National Congress, he opted for a 'golden mean' which has both Buddhist and Aristotelian connotations. *Hind Swaraj* in a way brought Gandhi onto the national arena and propelled him into an action which would inevitably lead him to his fateful destiny.

Gandhi must have been familiar with the prevailing discourses on nation and nationalism both in India and abroad when he started writing *Hind Swaraj* as an answer to many questions he was troubled with. Although his idea of a nation seems close to Renan's in so far as it is embedded in a spiritual principle, he was somewhat sceptical about nationalism because he was afraid that it might slip into parochialism and xenophobia if it is not carefully nurtured and directed. In *Hind Swaraj* he avoids to take an extreme position with regard to the cultivation of the English language. While he makes a bold assertion in support of education in a vernacular language, he does not denigrate English as a mode of knowledge, particularly for secular education. What he is opposed to is what he calls a 'fetish' of it.[10] He suggests that both English and the vernacular should be used for forging a balance between 'secular' education and 'ethical education', respectively. This clever strategy of forging a productive alliance between two modes of knowledge has prevented him from being appropriated by either of the two groups: the extremists and moderates.

In a profound way, *Hind Swaraj* makes a trenchant critique of the Enlightenment ideology of nation, premised on the philosophy of progress through instrumental modernity without appearing to do so. This 'instrumental modernity' is laden with a 'value' with so much certainty that appears to offer a panacea to those countries who have yet to become nations in the Western sense. Gandhi is opposed to most of what this philosophy stood for, and in a systematic way while answering the questions of the 'Reader', he demolished the myth of the Western civilization

---

[10] Gandhi, *Hind Swaraj*, 103.

and its various agencies. First, he questions the tenor of the word 'civilization', which is opposed to 'savagery' and deployed as a mode of self-valorization. He calls 'civilization' a 'disease', a word he borrowed from the English writer Edward Carpenter's work,[11] to suggest that it needs a 'cure'. This is a brilliant move of critiquing the other in its own rhetoric, which also serves the purpose of absolving the transmitter of that rhetoric of any intentional ill-will for the other. 'Health' and 'disease' are, in a way, master tropes which Gandhi utilized in many ways to underscore his seminal ideas. His critique of modernity is in fact a critique of 'body-politic' which is infected by a disease. This disease is caused by the industrial culture's obsessive celebration of bodily pleasure directly or through its metonymic or metaphoric substitutions.

An important facet of the new nation engendered on the principles of industrialism is its faith in a progressive ideology which believes in forward movement by turning the artefacts of the past into their obsolescence. The Enlightenment envisioned the new nation in Europe in terms of a historical rupture. The new nation was born in specific time, and even in a specific place, it was assumed. So there was no question of continuity of time in terms of its cumulative effect. In order to progress, one has to bury the past. Gandhi is opposed to this epistemology. One of his major tasks as a political reformer has been to resuscitate the past in all its 'pristine condition' and bring it face to face with the present and to place both in their dynamic relationship. So as an act of such resuscitation he revived the *charkha* (the spinning wheel), which had been made obsolete under the impact of new technology, an act which was not merely a symbolic gesture of cultural revival but an audacious act of self-assertion through a strategy of saving indigenous technology from a threat of extinction by the new technology. A nation that prides itself in its legacy of a rich heritage, he implies, could not afford any disruption of its cultural continuity. So by these so-called small gestures, Gandhi was trying to re-connect himself to his nation that, he felt, was

---

[11] Carpenter, Edward. 2015. *Civilization: Its Cause and Cure*. Dubai: Palala Press.

slowly drifting away from its moorings. It does not mean that he was fascinated by an attitude of longing for a return to nature as an escape from urban squalor; it has a more profound meaning, implying that he was able to recognize in nature and other objects connected with it their intrinsic value, and not for their utility only. In a similar way, Gandhi suggests that a nation is a valuable concept, not because it makes us aware of our 'rights', but because its intrinsic value makes a spiritual claim on our 'duties' towards it in an imperceptible way. So the onus is on us to conceptualize the nation in whatever way we want, as long as this basic premise is kept in mind. So Gandhi wanted every Indian to be proud of his/her national duty without becoming a narrow-minded promoter of ethnic nationalism derived from a perverse sense of the superiority of the Aryans over the other indigenous communities. If nationalism promotes racial and ethnic superiority, it poses a danger to the idea of a nation.

But a healthy nationalism grown from one's inherent love for one's nation and its presence in narratives, both oral and written, is a desirable impulse to be cultivated among those who are ignorant about the wisdom of his/her country. This cultivation, however, needs to be undertaken in a spirit of detachment, allowing maximum freedom to the uninitiated to probe the mystery of his heritage and to feel proud of its spiritual content. The question regarding whether nationalism is healthy or perverse need not be pushed too far to complicate its intentionality, but should be tackled within the framework of one's duties to their country with which one has entered into an emotional contract which cannot be defined in merely linguistic, religious or territorial terms. The genuine spirit of nationalism transcends these terms and is more than the combination of all its manifest expressions. It stems from a profound faith in oneself, capable of perceiving beneath the surface of things the values that sustain the spirit of the nation through its period of stress and strain. That is perhaps the reason why Renan says that a 'nation is a soul',[12] whereas race is a

---

[12] Renan, 'What Is a Nation?' 19.

'chimera'. Therefore, one is not ready to accept the radical liberal view that nationalism as an offshoot of religion is a perversion. Gandhi subscribes, to a large extent, to this view.

Gandhi is inclined to accept the so-called conservative view that the core principle of nationalism derives from its religious source. This source, however, should not be confused with the doctrinaire position of a religion, which leads to a dogma. The source we are talking about is saturated with certain perennial values that continue to nourish one's faith in the humanity and to keep the dialogue with nations alive. This religious spirit is what makes nationalism a genuine feeling to imbibe, preventing it from slipping into a frenzy of self-obsession. The idea that the nation in Europe emerged from a decline of religious spirit is not what Gandhi would subscribe to. He would rather be happy to endorse T. S. Eliot's unconventional endorsement of Baudelaire's faith in Satanism as akin to such a religious faith: 'His [Baudelaire's] business is not to practice Christianity, but—what was more important for his time—to assert its *necessity*'.[13] What Eliot meant here was that even though Baudelaire was not a practicing Christian, he had a Christian spirit which was evident in his attachment to the deviant characters he depicted in his work. One could say a similar thing about Shakespeare.

Gandhi had this kind of religious faith in mind when he talked about the primacy of a religious point of view in the development of a national spirit. Although he derived most of his ideas from the core principles of Hinduism, he was well versed in other religions too. He extracted the essences from all the religions he was familiar with and utilized them, in large measure, to develop many of his seminal ideas. But he continued to remain profoundly attached to Hinduism, which he did not consider as a religion, but a way of life, a vestigial spirit that pervades the spirit of the nation. Like Annie Besant, who had thought that the spirit of Indian literature came from Hinduism, Gandhi felt that a creative

---

[13] Eliot, T. S. 1932. 'Baudelaire.' *Selected Essays*. London: Faber and Faber, 422.

engagement with Hinduism would provide the necessary strength for an Indian to confront the challenges of Western modernity. He returns to religion from time to time in his political writings to underscore the point that a strong religious conviction is needed to counter Western civilization which has drifted away from its religious origins. His principle of 'passive resistance' (a sort of oxymoron) is a combination of the quintessential principles of several religions put to political use. This principle, which is also an effective political strategy, will remain with him for the rest of his life.

I would like to return to the questions of nationalism and religion and the critique of modernity via the detour of the episteme of passivity. *Hind Swaraj* is a text about 'home rule', a phrase that gives a fresh twist to the concept of freedom as an essential attribute of nationalism. According to Gandhi, freedom is something one is endowed with, and to get back to it one must need to search within to discover the 'pristine condition' of his self, hidden behind the cloud of ignorance. I think Gandhi's notion of freedom provides a corrective to the Enlightenment notion predicated on the thesis that freedom is always from something, and not to something. The Enlightenment notion takes an escape route, and is thus a retreat from a condition; Gandhi's notion, on the other hand, is based upon a proactive move, a return to the past, to a condition of its subliminal presence. Therefore, Gandhi anchors his nationalism more on the strength of inner freedom than on the external need to overthrow the British from the Indian soil. By merely overthrowing the British but continuing to retain the institutions they had set up is not enough to vindicate one's nationalism. Gandhi prefers a passive acceptance of suffering to an active struggle for freedom: 'Passive resistance is a method of securing rights by personal suffering'.[14] For him, suffering that is caused by passive resistance strengthens one's spirit and prepares him to face the colonial power with courage and conviction. He emphasizes the need for abjuring the pleasure

---

[14] Gandhi, *Hind Swaraj*, 90.

of the body and other types of material pleasure in order to build an inner strength needed to pursue higher goals. He calls the Western civilization a 'disease' for its obsessive preoccupation with materialism and hedonism, which were spurred by the success of the Industrial Revolution. That is why he does not favour the continuance of Western institutions in India after the British have left.

The spirit of nationalism, according to him, lies in the accumulated wisdom of its religions founded on ethical principles of harmony and good conduct. The religions may have taken different roads, but they have eventually 'converged to the same point'. Therefore, it is the 'duty' of every Indian to appreciate this aspect of nationalism and to work towards achieving this goal. The goal can be achieved only by an act of living the truth, not through professing it. Gandhi's experiments with 'truth' are aimed at showing to the world that truth is not a matter of theoretical speculation but a liveable force that enables one to live a life of peace and harmony in the company of others, despite their different religious persuasions. If India has acquired a special status as a nation with varieties of religious attitudes available to her, it is because of its inherent capacity for openness to accept those who have knocked at it door from time to time. This history and tradition must be kept in mind while thinking of national imperatives. The facility that India has offered to many communities and religious groups to blend with each other culturally while maintaining their otherwise unique distinctions is a sign of its largeness of spirit, which has been denuded under the impact of Western imperialism and its various instruments of power. Gandhi wants that denuded spirit be recharged so that whatever was considered obsolete and unusable could be recycled and become part of the process of self-renewal. Religion is one such idea that still persists in our time, despite the skewed epistemological assertion of some scholars that it belonged to a bygone era. Gandhi brings religion back to the centre stage of his philosophical thought and accords it a new dimension. However, his notion of religion has nothing do with its institutional or ceremonial aspect; he views religion for its entrenched ethical values and practical lessons for living through good conduct. That is why he thinks the strength of nationalism lies in its religious spirit. One cannot have that spirit without having lived in a religious atmosphere at home. One needs to have a strong religious grounding to think of religious transcendence. That is why Gandhi returns to Hinduism again and again for sustaining his grand edifice of the nation. He believes strongly that a person imbued with religious spirit coming out of his specific religious environment can appreciate others from different persuasions. Dialogue is possible only when such a situation prevails. But under the impact of industrial modernity, the British have lost their religious moorings, and therefore, Gandhi thinks that a proper dialogue with them is not possible in such a situation. He is not against the British choosing to stay on in India even after the end of their rule, but in order to make their stay meaningful they must return to their religious fold. He tells them, '...we shall learn several things from you, and you will learn many from us. So doing, we shall benefit each other and the world. But that will happen only when the root of our relationship is sunk in a religious soil'.[15]

This may sound somewhat obscurantist to a liberal intellectual brought up on the Western tradition of modernity, but by close scrutiny, one will certainly find in it a philosophical position which is not only germane to Gandhi's overall vision as a political philosopher engaged in an arduous task of nation-building while working towards the political liberation of India, but more importantly a strategy for redefining the nature of a nationalist ideology for India that would not alienate any group, including the colonial power, from being associated with it. An important aspect of that ideology is its inclusiveness and 'hospitality', to use a Derridean word, which create a congenial environment for the integration of divergent cultural and religious groups into its

---

[15] Ibid., 115.

fold. He cautions the Hindu zealots against dreaming to establish a pure Hindu Rashtra:

> ... the introduction of foreigners does not necessarily destroy the nation, they merge in it. A country is one nation only when such a condition obtains in it. That country must have a faculty for assimilation ... those who are conscious of the spirit of nationality do not interfere with one another's religion. If they do, they are not fit to be considered a nation. If Hindus believe that India should be peopled only by Hindus, they are living in a dreamland.[16]

This is by far the most clear definition of what the Indian nation ought to be, and a proleptic advice to those in the future whose politics is likely to be influenced by fundamentalism and xenophobia.

As is made clear from the above statements, Gandhi's concept of nationalism is based neither upon religion in the fundamentalist sense nor on secularism in the modernist sense. The kind of secularism which Western modernity promotes views a religious sense of life as detrimental to the spirit of the nation. Gandhi is opposed to a sanitized version of secularism bereft of any traces of quintessential religiosity; he would rather prefer a religious attitude tempered by a gentle mix of some secular elements. He is opposed to modern Western civilization because it not only because has replaced religion with secularism, but has also valorized the primacy of individualism. Under the impact of individualism, community life has disintegrated. The most baneful aspect of individualism is the pursuit of bodily pleasure, which Gandhi thinks, is the root of all kinds of degeneration.

Why does Gandhi oppose modern Western civilization so forcefully? To answer this question, one needs to carefully examine the essence of his philosophical vision from which his political ideas have emanated. This vision is tempered with a rich ingredient of romantic thought, which is basically earth-bound.

---

[16] Ibid., 52.

It is a romanticism that opposes technology as a controlling force in life and supports a way of life that is oriented towards community and agrarianism. His oft-quoted statement, 'India lives in the villages', aptly sums up his nationalist *oeuvre*. Those who champion the case of the progressive ideology of modernity for its possible transplantation into India after the end of colonial rule are misdirected, according Gandhi. The most of *Hind Swaraj* is in fact directed against them and their agents such as doctors and lawyers. The railways, by facilitating migration of people from the villages to cities, have contributed to the breakdown of community living and to overcrowding of cities. The speed of technology has disrupted the leisurely pace of life and its capacity for reflection. Gandhi wants people of India to be aware of all these evils coming from Western modernity so that they will not fall prey to its allurements. In other words, he cautions Indians against falling into the imminent danger of cognitive enslavement under the impact of technology.

Reading *Hind Swaraj* in the 100th year of its publication, one is still amazed how contemporary Gandhi sounds in the overall tenor of his thesis, although one may like to differ with him with regard to certain specifics. Today when there is a worldwide movement against industrial pollution, global warming, environmental depredation and urban overcrowding and other such issues, Gandhi's call for a return to nature and to the economy of simple village community provides a possible answer to the myriad challenges that humanity has been facing. His vision is like Thoreau's; he admired Thoreau's concept of 'civil disobedience', which he transformed into the political praxis of satyagraha (truth force). As I have implied above, for him truth is not only a laudable idea; it is performative, and an exemplary model to follow. Truth, to him, is what is true to one's heart, which cannot be corrupted by the false trappings of civilization. His concept of freedom is a return to truth. Civilization, particularly Western civilization, is, for him, a false consciousness. His opposition to such a civilization is made from a strong conviction that it needs to be cured of its disease. One way of curing it is to return it to its earlier Christian roots. Gandhi does not, therefore, speak against the British as such for colonizing India; he rather pities them for their distressing condition.

In a profoundly philosophical way, Gandhi provides a radical alternative to Western modernity spawned by the Enlightenment by proposing a return to rural technology which was in use for a long time but was subsequently discarded as a result of the impact of scientifically advanced technology, imported from the West. Modernity brings with it an attitude of disenchantment with the world having an intrinsic value in it, and proclaims that only when an external agent acts upon the world is it invested with a value, a thesis which finds eloquent expression in Newton's first law of motion, which states that 'a body continues to be in the state of rest or of uniform motion as long as it is impressed upon by an external force to change that state.' Gandhi should not be judged for only his disparagement of the Western modernity, but more importantly for his subtle move to provide a different blueprint of a nation to India in a new century which will see its independence. That blueprint is devoid of Western trappings; it is conceived not as an alternative to Western nationalism because an alternative picture always carries its affiliation with the original it has deviated from, but as coeval with its adversary. In other words, Gandhi is not averse to modernity *per se*, but to the form it has taken in its trajectory in the West. I would say by way of conclusion Gandhi, too, is modern in a new way, and that modernity has to be understood in a different register.

2

Some Contextual Reflections on *Hind Swaraj*

A Critique of 'Modernity' and an Argument for Indian Modern Consciousness

Alok Bajpai

It is unjust to a writer to quote against him passages from his writings without reference to the context.[1]

Here at the very outset I wish to clear my vantage point about *Hind Swaraj*. Gandhi was essentially a mass political leader. So, as a prolific writer he wrote and spoke always within a context and according to demands of the situation as he perceived them. Thus, all his writings have an inevitable context and tearing them from their concrete settings would simply not do justice to understand his multifaceted, multidimensional and highly complex personality. *Hind Swaraj* is no exception to this. It was written by Gandhi not as an independent philosophic text. The purpose of this chapter is to shed some light on its context keeping in view Gandhi's own understanding on the issue of being modernized.

---

[1] Mahatma Gandhi, 'Collected Works of Mahatma Gandhi' (hereafter CWMG), Vol. 54, *Harijan*, 1 April 1933, p. 259.

Of course, *Hind Swaraj* is an important work of Gandhi, but it is also not like 'swan song' or 'most fundamental work', 'seed', 'right place to start' or similar sentiments expressed by the scholars in recent times.[2] For making any broad generalization about Gandhi, we have to understand that Gandhiana has also to its credit other very important and crucial writings which shaped not only the future course of the Indian National Movement but also the future of democratic movements all over the world.[3]

While dealing with *Hind Swaraj* it must be kept in mind that it is not a 'Programmatic Statement' or 'Political Action Plan Chart' of Gandhi. Gandhi did not write it as a definitive work on the issues of Future Model of Independent India. It never found a place in any of his political programmes or campaigns. Even in his indirect political activities like Constructive Programme and other social reform drives, he never used *Hind Swaraj* as a help tool or guide book to propagate his ideas and vision.[4]

---

[2] Anthony Parel's edited book *Gandhi Hind Swaraj and Other Writings* (1997) is the best representative of this trend. In his analysis of *Hind Swaraj*, Parel treats it as a fundamental book to understand Gandhi. His analysis has provided some valuable insights to understand *Hind Swaraj*. I have used his coined term 'Expatriate Indians' in a slightly different mode and orientation in this chapter. However, his generalization about Gandhi and his reliance on literary interpretation is problematic. He also does not give weight to anti-colonial nationalist instinct of Gandhi. He also relies heavily on the cultural discourse of *Hind Swaraj* while neglecting the political understanding of Gandhi that is evident in the booklet.

[3] It is not possible here to refer all his other significant writings. His London Diary, BHU Inauguration speech, Champaran speeches, Non-Cooperation phase speeches and writings, his lifelong crusade against religious orthodoxy and Communalism, Round Table Conference speeches, Salt Satyagraha phase speeches, Anti-untouchability campaign utterances, Quit Indian Resolution speeches, Reply to Linlithgow reports on violence in the 1942 movement are some of the very significant speeches and writings which are crucial to understand Gandhi's multifaceted personality and politics.

[4] Please do not infer by these arguments that I am, in any way, trying to undermine the value of a classic of Gandhi. Of course, it, like any other classic work, may be legitimately interpreted in more than one way, but to claim to understand Gandhi on the sheer basis Hind Swaraj by making it a 'Vantage Point' is not tenable in my view.

It is interesting to note that his antagonists and admirers both have been fascinated by the overtures of 'no Railways, no Hospitals, no Machinery, no Army and no Law-Courts' over the years. During his lifetime, Gandhi was also forced to reply on similar literal interpretations of *Hind Swaraj*. In 1922, during the Non-Cooperation Movement, the booklet was misquoted by some. He cleared the cobwebs regarding *Hind Swaraj* in his mouthpiece *Young India*. The propaganda leaflet against Gandhi contained a mocking question answer:

What would India be like when Gandhi-Raj comes? .... No Railways. No Hospitals. No Machinery. No army and navy will be wanted, because Gandhi will assure other nations that India would not interfere with them, and so they will not interfere with India!... No laws necessary, no courts necessary, because everyone will be law unto himself. Everybody will be free to do what he likes. It will be a very easy life, because everybody will have to go about in a khaddar *langoti* and sleep in the open....

What Gandhi wrote in reply is very important to gauge his mind in general and understand the concrete context of *Hind Swaraj* in particular. He replied:

I cannot say that this is an exaggeration. It is a clever caricature permissible in Western warfare. It is only suggestively false. Let me say what I mean.... Under swaraj nobody ever dreams, certainly I do not dream, of no railways, no hospitals, no machinery, no army and navy, no laws and no law-courts. On the contrary, there will be railways: only they will not be intended for military or the economic exploitation of India, but they will be used for promoting internal trade and will make the lives of third-class passengers fairly comfortable.... Nobody anticipates complete absence of diseases during swaraj: there will therefore certainly be hospitals.... Machinery there certainly will be in the shape of spinning-wheel, which is after all a delicate piece of machinery, but I have no doubt that several factories will grow up in India under swaraj intended for the benefit of the people, not as now for draining the masses dry.... Army of India of the future will not consist of hirelings to be utilized for keeping India under subjection and for depriving other nations of their liberty, but it would be largely cut down, will consist largely of volunteers and will be utilized for policing India.... There will be law and law-courts also under swaraj, but they will be custodians of the people's liberty, not—as they now are—instruments in the hands of a bureaucracy which has emasculated and is intent upon further emasculating a whole nation.... It is not right therefore to tear some ideas expressed in *Indian Home Rule* from their proper setting, caricature them and put them before the people as if I was preaching these ideas for anybody's acceptance....[5]

During the Non-Cooperation Movement, Gandhi warned the readers of his journal and political activists against the thinking that he was anyway aiming at the Swaraj described in *Hind Swaraj* and commented that it was not right to scare away people by reproducing from his writings passages that were irrelevant to the issues before the country.[6] In 1925, during his Bengal tour for the Khadi propaganda, he was asked whether he proposed to replace the railways with country-carts as he expected to replace mills with wheels. Gandhi in reply wrote:

It is remarkable how false or incomplete analogies deceive people. In the case in point, the difference between mills and railways on the one hand and wheels and country-carts on the other, is so obvious that the comparison should never have been made. But probably the friend thought I was against all machinery in every conceivable circumstance. Probably he had in mind my objections to railways stated in my *Indian Home Rule* though I have repeatedly said that I am not working out the different fundamental problems raised in that booklet....[7]

On another occasion, replying to objections in 1924, he said:

It must be remembered that it is not Indian Hole Rule depicted in that book that I am placing before India. I am placing before the nation parliamentary, that is, democratic swaraj.[8]

[5] CWMG, Vol. 23, *Young India*, 9 March 1922, pp. 37–39.
[6] See, CWMG, Vol. 19, pp. 277–78.
[7] CWMG, Vol. 27, *Young India*, 28 May 1925, pp. 163–64.
[8] CWMG, Vol. 24, *Young India*, 14 August 1924, p. 548.

So, the point is that whenever anyone tried to locate Gandhi in the company of anti-modernism, anti-industrialism and glorious past rhetoric, he dismissed the charge with enlightened modern logic. For another example, in 1939, he retorted to an 'estranged friend' who failed in following the rich humour behind his writing in which Gandhi exposed himself to ridicule by referring to *Hind Swaraj* and 'beauty of slowness' while himself travelling by train.

> The key to understand that incredibly simple (so simple as to be regarded foolish) booklet is to realize that it is not an attempt to go back to the so-called ignorant, dark ages. But it is an attempt to see beauty in voluntary simplicity, poverty and slowness.[9]

On another occasion, in 1945, he sought to differentiate between 'ideal' and 'practice' to a distinguished fellow worker with reference to *Hind Swaraj*:

> I still abide by whatever I wrote about railways, etc., in Hind Swaraj. But that applies to an ideal state. It is possible that we may never reach that state. Let us not worry about it. It is for this reason that I have said that if we do not have railways and other such facilities, we should not feel unhappy. We should never make it our duty to multiply such facilities. At the same time we should also not make a duty of giving up these things. We should have a free and easy attitude in such matters. We must use these facilities as little as possible. There will be all types of people in our society. There certainly are today. We have to live with them. Non-attachment is the only proper dharma under these circumstances. The only thing we must be careful about is that we do not deceive ourselves. Your statement that trains, etc., should be shunned even as theft, adultery and falsehood is not correct. The important reason for this is that every society considers theft, etc., to be immoral. Trains, etc., have not been, nor need they be so considered. All that we may say is that we should not consider trains, etc., as means of enjoyment. I have repeatedly pointed out

---

[9] CWMG, Vol. 70, *Harijan*, 14 October 1939, pp. 241–243. In this article, Gandhi said that speed was not the aim of life and man sees more and more lives truly by walking to his duty. At the end of article, he conceded that he was on a train to Simla.

in my articles where to draw the line. Read them and if you give a little thought you will easily be able to draw the line.[10]

In 1926, when two American correspondents asked Gandhi, 'How can we get back to the ideal condition of things?', Gandhi replied them in a reflective way:

> Not easily. It is an express moving at a terrific speed that we are in. We cannot all of a sudden jump out of it. We cannot go back to the ideal state all at a jump. We can look forward to reaching it some day.[11]

The purpose of above quotes is to argue that any generalization about Gandhi on the basis of literal interpretation of *Hind Swaraj* is not the fair way to claim to understand Gandhi. In fact, he was fed up with those hard-core Gandhians who lacked the skill of 'discriminatory knowledge' to feel the essence of his utterances. He was very fond of referring Emerson's famous line that 'foolish consistency is the habit of smaller minds'.

The main plea of *Hind Swaraj*–based generalization about Gandhi has been Gandhi's lifelong adherence to it. As a matter of fact, Gandhi, in reality, never condemned or rejected any of his major writings or statements.[12] He always held that his basic

---

[10] CWMG-80, *Letter to Krishnachandra*, 14 June 1945, pp. 325–26. Interestingly, in this letter, he advised him to read some books written as an aid to restudy of Karl Marx's *Das Capital* because reading them would help.

[11] CWMG-29, *Interview to Langeloth and Kelly, Young India*, 21 January 1926, pp. 417–18.

[12] I have given instances in this chapter that show that *Hind Swaraj*, more than any other writing of his, was repeatedly made a target to malign Gandhi's organic politics of social change. Gandhi, to counter these false propagandas, defended the content and intent of the booklet. He also interpreted it in deeper sense than his objectors. His interactions with Jawaharlal Nehru are quite revealing in this regard, which I shall elaborate in later part of this chapter. It is important to note that Gandhi also defended his other writings whenever any controversy arose over them. The main reason for defending *Hind Swaraj* has been explained in the later pages of this chapter.

values have been the same throughout his life, and the contradictions or differences are only apparent so. Moreover, whenever any confusion occurred over his previous writings, Gandhi emphatically told the audience to rely more on latest utterance. He did not say this due to any basic change of his ideas but rather in the hope that the latter statement would be more strategically fitting to the current situations. It is important to emphasize that Gandhi disliked the way of taking his writings literally. He expected from fellow workers and comrades to understand his words with their real essence and not follow them blindly in a sheepish way. In fact, his famous quote that all his writings should be buried was a reflection of his agony over the inability of even his staunch followers to understand his complex and intricate insights.

Moreover, *Hind Swaraj* was written in 1909, and so it was still the formative stage of Gandhi at least as far as Indian affairs are concerned. He was yet to acquaint himself with the complex realities, priorities of Indian masses and engage himself with the aspirations of Indian people. Gandhi in this period was also preparing himself to be able to make a shift from the South African Struggle to the Indian National Movement. As he was a thorough democratic leader in his approach towards contemporary affairs, he met, discussed, agreed and disagreed over issues with a variety of people. *Hind Swaraj* is a natural output of that transformation phase of Gandhi. The transformation was an evolution in his body politic, but we should not ignore that evolution was a continuous process in Gandhi's case, and he never claimed the finally of his truth in his entire life. In this context, many insights and undercurrents of the Gandhian ideology and political understanding are evident in *Hind Swaraj*, but much more is obviously missing in *Hind Swaraj*. His satyagraha technique, Constructive

---

But Gandhi's defence of it should not be taken as a proof to give it centrality in the ocean of Gandhiana. One has to dive deeper and travel a lot to grasp Gandhi's ideology.

Programme, his unique way of tackling sub-contradiction and their incorporation into the Main Contradiction, his organizational acumen and strategy of Mass Movements is quite absent in *Hind Swaraj*.[13] Even Gandhi occasionally referred to his tentativeness and inferential approach while writing of *Hind Swaraj*'s some arguments.[14]

Now, in an attempt to grasp the essence of contention in *Hind Swaraj*, it would be pertinent to reflect over Gandhi's peculiar dialectic or discourse. While dealing with philosophic and transcendental issues, Gandhi preferred to argue in 'extremes' combined with complex and subtle notions.[15] In the context of *Hind Swaraj*, Gandhi argued about nonviolence and truthfulness (in public and private lives both) in extreme rhetoric to counter the arguments of violent school. These arguments were not put forward for any Concrete Political Action or Programme but only to ideologically disarm the proponents of violent school who advocated individual violence to uproot the British.

In fact, *Hind Swaraj* is the argumentative and dialogic side of Gandhi. He argued on societal issues with the objective of making a purposeful ideological intervention. In these matters,

---

[13] By referring to them, I do not mean anyway to belittle the significance of the booklet, but only to mention the context and limitation of using Hind Swaraj for making an attempt to understand Gandhi organically.

[14] For example, about spinning wheel in *Hind Swaraj*, he said in 1939, 'I had not seen even a single spinning-wheel at the time. Not only this, I had even confused a loom with a spinning-wheel.' That was exactly why I had mentioned the loom rather than the spinning-wheel in that book (CWMG-69, Speech at Gandhi Seva Sangh Meeting, Brindaban, 3 May 1939, p. 197). Also see, Mahatma Gandhi, *An Autobiography*, Part V, Chapter 39, 'The Birth of Khadi', p. 389; CWMG-26, Speech at Bagasara, 2 April 1925, Navajivan, 19 April 1925, p. 458; CWMG-68, Talk to Khudai Khidmatgars, 26 October 1938, p. 60; CWMG-71, The Charkha, *Harijan*, 13 January 1940, p. 95.

[15] In the domain of politics, there has to be difference between ideological struggle and concrete political action. Of course, they are interdependent and complementary to each other.

he recognized the importance of ideological struggles and contemplated for constructive intervention in action mode, but his ideological struggles were not meant for immediate literal actions corresponding to those ideas. Further, Gandhi enriched his content of ideological struggles with the prevailing mass-consciousness and viewpoints of other positive trends in the contemporary society. As a mass political leader, Gandhi implied inclusiveness in his approach and political discourse, and the extremist rhetoric is almost non-existent in action domain. In this way, he succeeded in transforming many violent revolutionaries into topmost non-violent soldiers in his non-violent army. Kaka Saheb Kalelkar is one such prominent example of this transformation technique. Only due to his sound but flexible strategy could he evolve a 'Grand Front' in the anti-imperialist struggle in India in which diverse political ideologies and currents could be incorporated.

It is necessary to keep in mind that the Gandhian discourse is basically self-introspective. *Hind Swaraj* is imbued with deep sense of introspection combined with self-esteem for Indian consciousness. His style is dialogically argumentative, which is also meant to emphasize the fundamental truths in relative terms. For example, he wrote in *Hind Swaraj* in self-analysis mode:

> If I am in the habit of drinking Bhang and a seller thereof sells it to me, am I to blame him or myself? By blaming the seller shall I be able to avoid the habit? And if a particular retailer is driven away, will not another take his place? A true servant of India will have to go the root of the matter. It is 'we' who are responsible for our bad fortunes; the enemy is only taking advantage of our self created misfortunes.[16]

Here, it is pertinent to point out that there is a difference between self-criticism coming out of depressed mindset and the self-criticism which invokes constructive intervention in a grim

---

[16] CWMG-10, p. 22.

situation. Gandhi's introspective tone does not culminate into inferiority syndrome or meek acquiescence for surrendering to subjugated position. It culminates into constructive exploration and self-activity. That is why Gandhian introspective rhetoric could encourage concrete sociopolitical activism. He was very quick to recognize the difference between genuine democratic discourse and pseudo-arguments or pass-time Sudoku-type brain activities. As in *Hind Swaraj* chapter 'Truth Force', he retorts:

> In this connection, academic questions such as whether a man may not lie in order to save a life, etc., arise, but these questions occur only to those who wish to justify lying.[17]

Of course, Gandhian dialectic is simple, but the ideas it imbues are not always so. His ideas are highly contextual, complex and often subtle. Gandhi was aware of it. For instance, for the language of *Hind Swaraj*, which was originally written in Gujarati, he acknowledged to its English readers constraints of language to convey the exact meanings and aspirations. He wrote in the preface of English version of *Hind Swaraj*:

> I am quite aware of the many imperfections in the original. The English rendering besides sharing these must naturally exaggerate them, owing to my inability to convey the exact meaning of the original…. Had I written for English readers in the first instance the subject would have been handled in a different manner.[18]

Interestingly, even his Gujarati-speaking colleagues often got confused over the exact meaning and intentions of the words used in it. For example, Gandhi, clarifying the meaning of 'civilization' used in the booklet, wrote:

> The Gujarati word generally used for 'Civilization' means 'a good way of life.' That is what I had meant to say. The sentence 'The

---

[17] CWMG-10, p. 53.
[18] CWMG, Vol. 10, *Indian Opinion*, 2 April 1910, pp. 188–90.

Gujarati equivalent for civilization is sudharo' is quite correct. But that is not what I intended to say.[19]

To make my point clearer, I refer to a Gandhi Seva Sangh meeting in 1937 in which Gandhi addressed many complex issues of radical politics within democratic domain and their relation with political discourse. The issue of contention was the content of the Manifesto of the Indian National Congress for contesting elections. Gandhi played a prominent role in drafting it. Hei took a decision that Gandhi Seva Sangh should engage with elections. It made uproar in the minds of hard-core Gandhians such as Kishorelal Mashruwala. They doubted that Gandhi had been reversing the previous line of outright rejection of Political Power. Gandhi found the real point of difficulty in the minds of workers. He realized that it was basically due to their inability to grasp the dynamic essence of Gandhian dialectic. He thoroughly explained the workers of the complex functioning of his political discourses and its democratic and multidimensional approach. A detailed quote will suffice the thinking mode of Gandhi, which, from hindsight, is very insightful also to understand the complex booklet like *Hind Swaraj*. He said:

All this is being said with reference to the manifesto of the Congress. How can we consider the language of the manifesto? The manifesto is not that of Jawaharlal alone. Vallabhbhai, Rajendra Babu and I have our share in it. I have not forgotten it.... The practical part of that resolution has been drafted by me.... He (Jawaharlal) interprets the manifesto in one way, I in another. I see nothing wrong in it. The language is open to two different interpretations; of this there is no doubt. But a satyagrahi can use language which may be interpreted in two different ways. Truth, as I know it, does not demand that the words a satyagrahi utters should have only one meaning. What he says may have not two but several different meanings. The condition merely is that the meaning should not be hidden; words should not be used for

---

[19] CWMG, Vol. 11, Letter to Jamnadas Gandhi, 28 August 1911, pp. 153–54.

deception and should be necessary [to convey the meaning]. The intention in using the language should not be to hide truth. When we frankly speak a language admitting two interpretations, we are not giving up truth. Sometimes it also happens that we intend only one meaning but those who hear us read two meanings in what we say. Here also truth is not violated.... The language of the servant of truth does not always yield only one meaning.... Last evening the language used was different but that is the way with language. Language acquires lucidity in the course of work. There is no doubt that harmony of thought, word and deed is the sign of truth. But ideas advance and language is left behind. I wondered why I was not able to convince Kishorelal. My language was vague. I listened to the discussion and my ideas became clear. But the language did not become clear. When I meditate after giving thought to a matter my language becomes clearer and clearer each day.... I speak the language of the Jains. They say that the rule should admit of no exception. This is also the language of geometry.... If what I have said has not satisfied you entirely, the reason can only be that I have not been able to couch my language in legalistic phraseology. But it is clearer than day before yesterday. My language is imperfect. The language of one who is himself imperfect must be imperfect, too. If after 17 years of explaining I have not been able to explain myself, then I am imperfect and so are you who cannot understand....[20]

As I have argued in this chapter, *Hind Swaraj* was not written by Gandhi as an independent philosophic text. Its vantage points are the concrete context of political understanding about India of those times. Gandhi was, by instinct, a very argumentative, compassionate and open-minded person. His main method of convincing people over his politics was through open heart–to–heart

---

[20] CWMG, Vol. 65, Speech at Gandhi Seva Sangh Meeting, Hudli III, 20 April 1937, pp. 118–34. My point is that if Gandhi's utterances, in this case *Hind Swaraj*, are read and used with a naïve approach of puritanical literary mindset, its contents might easily be distorted to praising Gandhi: Gandhi as a supra-human who is against the Modern Civilization in its totality and whose destruction is his long cherished secret mission. In our view, this understanding of *Hind Swaraj* and Gandhi is not historically appropriate or academically legitimate.

discussions and dialogues. Even for his political opponents, Gandhi used similar devices to change their hostile mindsets.

Of course, Gandhi's sojourn in England in 1909 played a crucial role in writing *Hind Swaraj*. Namely, the murder of Curzon Willie and his intense interaction with many proponents of violent methods in politics and other revolutionaries provided Gandhi stimulation to systematically reply to the larger issues. In fact, during South Africa struggle, Gandhi sensed the crucial importance of organized political activities, systematic political moves; complex question of mobilization of masses and the need of enhancing their fighting spirits; influence formation techniques; spreading self-awareness; role of sacrifice in weaving social fabric through various activities, and so on. All these worries find an echo in *Hind Swaraj*.

Thus, these above factors and the final push of England sojourn culminated in *Hind Swaraj*.

As I have said, Gandhi met and interacted with various persons of other ideological orientations. Most importantly, apart from British officials and British Parliament members, it included 'Expatriate Indians' living there.[21] Before analysing this factor, it is necessary to reflect over Gandhi's take on modernity-related issues.

Gandhi was a great political strategist, and his dialectic also had to be strategic. He did not use the word 'modernity' to address the realities of contemporary modern world. Rather, he preferred the notions of modern civilization to analyse the harsh

---

[21] With hindsight, it is befitting to write about Gandhi's testimony of writing *Hind Swaraj*, which he gave in 1940. It helps to contextualize *Hind Swaraj* in democratic-argumentative mode. He said, 'You may not perhaps be knowing for whom I wrote Hind Swaraj. The person is no more and hence there is no harm in disclosing his name. I wrote the entire Hind Swaraj for my dear friend Dr Pranjivan Mehta. All the argument in the book is reproduced almost as it took place with him.' CWMG, Vol. 71, Gandhi Seva Sangh Ke Chhate Adhiveshan Ka Vivran, Malikanda, 21 February 1940, p. 238.

facts which colonial people of India were facing. It is important to note that during his South African struggle, Gandhi experienced many faces of imperialism. He also sensed the duality of innocent-looking imperialist notions and harsh real practices. He also saw the real face of the pro-pounders of the theory of modernization. This all forced him to reassess and critically examine the so-called nations of modern civilization. He tried to evaluate and examine main apparatuses of imperialism through which it got the hegemonic sanction of ruling over the minds and psyche of subjugated masses. While talking of modern civilization, he focused on its negative aspects and he often made it synonymous with Western civilization. In 1929, he wrote to highlight its negative features,

> As for the Empire, wherever I turn I see lies, fraud, arrogance, tyranny, drunkenness, gambling, lechery, plunder by day and by night and Dyerism. All are sacrificed at its altar. Its benefits are only apparent. It lives for its trade, it will die in trying to safeguard it. None should misconstrue these strong words. The Western civilization which passes for civilization is disgusting to me. I have given a rough picture of it in *Hind Swaraj*. Time has brought no change in it. It is not my purpose even to imply that everything Western is bad. I have learnt a lot from the West. There are a number of pure and holy men there. I have many friends in the West. But what the Westerners worship under the name of civilization is a golden vessel. I find that the questioner and others have been dazzled by its glitter.[22]

Gandhi had been convinced until when the chief driving force of Western societies is imperialistic and its agenda purpose for colonized people is to exploit the wealth and other resources from colonial land for the benefit of the West. His emphasizing in the negative features of modern civilization has this concrete context. He was aware of the fact that many Indian expatriates and other intellectuals and political persons were in the hypnotic grip of all-pervading Westernized wisdom and its offshoots, which were not good for the welfare of humanity in general and for India in particular. London at that time was a great centre of

---

[22] CWMG, *The Suzerain and Vasslas, Navajivan*, 28 April 1929, p. 300.

that type of thinking. Most of the expatriates (who, in present vocabulary, may be called Diaspora intellectuals or NRIs) were patriots in spirit, but their patriotism was constrained and limited due to their wrong political understandings. Two points need to be stated here:

1. At that time, the revolutionary activities were meant only as individualistic violent activities. Expatriate Indians were the votaries and supporter of individual violence-centred political action who often indulged themselves in sensational, individualistic, sentimental and opportunistic ways of thought. Tacit sentimental support and high praises for individual violence were there among expatriate Indians. Gandhi found it funny that these types of patriots desired to extinguish British people from India through individual violent acts but they had no sincere objections for the very exploitative structures established by same British government. Gandhi felt it was like that we want British rule minus British people. Gandhi found a fundamental fault and double speaking in this type of thinking. He also sensed that they eluded the crucial importance of 'introspection based thinking' and tried to hide their cowardly passivity through high-sounding emotive words.

2. Expatriate Indians' thinking was dominated by the so-called modernist achievements of the West, and it prevented them to think independently and originally on the core issues of the day. Their contradiction was that they hated British officials in individualistic sense but loved the system designed by same British officials. They also did not understand the real nature of colonialism. They wanted to copy the West without using the discriminatory faculty.

Gandhi himself was a historic product of modern times, and he had acquired his knowledge of contemporary society and its peculiarities within the parameters of modern political consciousness. The suggested reading list given in *Hind Swaraj* is an ample proof of Gandhi's concerns about India and the world. If we go through his writings and life work, we may easily find out the essential modern vantage points in his comprehensive ideology. He was basically a revolutionary political leader in the domain of democratic consciousness who took it his historic duty to ideologically explore the imperialistic realities for a colonized nation. The very tools of colonialism were the Pax-Britannica drives which often got the legitimacy from modernity-based currents. Gandhi understood this complex phenomenon that, on the one hand, India was to be modernized in real sense, on the other, it could not afford to be plundered by imperialistic structures for the sake of modernization because that modernization would culminate and strengthen only the colonialization of Indian society. So like any vigilant leader, he made a distinction between positive historical renaissance-inspired features of modern political consciousness and the negative imperialistic tendencies of exploitation of subjugated nations by the proponents of Western civilization. So he made a critique of modern civilization without accepting or rejecting it outright. In a way, he was for the original derivation of modernity keeping in view Indian conditions and interests.

Thus, Gandhi's criticism of modern civilization, which he makes synonymous with Westernized notions, has a concrete colonial context. He was an avid book reader and keen observer. As pointed out, through scholarly studies and acute observations, he had convinced himself that India was witnessing a unique case of colonial exploitation in the name of modernization of India. Colonialism in India had created a massive and definite colonial structure which was being used to exploit and emasculate the real strength of India. Whenever he found an occasion to analyse the cultural and other tools of colonialism, he strongly criticized those apparatuses of it that were the main weapons for gaining hegemony over the Indian mind.[23]

---

[23] But it should be kept in mind that he did not reject its positive features in anyway and in fact cherished the hope of inculcating those modern values which were of universal mankind.

The real reason for Gandhi's adherence to *Hind Swaraj* lies in the fact that he, over time, used it to emphasize the crucial need of decolonization of Indian society and structure. Similarly, his take on the decolonization drive was not anti-modern in all respects. In fact, it was anti-modern as far as the issues of imperialism and its offshoots were concerned. As I have argued that the basic premise of Gandhi's consciousness was modern, *Hind Swaraj* has some deep connotations with his sense of modern consciousness. Here, modern consciousness should not be mixed up with Westernized capitalism mode consciousness. For Gandhi, the main features of modern consciousness lie in the domain of mass-based political consciousness and Modern Democratic Politics.

Now, a brief (inevitably selective) analytical paraphrasing of *Hind Swaraj* is being attempted to highlight its Indian modern consciousness. *Hind Swaraj* starts with the appreciation of the Indian National Congress and its leaders.[24] In it, Gandhi fully grasps the historic value of Nationalism and Congress's historic role in propagating it.[25] Gandhi emphasized that the role of ideology and ideological struggle was the key factor in this direction.[26]

---

[24] The questioner asks about the construction of desire for Home Rule. Gandhi replied 'That desire gave rise to the National Congress.' CWMG, Vol. 10, 'Hind Swaraj', 'The Congress and its officials', p. 8.

[25] The questioner posed the doubt that he does not understand how the Congress laid the foundation of Home Rule. Gandhi explains him, 'Let us see. The Congress brought together Indians from different parts of India, and enthused us with the idea of nationality. The Government used to look upon it with disfavour.' Ibid., p. 11.

In the reply, he adds, in the end, 'To treat the Congress as an institution inimical to our growth as a nation would disable us from using that body.' Ibid.

In this way, Gandhi linked the choice of nationalism, indispensability of the Indian National Congress and desire of Home Rule in one fabric.

[26] The questioner says that the Congress is considered an instrument for perpetuating British rule. Gandhi repudiates this charge and argues, 'Had not the Grand Old Man of India prepared the soil, our young men could not have even spoken about Home Rule.' Ibid., p. 8. He also refers the writings and deeds of A.O. Hume, Willium Wedderburn, Gopal Krishna Gokhale, Justice Budruddin Tyebji in this regard. See, ibid., pp. 8–9.

He also understood the long-term strategic perspective in finding the Home Rule imperative.[27] Rejection of tradition and arrogance of 'starting a new thing' was repugnant to him.[28]

From it, we can say that Gandhi, in his early political career, recognized the historic role of Congress in propagating anti-colonial instincts. He also fully grasped the enduring importance of concrete analysis by Early Nationalist Scholars and the Nationalist Political Leaders. Apart from that, he also understood the real tenets of foundation of nationalism in India. He did not fall in the trap of 'eternity' logic in recognizing nationalism

---

[27] When the questioner shows sign of impatience about Gandhi's appreciation of early Congress leaders, Gandhi bluntly rebukes him in strong words, 'You are impatient. I cannot afford to be likewise.... Remember the old proverb that tree does not grow in one day. The fact that you have checked me and that you do not want to hear about the well wishers of India.... If we had many like you, we would never make any advance.' Ibid., p. 9. Further, he emphasizes, 'The seed is never seen. It works underneath the ground, is itself destroyed, and the tree which rises above the ground is alone seen. Such is the case with the Congress'. Ibid., 'Partition of Bengal', p. 12. He tries to convince the questioner about nationalism and nation, by saying, 'Nations are not formed in a day; the formation requires years.' Ibid., p. 12.

[28] The questioner shows disrespect for Naoroji whom Gandhi considered the best-suited person to be called the 'Father of the Nation'. He did some plain speaking to correct the questioner by saying, 'I must tell you, with all gentleness, that it must be a matter of shame for us that you should speak about that great man in terms of this respect. Just look at his work. He has dedicated his life to the service of India. We have learnt what we know from him. It was the respected Dadabhai who taught us that the English had sucked our life-blood.... Is Dadabhai less to be honoured because, in our exuberance of youth, we are prepared to go a step further? Are we, on that account, wiser than he? It is a mark of wisdom not to pick away the very step from which we have risen higher. The removal of a step from a staircase brings down the whole of it. When, out of infancy, we grow in to youth, we do not despise infancy, but, on the contrary, we recall with affection the days of our childhood. If after many years of study, a teacher were to teach me something, and if I were to build a little more on the foundation laid by that teacher, I would not, on that account, be considered wiser than the teacher. He would always command my respect. Such is the case with the Grand Old Man of India. We must admit that he is the author of Nationalism'. Ibid., pp. 9–10.

and nation in India.[29] In this respect, two points are of crucial importance.

First, Gandhi never adhered to the view that practice of different religions in India was anyway a hindrance to the healthy growth of nationalism in India. He thoroughly argued in *Hind Swaraj* the non-religious secular character of nation formation in India. For example, he replied to the questioner about it with precision, when the questioner showed signs of Hindu identity of nationalism in India and blamed Muslim religion practitioners for unmaking the nation, Gandhi replied him in clearest terms which reflect his deep understanding of Indian secularism. He retorted:

India cannot cease to be one nation because people belonging to different religions live in it.... In reality, there are as many religions as there are individuals; but those who are conscious of the spirit of the nationality do not interfere with one another's religion. If they do, they are not fit to be considered a nation.[30]

Second, Gandhi argued that the basic tenets of nationalism have to be drawn by concrete Indian conditions and contexts. Western notions of nationalism are not to be copied for narrating Indian Nationalism. He writes, in *Hind Swaraj*:

All countries are not similarly conditioned. The condition of India is unique. Its strength is immeasurable. We need not, therefore, refer to the history of other countries.... It is well that you have instanced Italy. Mazzini was a great and good man; Garibaldi was a great warrior. Both are adorable; from their lives we can learn much. But the condition of Italy was different from that of India.[31]

Gandhi did not differentiate between India and Italy on any jingoistic grounds. He further narrated the nature of difference

---

[29] In this regard, Gandhi differs from cultural revivalism and their theoreticians of Hindu nation or Muslim nation and so on.

[30] Ibid., 'The Condition of India (Continued): The Hindus and the Mahomedans', p. 29.

[31] Ibid., 'How Can India' Become Free' and 'Italy and India', p. 40. (For continuation of my argument, I have used citations from both chapters.)

between these two countries on peculiarity of the situation, which had to be different for both countries. So any copious comparison be only a false anomaly. He writes:

> Again, India can fight like Italy only when she has arms. You have not considered this problem at all. The English are splendidly armed; that does not frighten me, but it is clear that, to pit ourselves against them in arms, thousands of Indians must be armed. If such a thing be possible, how many years will it take? Moreover, to arm India on a large scale is to Europeanize.... This means, in short, that India must accept European civilization, and if that is what we want, the best thing is that we have among us those who are so well trained in that civilization. We will then fight for a few rights, will get what we can and so pass our days.[32]

Hind Swaraj is a strong case of argument for 'mass-empowerment through democratic means'. Gandhi's concrete understanding of mass-consciousness is intricately related with this objective of social change, because without it any attempt to mass-empowerment might be derailed.[33] For a constructive organic politics, all these aspects have to be properly understood in formulating a viable political line. While arguing with the questioner over the issue of best-suited politics in India, Gandhi based his arguments on the above-mentioned method of deriving a workable political understanding.

Gandhi, in *Hind Swaraj* and in other writings also, treats mass-consciousness as tantamount to Soul Force or Truth Force. Gandhi's specific emphasis on this aspect is basically his emphasis on modern consciousness of the masses. He was a great believer in the capacity of man to struggle and survive even after oddest circumstances. Conservation of self-respect was, according to Gandhi, an indispensable necessity. Refusal to follow anything against conscience was a motto in Gandhi's own

---

[32] Ibid., pp. 41–42.

[33] Even in 1909, at the time of writing the booklet, Gandhi was aware of the dangers of massization of politics. About too much discontent, he concludes his argument by saying, 'All these may be considered good signs but they may also lead to bad results', ibid., 'Discontent and Unrest', p. 14.

life, and throughout his political career, he propagated it with a revolutionary zeal. To feel the interconnectivity of self-respect, mass-consciousness and soul force, two of his quotes are worth noting:

> When I refuse to do a thing that is repugnant to my conscience, I use soul force.[34]

Again he said:

> It is contrary to our manhood if we obey laws repugnant to our conscience.... A man who has realized its manhood, who fears only god, will fear no one else. Man-made laws are not necessarily binding on him.... If man only realizes that it is unmanly to obey laws that are unjust, no man's tyranny enslave him. This is the key to self-rule or home-rule.[35]

It is important to note that Gandhi's notions of mass-consciousness are not for blind eulogy of everything that masses might feel or understand. He was aware of the historic fact that mass-consciousness may or may not be correct at a particular time. Many times it needs to be ameliorated or transformed through constructive interventions of democratic leadership. In the booklet, he frankly says:

> To a certain extent the people's will has to be expressed; certain sentiments will need to be fostered, and defects will have to be brought to light.[36]

Mass-consciousness has to be understood in terms of the historical process. As for the state of mass-consciousness in modern India, he writes:

> When a man rises from sleep, he twists his limb and is restless. It takes some time before he is entirely awakened.... We are still twisting our limbs and are still restless, and just as the state

---

[34] Ibid., 'Passive Resistance', p. 48.
[35] Ibid., p. 49.
[36] Ibid., 'The Congress and Its Officials', p. 8.

between sleep and awakening must be considered to be necessary,
so may the present unrest in India be considered a necessary and
therefore a proper state.[37]

Gandhi considered discontent as a necessary raw ingredient for
further mass action for social change. He wrote in the booklet:

> The knowledge that there is unrest will, it is highly probable,
> enable us to outgrow it.... Mr Hume always said that the spread
> of this content in India was necessary. This discontent is a very
> useful thing. As long as a man is contented with his present lot, so
> long is it difficult to persuade him to come out of it. Therefore it
> is that every reform must be preceded by discontent. We through
> away things we have, only when we cease to like them. Such
> discontent has been produced among us after reading the great
> works of Indian and English men.[38]

The above quote also throws a very significant aspect of Gandhi's
thinking. He believed in well-informed ideological struggles by
using the works of the distinguished scholars. It was the academic
method he adopted in *Hind Swaraj*.

Hind Swaraj also points out one very distinct feature of
Gandhi's modern political mind. That is the 'exact timing' of a
movement and 'readiness of masses to struggle for the cause'. He
recognized the historic significance of Partition of Bengal as an
accurate indicator of starting of a mass movement phase of the
Indian National Movement. He wrote:

> This does not mean that the other injustices done to India are
> less glaring than that done by the Partition. The salt tax is not
> a small injustice. We shall see many such things later on. But
> the people were ready to resist the Partition. At that time feeling
> ran high.[39]

---

[37] Ibid., 'This Content and Unrest', p. 13.
[38] Ibid., pp. 13–14.
[39] Ibid., 'The Partition of Bengal', p. 12.

'Installation of fearless attitude' in mass-consciousness is another point in Gandhian politics, and it is fairly reflected in *Hind Swaraj*. With reference to the outcome of the Partition of Bengal Movement and its after-effects as in change in mass psyche, he wrote:

> Hitherto we have considered that for redress of grievances we must approach the thrown, and if we get no redress we must sit still, except that we may still petition. After the partition, people saw that petitions must be backed up by force, and that they must be capable of suffering. This new spirit must be considered to be the chief result of the Partition. That spirit was seen in the outspoken writings in the Press. That which the people said tremblingly and in secret began to be said and to be written publicly. The Swadeshi movement was inaugurated. People, young and old, used to run away at the sight of an English face; it no longer awes them. They do not fear even a row, or being imprisoned.[40]

In fact, *Hind Swaraj* is a strong argument in favour of complete decolonization of Indian society and culture. British rule in India had done some foundational work, which also formed the core of Pax-Britannica syndrome. These, in main, were judiciary,

---

[40] Ibid., pp. 12–13. (At another instance, he emphasized that 'strength lies in absence of fear, not in the quantity of flesh and muscle we may have on our bodies.' Ibid., 'The Condition of India', p. 25.) (In the last chapter of *Hind Swaraj*, Gandhi argued of the necessity of speaking fearlessly to the British by saying, 'We cannot tolerate the idea of your spending money on railways and the military. We have no occasion for either. You may fear Russia; we do not.... We do not need any European clothes. We shall manage with article produced and manufactured at home. You may not keep one eye on Manchester and the other on India. We can work together only if our interests are identical. This has not been said to you in arrogance. You have great military resources. Your naval power is matchless if we wanted to fight with you on your own ground, we should be unable to do so, but if the above submissions be not acceptable to you, we cease to play the part of the ruled. You may, if you like, cut us to pieces. You may shatter us at the cannon's mouth. If you act contrary to our will, we shall not help you; and without our help, we know that you cannot move one step forward.' Ibid., pp. 61–62.)

Westernized machinery-based Industrialization and penetration of capitalism. All these and other administrative set-ups were the chief tools of consolidation of colonialism and imperialism. Gandhi challenged these notions in *Hind Swaraj* in his typical dialectic.

I have argued in the context of Gandhian dialectic, Gandhi's style of taking extreme ideological positions in ideological struggles. In the booklet, there are certain signs of 'taking extreme positions'. But we should also keep in mind that it was written in a dialogue form, and for that reason it is highly contextual and has a desire to correct the questioner's attitude. As argued, *Hind Swaraj* is not a political programme or political action chart; so Gandhi's writings of *Hind Swaraj* can only be taken in a reflective mode as a keen desire to install the basic point of decolonization.

Gandhi connoted all the negative tendencies of British rule with the modern civilization. After all, India was witnessing the colonization in the name of modernization. Expatriate Indians often missed this very crucial point and deluded themselves in the lures of Westernized modernity. The questioner in the booklet is a specimen of this type of thinking. He is influenced by liberal thinkers like Mill and Spencer and says:

> ...if the works of Spencer and others be of any importance, and if the English Parliament be the mother of Parliaments, I certainly think that we should copy the English people.... It is, therefore, proper for us to import these institutions.[41]

Gandhi rebuked the questioner severely on his this remark. Gandhi criticized British Parliament in harshest terms. In fact, it is the context of the questioner's lack of understanding of colonialism and imperialism that provoked Gandhi to challenge his adored attitude for British Parliament. The questioner's anxiety to copy Western institutions per se without seeing any need of discrimination was the concrete context of Gandhi's criticism of

---

[41] Ibid., 'What Is Swaraj', pp. 15–16.

British Parliament. He argued that British Parliament needed to be examined more closely.[42] He said that it is assumed that, 'The best men are supposed to be elected by the people.'[43] But 'as a matter of fact, it is generally acknowledged that the members are hypocritical and selfish', and 'When the greatest questions are debated, its members have been seen to stress themselves and to doze'.[44] He referred to famous thinker Carlyle by saying:

> Carlyle has called it the 'talking shop of the World.' Members vote for their party without a thought. Their so-called discipline binds them to it. If any member, by way of exception, gives an independent vote, he is considered a renegade.... Parliament is simply a costly toy of the nation. These views are by no means peculiar to me. Some great English thinkers have expressed them.[45]

It is important to note that Gandhi's criticism of British Parliament would be a natural choice for an Indian nationalist who had been experiencing the colonial and imperialist colours of British Parliament which had identical interests among Britishers and had a deep-rooted contradiction with Indian interests. Moreover, Gandhi's remarks are also the remarks of a revolutionary mass leader whose ultimate vantage points and ideology are of constructive mass-empowerment and social transformation drives irrespective of petty constitutionalism. However, Gandhi advocated the parliamentary system of democracy in India, which I have mentioned earlier.

---

[42] Gandhi's arguments of criticism of British Parliament should not be taken as his rejection of the parliamentary system as such. Gandhi was a great supporter of parliamentarian democracy. His politics and mass movements in India are ample proof of this. Since the questioner in *Hind Swaraj* portrays British Parliament in blind-faith terms, Gandhi as a vigilant mass leader could feel the possible political outcome of this mode of thinking. It would culminate in either to be a passive constitutionalist or to be a supporter of British rule in India.

[43] Ibid., 'The Condition of England', p. 15.

[44] Ibid., p. 17.

[45] Ibid., p. 17.

The main theme of argument in *Hind Swaraj* is that India needs a change of colonial structure; only change of individuals from one post to another will not bring any change in the fortunes of Indian people. The questioner in *Hind Swaraj* is greatly influenced by the achievements of the West and cherishes the hope that India will also become such one day. Replying to him, Gandhi said:

> You have drawn the picture well. In effect it means this: That we want English Rule without the English Man. You want a tiger's nature, but not the tiger; that is to say, you would make India English.[46]

Gandhi's blunt critique of the Westernized model of modern civilization is also due to the fact that in their self-righteous arrogance combined with imperialistic motivations, their proponents inherently lacked the desire for any self-introspection. He said in this regard:

> We rarely find people arguing against themselves. Those who are intoxicated by modern civilization are not likely to write against it. Their care will be to find out facts and arguments in support of it, and this they do unconsciously, believing it to be true.... Their writings hypnotize us. And so, one by one we are drawn into the vortex.[47]

Gandhi criticized the very nature of Western modernity, which he found deeply drowned in pleasure mode hypocrite life styles and making bodily sensual pleasures as their aim of life. For an instance, he referred to excessive fashion mode clothing as an accepted notion of being civilized.[48]

---

[46] Ibid., 'What Is Swaraj', p. 15.

[47] Ibid., 'Civilization', p. 19.

[48] He said, 'If people of a certain country, who have hitherto not been in the habit of wearing much clothing, boots, etc., adopt European clothing, they are supposed to have become civilized out of savagery.' Gandhi had a knack for naturalness and common sense in all aspects of life. He was by instinct a great rationalist who rarely accepted things without using discriminatory skills. It was also his endeavour to decolonize the culture of colonized.

In the end, I would refer to a very interesting interaction between Gandhi and Jawaharlal Nehru in the context of the essence of modern consciousness in *Hind Swaraj*.[49] While dealing with Nehru's criticism, Gandhi often used to say that their languages were different, but their essence was almost the same. The difference was only apparently so and it was only due to emphasis. Since Nehruvian dialect is less complex and more modern to comprehend for 'university education trained modern intelligentsia', Gandhian dialectic, as I have argued, is somewhat of different genre. So a detailed narration of their correspondence about *Hind Swaraj* is quite interesting to understand Gandhi's mind regarding the message of the booklet and their dynamic evolution of it.

In 1933, Nehru met Gandhi at Poona. There, both had a long conversation over political and other issues. They exchanged letters, which were published later as the Poona statements in September 1933. Tendulkar writes that 'the central idea running through their letter was the economic programme of the Congress, particularly as expressed in the enunciation of the Fundamental Rights at the Karachi Congress, should be stressed'. In it, Gandhi observed:

> I have no doubt that our goal can be no less than Complete Independence. I am also in the whole agreement with you, when you say that without a material revision of the vested interests the condition of the masses can never be improved.[50]

Nehru insisted Gandhi to define clearly his political objective. In reply, Gandhi wrote that, 'that once having fixed the goal, he was not interested in its repetition, but only in devising the means of its progressive realization. That goal was set forth in

---

[49] It needs to be emphasized here that Nehru was Gandhi's chosen political heir.

[50] Tendulkar, D. G. *Life of Mohandas Karamchand Gandhi*, Vol. 3, p. 216. New Delhi: Publication Division, 1992.

his *Hind Swaraj*, as an exploitation-free society in which the supreme instrument of defending just rights lay within the grasp of the common unarmed individual.'[51]

On another occasion, in 1945, a discussion occurred in the high leadership of Congress and in it Gandhi and Nehru took their shares. They both started discussion and correspondence. In it, Gandhi referred to *Hind Swaraj* saying:

> I have not Hind Swaraj before me as I write. It is really better for me to draw the picture a new in my own words. And whether it is the same as I drew in Hind Swaraj or not is immaterial for both you and me. It is not necessary to prove the rightness of what I said then. It is essential only to know what I feel today.[52]

In that letter, Gandhi elaborated his ideas about Swaraj and referred to his notions with it. Nehru, in reply, rejected *Hind Swaraj*, saying it is very old and unreal and elaborated his views for the future Cause about Independent India.[53] Gandhi did not mind his condemning of *Hind Swaraj* and endorsed Nehru's ideas in his typical manner. Very quickly, he recognized the similarity of objectives between *Hind Swaraj* and Nehru's vision for future India. He wrote:

> The impression that I have gathered from on yesterdays' talk is that there is not much difference in our outlook. To test this I put down below the gist of what I have understood. Please correct me if there is any discrepancy.

---

[51] Ibid., 216. Here Gandhi emphasized the centrality of mass empowerment imperative in *Hind Swaraj*. In fact, he found it an ideological device to promote mass empowerment objective.

[52] Jawaharlal Nehru (ed.). 'A Bunch of Old Letters', 5 October 1945, pp. 509–511. Penguin Books: New Delhi, 2005.

[53] Ibid., 9 October 1945, pp. 511–14.

(1) The real question, according to you, is how to bring about man's highest intellectual, economic, political and moral development. I agree entirely.

(2) In this there should be an equal right and opportunity for all.

(3) In other words, there should be equality between the town-dwellers and the villagers in the standard of food and drink, clothing and other living conditions. In order to achieve this equality today people should be able to produce for themselves the necessaries of life, that is, clothing, food-stuffs, dwelling and lighting and water.

(4) Man is not born to live in isolation but is essentially a social animal independent and interdependent. No one can or should ride on another's back. If we try to work out the necessary conditions for such a life, we are forced to the conclusion that the unit of society should be a village, or call it a small and manageable group of people who would, in the ideal, be self-sufficient (in the matter of their vital requirements) as a unit and bound together in bonds of mutual co-operation and inter-dependence.[54]

The gist of this historical correspondence is that Gandhi was ever receptive to a modern constructive interpretation of his utterances. In fact, in what was he against modern intellectuality was intellectual dissipation or modernity infatuated capitalist temptations and imperialistic liberal model of 'pleasure mode thinking'. His lifelong love for *Hind Swaraj* was due to its pro-poor orientation, anti-imperialist, anti-colonial essence, mass-based organized democratic politics, secularism and the all-inclusive nationalistic orientations. After all, by *Hind Swaraj* he had succeeded in winning over the mind of a person who was till now a supporter of individualistic violent politics. Throughout his life, Gandhi struggled to remind the political class 'what is real and

---

[54] Ibid., 515. In fact, Gandhi's ideal village vision has nothing to do with the medievalist type of village system or any agrarianism-centred politics. It is, in fact, a vision for the horizontal development of India with least discrimination and exploitation for a majority of the inhabitants of the land.

what is transitory in this highly complex World'. The booklet was an attempt in that life quest. The basis of his adherence to *Hind Swaraj* lies in this context of above narrated Indian modern consciousness. It was the reason for Gandhi's consistent effort to defend the intent of the booklet despite so many strategic deficiencies in it.

3

Confession as Public Communication
Reflections on Gandhi's The Story of My Experiments with Truth

Ratnakar Tripathy

Between Fatherhood and Sonhood: The Urgencies of Communication

This chapter has been distilled from three separate readings of Gandhi's autobiography done at different stages of my life. Understandably, the three readings involved differing degrees of passive reception and active interpretation of the text in the larger backdrop of Gandhi's personal and public life. My latest reading of Gandhi's autobiography is informed by the wider traffic of ideas and themes from other external events and sources, specifically the Lokpal movement led by Anna Hazare and the practice of janata durbar by Nitish Kumar during 2010–2013, the chief minister (CM) of Bihar since 2010. The two episodes from recent Indian history have, however, not been analysed as full-blown case studies on their own. They have instead been selectively used for the purpose of illustrating what I believe to represent the Gandhian strain of thinking in the broader context of modern Indian political thought. In my reading, the Gandhian philosophical disposition reflected in his autobiography raises some fundamental questions over the extant communication processes and the functioning of modern democratic systems. These questions help us contextualize some of the seminal failings of democracy, as we have known it, requiring new remedies and institutional innovations a democracy in its present form may not be able to provide. Readings of Gandhi, I believe, enable us to explore those uneven and tortuous topographies of modern democracy in an era when the core problems of democracy and its characteristic procedures seem insurmountable globally. This chapter is thus more about the Gandhian philosophical urges and search for a just society and a more meaningful democracy rather than the glaringly sparse solutions, if any, offered by Gandhian thought in a direct sense.

My earlier readings of *My Experiments* ... are based on unstinted, though episodic, recall, that may, of course, be tainted by my current stances, but my earlier reactions to Gandhi's autobiography have been made easier to cull out thanks to the hermeneutic nudges and steering provided by the present. I am not sure I would have remembered them with the same clarity or intensity without the secure perch of my present concerns. My present concerns are centred, of course, around the idea of democracy and the style and substance of communication it seems to require in our time. This chapter has a certain circularity in that after all my philosophical, conceptual and narrative detours I shall keep coming back to the question of Gandhi's insights and their relation to democracy in our own time.

Let me begin right away with the admission that reading *My Experiments...*[1] can be a very overwhelming experience and a

---

[1] The few verbatim quotes used in the chapter have been taken from the volume Gandhi, M. K. *The Story of My Experiments with Truth*. New Delhi: Prakash Books, 2010. My memory of the editions read earlier is not

task that places perhaps an unduly heavy responsibility on the most casual reader. It is a responsibility that a younger reader with slighter shoulders may even refuse to accept! As I read the autobiography recently for the third time in my life, I felt I was being addressed by Gandhi in two contrasting capacities and roles—first incredibly as a father, a priest or a higher authority across a mesh who must patiently listen to a series of confessions from half a lifetime. This is somewhat akin to what Gandhi once did to his father in his childhood. After a series of petty thefts, Gandhi could bear the guilt no longer and, unable to speak up, went to his father with a written note of confession. Gandhi says in his autobiography that the ailing father did not say a word and just wept copiously. What may have gone back and forth between the father and the son with a great deal of intensity is anyone's guess with no words spoken. Instead, the incident was deleted out of the database of memory or the forever accumulating and ever-crowding stack of human *karma*! Isn't it ironic that a would-be father of a nation should approach his reader in the capacity of a child laying down his life story in the manner of both a submission and an appeal? The solicitous tone may not perhaps run continuously throughout the book, but time and again it flatters the reader into believing that he has been placed in a lofty position from where he must judge the thoughts and deeds of a confessor of the most ordinary sort.

If such a condescending approach to Gandhi's autobiography could be maintained consistently, there was no need to feel overwhelmed. There is a contrary and inescapable perception however, which I must now discuss. Reading the book, I also felt like a common member of the vast sea of humanity, listening to another fellow being, albeit a senior father-like figure, deliver a murmuring discourse on the most mundane of human affairs ranging from diet, hygiene, sexual jealousy, adolescent rebellion, shyness of temperament, use of tobacco to tasting of the forbidden mutton! After the confessional mode of address, the message

---

very clear or definite. Since the essay does not indulge in a dense exegetic exercise over the text, the matter of editions does not seem very vital to me.

now seems to be rather trivial—as human beings, let us just keep talking of the simplest of things over time and see what comes of it. Even when you itemize all the significant matters brought up in the autobiography, you will find it near impossible to arrange them in a hierarchic order of importance where the author and the reader seem to concur. So suddenly, the tone and the feel of Gandhi's natter change, and I am made to realize that now it is actually my father talking to his son, letting him choose his own priorities and preferences! This can be very disarming for an oedipal impulse if you carry one. Oedipal or non-oedipal, there are things that you do not want your father to tell you and have your worst fears come true!

Understandably, putting these two modes of communication and discrete channels together as an integral communicative event is a tough business and very distracting or even bewildering. Instead of focusing on the text, you end up gazing at your own ambivalent reactions to it. The question "what is Gandhi up to" seems to turn back on yourself and "what are you up to" becomes the relevant question. Namely, "what are you up to" listening to the life account of a man who in his very first public address in Pretoria, South Africa, most impudently started a discussion on standards of personal hygiene among the Indian community! He was supposed to address a vital issue on the agenda—the issue of dignity and self-respect among the Indians gathered in front of him. The very same crowd-shy Gandhi had repeatedly failed to read out his own prepared and rehearsed speeches in front of vegetarian societies in England some time ago. It requires a tremendous child-like innocence combined with the licence of unquestionable authority to make remarks of utterly personal nature. How and why could Gandhi get away with such impertinence! Isn't this an old fogy of a grandfather and an irrepressible infant packaged together into a unique composite persona? This is a question I have been asking for several decades since my adolescence into ripe adulthood, though not with the same clarity and focus. I will go back to my earlier readings through adolescence and late youth later on. But let me place my latest goods, or what I have, by way of an answer to the above question, right away as it occurs to me.

After having asked the above question long enough, and after all the giddy bewilderment caused by it, like the missing lines from an incomplete poem, the thought struck me that the central message of Gandhi's autobiography, with its Panini-like terseness may simply be—'let us talk', a platitude implemented in its fullness through a published volume of autobiography. Namely, there is indeed little that we human beings cannot or should not talk about or communicate about as part of public discourse! In a complete open-endedness of human conversation lies an ontology of communication that must be made explicit. Human conversations, though curtailed and punctuated by other activities, are essentially immortal or ever ending. They begin and end in certain contexts, of course, but their demise is not predetermined in the sense that no dialogue between two willing parties could ever reach a point of complete resolution or concurrence. An impasse, on the other hand, is quite likely, but most often we just have to get up and leave before a conversation can come to an end. To put it more rigorously, what should and what should not be said as part of public discourse cannot be determined beforehand and forms an integral part of the conversation itself. Unlike a human life, the birth of a conversation by no means presumes an end or a clear point of termination. Whether a story lies beyond the story told already, is a matter for an individual to decide in the light of his or her own life experiences and a felt urgency to express and communicate. If you interrupt the palaver and ask, what next, Gandhi would cheerfully say let us wait and watch for the actual outcome as we talk—this was just an experiment.

The claim I make here is not my own. Gandhi makes it in his own introduction to the book. The very purpose of the autobiography, according to Gandhi, was as follows:

> I hope and pray that no one will regard the advice interspersed in the following chapters as authoritative. The experiments narrated should be regarded as illustrations, in the light of which every one

may carry on his own experiments according to his own inclination and capacity.

Indeed, I am not sure how many of Gandhi's answers to questions I agree with. I am not even sure if I wish to, or am capable of, replicating the Gandhian experiments, by way of either scientific trial or just plain existential adventure. And yet, the questions raised by Gandhi are a wonderful mix of everything we have been dying to say and everything we compulsively avoid discussing in daily lives because of known and unknown fears or avoidable awkwardness in society or indeed due to the deep and lurking fear of one's own self. The reader of *My Experiments...* may thus react to its confessional mode with an empathy that may turn him/her into a Gandhian for the duration it takes to read the book, if nothing else. This disarming or complicit quality of the confessional work is corrected partly by the use of the word 'experiment'. 'Experiment' is a hard-edged and objective sounding word unlike its softer and sentimental variants such as 'life experience' or 'story' and so on that are associated with literary autobiographies, which when successful often make you fall irretrievably in love with the author on the very first page.

Gandhi's usage of the word 'experiment' is thus interesting in that he does not use the commoner word 'experience', but only the carefully selected highlights or 'experiments' from his stock of experience that he is compelled to share. The word 'experiment' is open to many interpretations of course, but I only wish to emphasize its two vital aspects here. First, the word 'experiment' may seem to carry a warning, an appeal not to react with total empathy and instead listen to the man with a sense of detachment, and in the process perhaps learn to distance oneself from one's own experiences. Second, the experimental language would also seem to convey a strong sense of conscious selection which turns his autobiography into a series of carefully and closely focused life accounts underlined in red. Free communication here does not mean idle babble or a general or indiscriminate exposure of one's life events, the reason being there is a sense of urgency attached to Gandhi's autobiographical outpourings. All his experiments are part of experience, but not all experiences may be called experiments. This is why Gandhi would seem to choose those life events that are to be brought into relief as the outstanding acts and experiences he wishes to share with great urgency. How urgent the need to communicate them may be becomes clear in the following passage:

'My experiments in the political fields are now known, not only to India, but to a certain extent to the "civilized" world. For me, they have not much value; and the title of 'mahatma' that they have won for me has, therefore even less.' It, thus, seems that this is an autobiography of a Gandhi who was not known widely. Clearly, according to Gandhi, his autobiography addresses matters undisclosed but also of utmost importance and urgency to him, even more so than his political work. Gandhi's near dismissal of his political work should not be taken literally, though. What he probably means is that the values at the core of his politics did not come from politics itself, and instead originated in the several other spheres of his life. Having thus stated and underlined the above premise and the urgency to communicate, Gandhi goes on to talk about his own bewilderments, confusions, traumas and even dead ends such as closure of intimate relationships with utmost candour. The great autonomy attributed to the realm and the category of 'politics' in the era of democracy would thus begin to seem baseless in a Gandhian universe. It would seem, instead, that politics, like many other realms of life, must seek its fundamental values from other aspects of life even when it acquires the status of a somewhat autonomous realm of praxis. This central issue of political philosophy in the era of democracy will crop up again in the following pages. To reiterate, are fundamental political values to be derived from several other fields of life or is politics an autonomous realm, either entirely watertight or somewhat porous with its own springs and sources of core values? In case the realm of democratic politics must generate and follow its own domain-specific values, do they or should they, in turn, make reverse inroads into other areas of human lives through a flowback, is another unavoidable question. These are questions and debates we cannot settle in a hurry, but a wilful neglect of such debates in public life is certainly a sure sign of decline in the communicative inclinations of a democratic system. Here we also have, according to me, a valid point of departure for further forays into the philosophical and operational aspects of modern democracy.

The Nation State as Society: A Politics of Communicative Inclusion

Significantly, even the chapter divisions in Gandhi's autobiography indicate a snapshot-like selection of life material—in the edition of 447 pages that I refer to, the five parts have above 160 snapshot-like sub-chapters or sections with separate titles indicating places, people and the general nature of the topics raised. It is thus indeed possible to claim that Gandhi discusses above 160 experiments from life in his modest-size life story. There is no point, however, in focusing on the quantitative aspect of the text, as if it was a logbook from a laboratory.

Being acutely aware of my own removedness from the Gandhian era, I will now quote from someone who grew up during the period—the well-known Hindi writer Harishankar Parsai (1924–1995). In his memoir *Hum ik Umra se Vaqif Hain*, he has a small chapter titled '*Gandhi ji rasoi ghar me*' (Gandhi in the kitchen), where one of the best-known satirists from Hindi literature affectionately says:

> Those days Gandhi was found not just on the meeting grounds. Gandhi's impact reached as far as the kitchen. Gandhi would intervene in all possible topics right from world of politics to the freedom movement and as far as the kitchen and the toilet. Women would say 'Gandhi Ji says we should lead simple lives, so we avoid fussing over our looks …', 'Gandhi likes cleanliness, so we pour buckets of water into the toilet every morning and evening'.[2]

---

[2] Parsai, Harishankar. *Hum ik Umra se Vaqif Hain*. New Delhi: Rajkamal Prakashan, 2018.

These somewhat comically exaggerated pictures tell us of an era (1920s) when the social divisions across caste, language, religion, community, colour and gender confined public discourse into tight compartments, allowing very little to escape into the wider social firmament. Gandhi's contribution lay in levelling up the public spaces as far as possible for a wider and freer public discourse—and he made a start with himself rather than offering to bare others or barging rebelliously through the countless social walls.

Before I go back to my own youthful readings of *My Experiments...*, allow me to make my unease with Gandhi a bit more explicit. I have always found Gandhi's communicative promiscuity, as I prefer to call it for the time being through the alarming coinage, both comical and jarring, but at times so sagely as to move one to tears. As I now slowly come to terms with it, let me illustrate this alleged promiscuity through a contemporary, if absurd, thought experiment. Suppose for a moment that a citizen of India sought an audience with the prime minister of the country. The prime minister's office (PMO) would ask him or her to state the purpose. What if the citizen replied that he has been very depressed of late and that he wishes to discuss it with the prime minister? Further, he says, lately he has also been afraid of darkness (a fear discussed more than once in *My Experiments...*), having to sleep in the full glare of lights and would like to hear what our PM has to say on such matters. The PMO will, in all likelihood, refuse to respond unless the eager citizen persists, which is when he will have government sleuths hovering in his neighbourhood to make inquiries about this disturbed little man's likely intent. The example is, of course, absurd in the extreme, but is it completely unimaginable even as a thought experiment? No, a perceptive student of political thought in the era of democracy and the nation state would instantly detect the conceptual slippage that explains its blatant absurdity—what the example does is to strip the modern nation state of India (which was yet to be formed independently) of its halo and treat it as society plain and simple. Not exactly a neighbourhood society, perhaps a society of enormous proportions with extremely high levels of anonymity. But a society nevertheless where the citizen member seems to have a minimal sense of context dependence for his communicative efforts! Family–friends–neighbourhood–college–workplace–village–town–country—all these are, after all, only instances of society, and however large they may be, they do not carry the stamp of the impersonal associated with the modern state. These numerous social contexts belong on a scale of acquaintance and anonymity in a deeply phenomenological sense as a graded scale of sociality. They carry with them different perspectives and measures of context dependence for every given magnitude of socialness.

If any talk, anytime, anywhere, with no sense of context dependence is how one might define communicative promiscuity, the above seems not a bad example. To go beyond hypothetical experiences and thought experiments however, let me now refer to an interesting political experiment that was carried out in the state of Bihar in India under the stewardship of the present CM Nitish Kumar soon after he came to power in 2010. I am referring to the unusual and unique practice of janata durbar, conceptualized as the government presenting itself at the informal court (durbar) of the people.[3] On a typical Monday, the scheduled day, Nitish Kumar would make early morning chirrups to the press as a statesman ought to do about Bihar being granted special status by the central government and then settle down to his durbar at his official residence. And typically, a young woman may narrate the harrowing tale of a beating she may have received from her husband three days ago, illustrating her forlorn tale with conspicuous bruises on her face. After dealing with many such major

---

[3] Sinha, Arun. *Nitish Kumar and the Rise of Bihar*. Delhi: Penguin Books India, 2011. This book is useful for contextualizing the janata durbar idea and the political climate that led to such an idea. For several years, newspaper reports on junta durbar sessions were fairly detailed, and the local Hindi press gave them a wide coverage. This volume captures some of the fresh enthusiasm of a new regime in Bihar and a new sense of hope that lasted throughout the first stint of Nitish Kumar as the chief minister of Bihar.

and minor upheavals in the lives of big and small men, Nitish may then go on to discuss with the attending reporters his demand to the central government for the little sum of ₹5,000 crores for a certain scheme devised by him. This transition from the 'paltry' to the grand theme may take less than a minute! But the transition also represents a shift from a state-like context to a society-like context where the CM talks and acts like a neutral neighbour or 'panch' capable of arbitrations of a nonlegal or semilegal sort.

For a number of years, not just Nitish Kumar, the CM, but simultaneously a superintendent of police (SP) in a district town in Bihar may have been holding his own durbar where an old widow complains that her brothers-in-law have lately been eyeing at her property. The SP, too, would have to figure out the relevant legal definitions and the culpability of 'eyeing at someone else's property' before getting down to sorting out a pressing and sensational murder case straight from the headlines![4]

But in either case, according to the standard practice, the CM or the SP did not ask the person to shut up or leave and instead tried to find inlets through which such suffering may begin to enter the highly restrictive discourse of daily governance. In brief, during the janata durbar, it did not occur to either of the two to utter the most vitiating line—'come through proper channels', a terminology from the governance of a state! In a society of any

---

[4] 'There was no past example of such a programme when a chief minister interacted directly with the common man. It was started in Bihar during my regime,' said Kumar, who since his first term as Chief Minister of NDA in November 2005 has been regularly holding the meets.

Earlier, Kumar's 'Janata ke darbar mein Mukhya Mantri' was held twice a week, but later it was made a once-a-week affair and is held on every Monday. Asked if he would like to give any tips to Kejriwal to make his janata darbar successful, the chief minister said, 'Everybody has his or her own style of functioning and it is not my nature to interfere or provide unsolicited advice.' 'Nitish Claims "Janata Darbar" His Brainchild.' *Jagran*, 14 January 2014. http://post.jagran.com/nitish-claims-janata-darbar-his-brainchild-1389669509 (accessed on 14 May 2019).

kind or proportions, the 'proper channels' are rarely given and must be negotiated for a given context with the aid of precedents.

To analyse the communicative value of the janata durbar practice, it has the following to show by way of achievement:

1. It refused in principle to place wider social suffering above individual suffering and the need to communicate it, thereby unburdening itself of superfluous ontological assumptions. To illustrate, the CM regards the battered woman's pain and problem such as earthshaking as the mega-problems of Bihar during the moments spent with her. This is what may be called bracketing together of the grand and the trivial! At a conceptual level, it means a profound and wilful conflation of the modern state and the society.

2. Apart from this, it would seem to imply that what is vital and what is trivial may depend on the context and the viewpoint of the subject concerned and is not something that could be presumed beforehand or imposed on the subject, the hallmark of a modern state with its rigid administrative procedures.

To illustrate the point after all, a citizen is mostly mentally gifted enough not to approach a chief minister when he is busy unfurling the national flag on a Republic day and start whispering in his ears urgent appeals to remedy the water shortage problems in his little 'Buncombe county'. Context dependence is an intuition natural to human beings, even infants. Unfortunately, the democracy of procedures through its endless series of rules tries to re-train us over and over again in the basic and almost congenital skill, instead of further extending opportunities and occasions for increasingly unstinted communication. Public discourse, when undemocratic or anti-democratic, thus creates a topography of communication where the highs and the lows, the significant and the trivial get decided by the authorities, even when the citizen lumped into the larger body of formal membership is empowered to vote and effect changes in regimes.

· In Gandhi's autobiography, the earthshaking matters and the trivia weave together in a much better semblance of daily life than the abstract hierarchies determined by our democratic institutions do. The philosophical implications here are nothing short of profound. While not denying the presence of the modern state, Gandhi's autobiography avoids the reification of the modern Indian state whether British or independent. This is unlike those who start their conceptual journey with firm roots in the abstraction of the state and then begin to carve and concretize their human beings by making place for the social when possible. The trouble with such conceptual journeys is that they resemble the well-known paradox of Zeno far too closely, and the statist mind never quite manages to reach its target, namely, the flesh and blood human beings, chasing as it does its abstraction of the 'citizen' of the modern nation state. The assumption in all this is, of course, that 'citizenship' is an enhanced form of humanness and that a human being is fortunate in being recognized as a citizen, a dubious and highly questionable claim at the best of times. To come back to *My Experiments...*, the democratic premise, to oversimplify, may go as follows: 'since we know that you have both the faculties—a fairly developed sense of significance and urgency that impels you to communicate, and a well-developed sense of context dependence, please go ahead and say anything you deem relevant'. It would now appear that what seemed like a hazardous invitation and encouragement to create a monstrous Babel (at least in theory) in an already noise-ridden communication channel just performs the task of social and communicative inclusion on an ever-ending basis. This is what *My Experiments...* has come to mean to me.

As against this, formal democracy, as we know it, insists on the precautionary measure of determining in advance both what is most significant and urgent and what is contextual or procedurally appropriate for a citizen. As against communicative inclusion, the system would seem to rely on a routine of communicative exclusion. Gandhi would instead seem to insist that the grand and the trivial, the urgent and the unimportant, the relevant and the inappropriate messages and information need to be aired freely before we make a judgement on their value. Isn't it ironic that the man who bore Gandhi's mantle as the co-founder of a new republic, Jawaharlal Nehru, wrote a tome titled 'Discovery of India' dealing with the sizable canvas of a whole subcontinent. Gandhi, the father of the nation, chose to focus on his own little follies and lessons instead. These two grand narratives—like a thin sound of an individual flute and a grand burst of the civilizational bugle now, of course—lie together but uncomfortably at the very core of our national imagination.

Just as Gandhi keeps coming back to us through an intimate autobiographical and self-reflective tug, we keep going back to him through a series of communing experiences. The fact is after wandering away from its unique inspirations, the Indian democracy indeed repeatedly keeps coming back to the Gandhian mode of discourse. The janata durbars in Bihar, a discourse that is in the process of trickling down from above to the block development officer's level, may well be one of the many comeback trails, however episodic or discontinuous.

True, janata durbar has a number of uses for a politician—it helps him keep his fingers on the public pulse, it creates a sense of intimacy with the voter apart from enhancing the image of the politician, not to forget the increasingly important task of media management.[5] There is no need to deny any of the obvious

---

[5] The following account of janata durbar may give a good idea of its present status—clearly, Nitish Kumar was ambivalent towards the value of janata durbar, veering between comprehensive implementation to sheer abandonment.

Patna: Chief secretary Deepak Kumar on Friday directed officials that interaction with the people was necessary, the order coming at a time chief minister Nitish Kumar's record of good governance (susashan) has taken a hit over law and order and accountability of officials.

'At a high-level meeting, Deepak said all officials—from top to bottom—must "interact with the people" every Friday. It resembles the janata durbar Nitish started after first coming to power in 2005 to listen to the people's grievances. District magistrates, superintendents

political gains made by the politician from janata durbar to make the simple point that the durbar discourse forms a parallel discourse in democracy that verges 'dangerously' on the informality found in a small population, possibly in an ancient republic in ancient India or Greece. Is this a simulation driven entirely by public relations or it may lead to a dynamic far beyond our present expectations? We will try to find an answer to this in the following sections.

Apart from the contrast between the grand style of politics and the utterly ordinary, we also need to face the informal and the intimate aspect of Gandhian politics. The question has to be asked in what sense Gandhi's autobiography, his spouting on hygiene and other matters in South Africa and elsewhere, as well as the janata durbar in Bihar and so on, belong to the category of the political at all. Seen from a philosophically inclusive viewpoint, it all seems obviously political, and yet paradoxically, when seen from the point of view of systemic politics, or indeed academic political science, none of the above seems to belong categorically to the 'political'. Is this just a problem of taxonomic labelling? I am afraid not. My intuition is that these experiences, experiments or empirical data, whatever you call them, stretch the category of the political towards a redefinition that seems unavoidable in the context of increasing democratization in the Indian society and well, tend to redefine the meaning of democracy in an Indian context.

---

of police and officers in-charge of police stations held the janata durbars. But Nitish stopped the janata durbars on the pretext that with the implementation of the Right to Public Service Act, the people no longer needed to come to the chief minister or the officials.... Many officials, however, remain sceptical at this move to regain Nitish's susashan image. "If officials stopped holding janata durbar, it is because the chief minister stopped holding his," said a senior official, who insisted that in spite of the RTPS Act, people would like to directly convey their complaints to the authorities.

'Chief Secy Orders Durbar Revival.' *Telegraph*, 24 August 2018. https://www.telegraphindia.com/states/bihar/chief-secy-orders-durbar-revival/cid/1444113 (accessed on 14 May 2019).

Informal Politics and the Category of the 'Political'

The 2010–2012 campaign and movement around the demand for a Lokpal (ombudsman) Bill and against corruption at all levels in India led by Anna Hazare illustrate the above point lucidly. Taking corruption in the government as the core issue, the movement ended up opening a virtual Pandora's box of political issues within a short span of time. I will, however, focus on a single fundamental issue that seems to me to be of seminal importance. Throughout the campaign that unfolded in fits and starts right till the 13-day fast by Hazare starting 16 August 2011 and following that, the political class in India was wondering how a group of political outsiders dare come to occupy the centre stage of Indian politics! Anna Hazare was accused of trying to haughtily rise above politics, above the parliament, and indeed above the Indian state itself. There is a good basis to believe that this episode created genuine bewilderment among the parliamentarians brought up on the straight and narrow grammar of the British and the American democracy, now largely internalized by them through several decades since independence. After all, a politician is willing to grant the common dignity of the average citizen. But the inflated hubris of the common man is a different matter altogether!

The media, the analysts and the agitators themselves took recourse to the misty phrase 'civil society' useful for its amorphousness rather than precision. But the professional politician instinctively reacted to Anna's fast as an intrusion from the outside, from a sphere beyond politics and resented it. This was most apparent in the parliamentary speeches from members of a wide range of political parties immediately after Anna's fast came to an end on 28 August 2011. I cannot think of another instance in modern democracy when the professional politician spent a long day on the floors of the parliament reflecting on their contribution to democracy and governance, trying hard to justify their very métier and existence. How does one understand the bewildered response of the professional politician to the Anna Hazare movement and its arrogant insistence?

Perhaps the most poignant moment of the Anna Hazare fast was when he declared his movement as the 'second freedom struggle', a rhetoric which many would dismiss as grandiloquent nonsense.[6] I, however, feel that for good or bad, the above phrase is an attempt to connect Hazare with the Gandhian past and the Gandhian strain in the independence movement. It is commonly understood that while Gandhi remained a key figure through much of the freedom movement of India, suddenly almost overnight on the 15th of August in 1947, he shifted to the very margins of mainstream politics in India. We do not know what role he may have played if he continued to live beyond 1948. But all too often Gandhi's sudden and wilful eclipse is seen by Gandhians as an act of great betrayal on part of the Nehruvian style of politics in India. It is almost as if with independence, the Gandhian and the Nehruvian modes, thus far yoked together for the several decades of the freedom struggle, abruptly bifurcated, with the Gandhian element being reduced to what we now call the civil society. The phrase civil society here would tend to mean something unstructured, brittle and fragmented, unlike the presumed stolidity of the modern Indian state.

This, of all questions, was my primary puzzle and fascination during my second reading of *My Experiments...* during my early 30s when I had recovered from a brief but intense phase of Marxian faith (not Marx so much) and was exploring the Gandhian path with a mixture of awe as well as revulsion. My interim answer for a long time was that Gandhian thought, despite its moral grandeur, is not fit for daily governance except as an inspiration meant to lie mostly in the background. It took me more than a decade to see the flaw in this 'use and throw' view of the Gandhian approach to the category of politics.

---

[6] 'It's the Beginning of Second Freedom Struggle: Hazare.' *The Hindu*, 11 August 2016. https://www.thehindu.com/news/national/its-the-beginning-of-second-freedom-struggle-hazare/article2361213.ece (accessed on 14 May 2019).

My second reading of *My Experiments...* is also associated with a prolonged attempt on my part to place Gandhian thought somewhere within the liberal–democratic socialist tradition as an ideological streak within the wider gamut. These theoretical manoeuvrings went on for some time till it became clear to me that what I termed Gandhian thought could not be fitted anywhere and was indeed an outsider to any kind of gamut though not in the sense of being politically irrelevant for practical governance. It occurred to me that despite his 'normal' political fight for independence, Gandhi leant heavily on the side of the flesh and blood world of people rather than the abstraction of the state, and on the side of people's sovereignty rather than the state's.

This is no place to reflect over the ontological import of political 'representation' or representation as such, and the strange merger of the self and the other engineered for the purpose of democratic governance. But we do need to understand that 'representation' despite lying at the very core of the idea of democracy is essentially a fraught notion simplified into a pragmatic instrument of democracy. To put it plainly, even though asking the question 'how can any human being represent another at all' may not be tantamount to challenging the basic democratic impulse, it does raise questions that the democratic idea cannot reconcile through tortuous procedures and institutional systems, however sophisticated. Popular movements have a way of throwing up leaders and 'representatives' through processes that can only be described as spontaneous. Daily governance associated with the state, however, devotes great attention to the selection of the representatives who legislate with ascribed authority through clearly laid down codes to be followed by the executive.

Given the philosophical problems with representation of the 'un-spontaneous' sort, if we swallow the idea of political representation willingly, it is for entirely pragmatic reasons, duly admitting its flaws and improvability. The synoptic and regrettably hurried conceptual analysis above aimed at providing us with the right context to put down my initial attempts at grappling with the Gandhian idea of politics during my second reading of the autobiography. Aware that the Gandhian idea indeed stood outside the gamut of mainstream democratic politics, I was still far from realizing that Gandhi's seminal idea of politics and non-violence could only be a product of the era of democracy and indeed made little sense outside the context of democracy. I will devote the next section trying to explain why I think so and come back to my present perception of *My Experiments....*

Indian Democracy and the Politics of the Apolitical

During the entire Anna Hazare episode (April–August 2011 and further), the tug of war between the professional politician and the Anna group revealed a number of subtle but vital dimensions crucial to the future of democracy in India which I now wish to bring into focus. I would like to underline one single feature of communication–cum-non-communication between mainstream politics and the Anna movement members, a communication channel of incomprehension that was joined widely by the educated Indians in metropolises and even remote small towns of India. During the entire episode, Anna Hazare, Kiran Bedi and Arvind Kejriwal were frequently taunted and asked to fight elections to the parliament to achieve their goal of a strong Lokpal Bill. Anna and others persistently refused to even consider joining politics. This led many commentators to characterize the Anna movement as undemocratic and an attempt to create a supra-constitutional body above the highest government authority and indeed the state itself. Through a process of a grave categorical confusion, there were instances when the movement was termed 'fascist' in its attempt to take over state power through extra-constitutional means. Interestingly, these exaggerated accusations came to an end abruptly when the Indian parliament conceded Anna's point in theory and promised to work for an appropriate Lokpal Bill.

All these developments could be interpreted in several ways. What I, however, wish to single-mindedly focus on is a persistent assertion by the participants of the Anna Hazare movement that they do not wish to enter politics but would like to influence it, keep a watch over it and also determine its basic course. Termed 'apolitical', this strain of the movement was found very disturbing by the commentators and critics who even saw elements of fascism in the movement. Peasant's struggles, tribal protests and workers' movements are commonly seen as cases of conflict requiring social, legislative and economic rearrangements of various degrees. But the mundane and even the longstanding and chronic issues such as the tribal and forest laws or laws concerning acquisition of land by the state even in their most problematic moment do not require redefinition of the 'political'. Indeed, the main task of democratic politics and politics such is to manage and resolve these conflicts through just means. But the perception that Anna's movement took matters 'above' politics and 'above' constitution is not altogether delusional or unjustified and has a core of truth in it.

That the political versus apolitical rhetoric and debate is now no longer the prerogative of learned discourse among political scientists became clear on an evening when a member of a public attending Arvind Kejriwal's public speech in Lucknow hurled footwear at him. Later on, the perpetrator admitted that he objects to the political turn taken by the Lokpal movement and that he holds Arvind Kejriwal responsible for this deviation. The assaulter felt that the Anna team is showing a tendency of developing political and electoral ambitions by intervening in the Hissar by-elections for the Haryana state assembly and felt disappointed and disturbed. This makes clear that the political–apolitical divide is very much part of the popular democratic consciousness. The question one may ask is why should a common citizen object to Kejriwal's entry into professional politics instead of welcoming it as a positive attempt to cleanse and transform the Indian political landscape?[7] We can thus see how the Anna

---

[7] Arvind Kejriwal and Aam Aadmi Party, https://arvindkejriwal.co.in. The website, of course, brings out the viewpoint of Arvind Kejriwal, and there may be other opinions and versions that would be relevant to the actual sequence of events and the forces that went behind the founding of

Hazare team has placed itself in a limbo with the professional politician challenging them to enter politics and their supporters objecting to any participation in the arena of party politics.

The curious predicament of the 'Anna team', as the small core group of activists came to be called, is characterized by the fact that every public statement and action taken up by the team seems to have dire political consequences, and yet the Anna team continues to claim it is not political or at least that its members do not have political ambitions. What seems here like a paradox or a limbo, however, becomes simpler to understand once we admit that the Team Anna is precisely in the same plight as that of a common citizen or voter of India, or in fact in any other democracy in the world. To elaborate on the point, the citizen in a mature democracy seems to suffer from the twin discomfort of wanting to control the destiny of the community and yet not wanting to take up 'political' career on a full-time basis. Thus,

---

the party. What is relevant here is the dilemma faced by a movement at a crucial point in its consolidation. As Kejriwal points out:

> The origins of the AAP can be traced to a difference of opinion between Arvind Kejriwal and Anna Hazare, social activists who had both been involved in Team Anna, a strand of the anti-corruption movement for Jan Lokpal Bill that had gained momentum in India during 2011 and 2012. Hazare had wanted to keep the movement politically neutral but Kejriwal considered that direct involvement in politics was necessary because attempts to obtain progress regarding the Jan Lokpal Bill through talks with existing political parties had, in his opinion, achieved nothing. ... On 2 October, the birth anniversary of Mahatma Gandhi, Kejriwal announced that he was forming a political party and that he intended the formal launch to be 26 November, coinciding with the anniversary of India's adoption of its constitution in 1949.

> 'Origin of Aam Aadmi Party.' 14 March 2014. https://arvindkejriwal. co.in/origin-of-aam-aadmi-party/ (accessed on 14 May 2019).

Notably, the Gandhian inspiration behind the movement and the party was acknowledged explicitly through the choice of the foundation day, namely Gandhi's birth anniversary on 2 October 2012.

there may be nothing bizarre about the plight of the Anna Team and in fact it would seem to be the common plight of humanity under democracies in general. But let us be clear that democracy is as much dependent on a cadre of professional politicians as on the willingness of the larger citizenry to abstain from full-time politics and to allow others to represent it, and not one or the other.

The Life Cycle of Democracy vis-à-vis the Life Cycle of the Voter

To further elaborate on the role of the apolitical within the political realm, we need to appreciate that a good part of the discomfort of the professional politician in India with the Anna team is that it was taking political contestation beyond the realm of the four- or five-yearly elections. The professional politician in a democracy is perfectly willing to be challenged on these occasions, and in fact it is the electoral 'anointment' as a ritual that lends meaning to his very profession. As a ruler, the democratic politician is perfectly willing to be questioned within the two houses of the parliament and the media and appreciates the reasonableness of demands to resign or step down in cases of malfeasance or lack of performance. In fact, these make the stuff of a political career on a daily basis. The question then may be—in which case, why object to the very idea of an Anna-like movement and why react to it with such fulsome antipathy?

By way of beginning to answer the above question, we need to look at some mundane facts of the human life cycle. The fact is if the periodic elections, the four-year cycle as the very norm of political representation, allow the voter a chance to renew his decision, they also seem to ensure that the four-year clause keeps her or him away from the handles of real power. Clearly, a society cannot have elections every morning and bring to standstill all human activities to ensure a perfect democracy with no time left for economic production, governance, self-defence or leisure. But this practical limitation should not stop us from freely admitting that the four- or five-year clause carries inherent hazards for democracy. The danger, put simply, is that after the elections, the chosen representatives, especially ones to form the government, regard the electoral approval as a licence to be used to the fullest possible extent for the next four years. Even if the word 'danger' seems alarmist in this context, one should be able to see the limiting nature of the time span and be willing to question its actual role.

If we place the high ideals of democracy in the real world of human life cycle, four years is a long time in human life, and four wrong decisions on voting may take a young man to a frustrated middle age. Thus, even within the ambit of democracy, the citizen and the representative get tangled in a contest—a contest between a sense of control over the representative's actions and the representative's agenda of fulfilling his/her own ambitions in a hurry necessitated by the four-year tenure. On an imaginary scale, one may thus conceive of a voter wanting the four-year period to shrink into as little time lapse as possible, preferably into a few days or hours, whereas the representative would wish for the exact opposite. The overall context for this contest is, of course, the exponentially growing information technology that allows both spread and accessibility of information, enabling the voter to try and turn a daydream into reality.

In brief, governance based on political promises that bring an individual or political party to power faces a new challenge from a body of voter that is increasingly unwilling to wait forever in an other-worldly democracy where fulfilment of desire-promise was seen to be possible only in another world, another generation or afterlife. Political audit is now seen to be a daily process that continues unstoppably and unceasingly, a task that every voter carries out for himself on the basis of right or wrong information received.

There is thus a need to focus on the representative–represented relationship in the age of democracy and its ever-changing equations. There is indeed a good basis to claim that despite the abstractness and the unquantifiability of such changes, it may just be the most basic measure for the maturation process of democracy. Even though the modern idea of the state carries within it vestiges of autocratic forms, being based as it is on the state–subject relation, the democratic representative or the government is in no position to look at the citizen as their own subject and must invoke the state in all its haloed symbolism in order to reduce the citizen-voter into subjecthood. Admittedly, this conceptual ploy is not just a sleight of hand on the part of the political representative, since it forms the very basis of the nation state. Ironically, as long as a nation state lasts, it must be seen as both immortal and the embodiment of the collective will, a myth essential to the idea of the state. The fickle idea of five-yearly political representation, on the other hand, has no such mythical burdens to carry.

Once we thus magnify the representative–voter relationship, we begin to notice the subtler shades within. It would appear that the entire political history of humankind forms part of this dynamic relation—monarchic or feudal obeisance, tribal and caste allegiances, religious affiliations, and a host of other loyalties make the stuff of this relationship, not simply as vestiges from the past but also as indispensable thresholds for new beginnings and as raw material for future allegiances. And yet all these loyalties are constrained by the voter's insistence that he can only wait so long before promises made to him are delivered. The ever-shortening time scale of the waiting period forms the basis for the apolitical voter to want to intervene in politics with greater frequency—the reason why once a vote is cast, the representative and the voter instantly enter a contestational relationship. No wonder politicians around the world are a hated lot—should this be happening in the age of democracy at all when for the first time in human history we choose our own leaders and should be primarily blaming ourselves and not the representative for making the wrong choice?

The First Encounter with *My Experiments*...

When I first encountered *My Experiments*... at the age of 14, I had no idea of the intellectual, ethical and emotional journey outlined above that it would take me through the decades. It all started way back on a 2nd October, when my school headmaster decided to make daily readings from the autobiography a part of the morning assembly in the school. Tired of daily moralizing and idealizing, he perhaps decided that he could outsource part of his job to Gandhi, also hoping that Gandhi's aura may be more effective than his dull disciplinarian forays into the juvenile consciousness. Allow me to trace the career of these readings over the period of several months after which the practice petered out.

Gandhi's autobiography is quite suited for a serial-like presentation—it has brief and crisp episodes that run through one after the other. Mostly in chronological sequence, the episodes or chapters take up specific themes and issues that may provide the reader-audience a decent sized morsel for chewing and digesting. The initial readings were thus a great hit and the assembly listened to the appointed reader with rapt attention.

The initial piety, however, began to dissipate very soon. If the teachers had planned to project Gandhi into a tall moral figure or an unquestionable authority, the readings were not having the expected results. Setting aside a small minority that listened carefully but laughed off any idea of a serious discussion, the readings seemed to be playing subversive rather than an ameliorative role. Despite having read the book himself, the headmaster had failed to see that *My Experiments*... was by no means an account of Gandhi's greatness. In its best moments, Gandhi only managed to convey the message that he was too much of a vulnerable mortal himself, and some of his struggles reminded students of serious though mundane handicaps rather than strengths.

The headmaster had got his motivational agendas badly mixed up—Gandhi's autobiography did not fit into the slot 'biographies of great men'. If the readings excited and charged up the students on many occasions, the students could not clearly articulate exactly why. Very often students borrowed their questions from Gandhi and then began to ramble for answers in many other misfitting contexts. In the process, the Gandhi who emerged was a very warm avuncular figure who created much mischief with his questioning wherever he went rather than the repository of profound wisdom that he was meant to be.

As usual, the discomfort started when a student would get up and raise a question related to the day's reading in the social studies or literature class—a question about celibacy and sex or another about caste system which were compared to the racism of South Africa, or a latter day variant of Gandhi's attempts to master ballroom dancing ('twist' was the rage then). This often made the whole class, including the sleepy backbenchers, tense with excitement. It was a big relief when a discussion followed and a big disappointment when the query was dismissed briefly. These discussions were not confined to the classroom and, to the alarm of the teachers, had gained immense respectability and validation from none other than the father of the nation. The schoolteacher's habitual references to the lives of great men, as examples to follow, have their known pitfalls anyway. Following all the ideals of all the great men did not seem a sensible thing to do, and comparisons between Nehru and Gandhi began to churn outlandish though inchoate political philosophies among the more eccentric lot. A tiny group of Nehru haters among these was the most active for a brief while, I remember. Such extremes were curbed only by the completely non-serious students who saw in Gandhi a funny outdated figure, a laughable anachronism.

As all these debates and jibes raged over the months, at some point, the student reader appointed for the daily task developed a serious eye problem threatening complete blindness and had to be sent home for advanced treatment for the entire academic session, bringing the readings to an abrupt end. The headmaster refused to appoint a standby or a substitute, as according to him he could find no one talented enough for the job, which was partly true. Our reader had a way of immersing in the text and taking the entire assembly along with him in a mesmeric spell that included the most cynical jeerers.

But my reading even then was all the teachers in the school was relieved to be rid of the daily ritual of readings from Gandhi. The school authorities had come to the definite conclusion that if you wish to raise regular children, it may be a good idea to keep them away from the autobiography of the father of our nation, though this parricidal sentiment could never be expressed overtly. The teachers could always argue that Gandhi was a special individual and what seemed right for him may not be applicable to the average mortals like us. This continues to be one of the most popular excuses also for shyster babas and saints in present-day India. Later on it occurred to me, the chief reason why the school headmaster's experiment came to an abrupt end was, while the students were excited about the 'experiments' carried out by Gandhi, the nervous teachers kept reminding us of the final outcomes and results of the experiments and the choices already made by Gandhi as a full-grown adult. They felt there was an obvious need to avoid duplication or repetition of Gandhian experiments and questioning. The students, however, fell most conveniently for the Gandhian experiments rather than the stated outcomes. Also, the Gandhian persistence in following a question to its very rock bottom was no part of the schoolteachers' brief who were there to simply raise us to follow successful careers. Such dogged persistence in the field of sciences was definitely encouraged in the school but matters of society and ethics required herding and hounding together of the unruly rather than independent questioning.

As I put together my three different readings of *My Experiments...* from different stages of life, I am struck by the unceasing and obsessive sense of subversion of illegitimate power that Gandhi's autobiography seems to convey. The subversive force of the Gandhian inquiry seems particularly effective when applied to politico-juridical abstractions and concepts. While other subversive ideologies like Marxism dream sweetly of the eventual elimination of the state, even as they erect an enormous megalith as a supposedly interim state, the Gandhian impulse is to keep sifting away all the chaff of pretences to power. This is why Gandhi keeps coming back to politics in the shape of a nibbling and nagging intervention rather than as a permanently dwelling 'ism' before vanishing again into the thin apolitical skies.

Myth, Metaphor and Strategy

4

An Unfinished Communication

Gandhi and the Ahmedabad Labour Strike, 1918

Shashi Bhushan Upadhyay

I

Although there were several forms of communication employed in the course of the resistance movements against British colonial rule as well as by the Indian nationalist movement, certain forms of communication used by Gandhi were quite unique to him. The use of press, pamphlets, petitions, open letters and public speeches had already been adopted. Most of these forms adopted during the earlier phase of the nationalist movement relied mostly on the modern British forms of communication. Although during the Swadeshi movement some new forms such as *prabhat pheri*s (morning processions) and street singing were used, they remained confined within certain regions, and their momentum petered out once the movement declined. During the Gandhian movements, the earlier forms continued and the participation of people in them rose massively. However, there were some entirely novel forms of communication devised by Gandhi.

Their novelty consisted not in their being modern, but in the fact that the earlier nationalist movement had not used them. In fact, they were mostly, at least in Gandhi's interpretation, derived from traditional Indian forms, and these are the characteristics that struck a chord with the masses. Satyagraha (lit. holding firm to truth) was one such polysemic agitational and communicational strategy which captured the imagination of the people. It encompassed several things such as agitation, demonstration, strikes, picketing, sit-in, protest, negotiation, economic boycott, emigration to escape oppression and non-cooperation. Other symbols in the network of Gandhian communication were spinning wheel, fasting, prayer meetings and *padyatra* (foot march). In this chapter, we will attempt to see how these channels of communication were used during one of Gandhi's earliest public engagements in India and how far they were successful in transmitting his views to the public, particularly the mill workers.

The general strike in the cotton mills of Ahmedabad in 1918 was important for various reasons. First, it was one of the earliest general strikes in the second largest production centre of cotton textiles, employing about 40,000 workers in 1918. Second, the involvement of Gandhi in the strike with his philosophy of satyagraha and non-violence made it different. And finally, the emergence of the Textile Labour Association out of this strike, which believed in the principle of arbitration and which lasted for very long, put the stamp of uniqueness on it. Throughout its career, it was distinguished from other trade unions in the country. The single most important factor which made this possible was the influence of Gandhi on its formation and growth. There are some significant writings on this strike as well as on the labour movement in Ahmedabad as a whole. But their focus, quite understandably, has been more on labour than on Gandhi. In these works, the analysis of Gandhi's role varies from criticism to praise. But there has not been the required effort to understand Gandhi's involvement from his point of view. In this chapter, I would try to view this strike from Gandhi's point of view, the way he felt and thought throughout the progress of the strike and its largely satisfactory conclusion.

II

When Gandhi was first approached by Anusuya Sarabhai to intervene in the labour struggle, he was a little reluctant. There was a significant concentration of labour in the Ahmedabad textile industry. The city has been a major commercial hub for many centuries and an important centre for production of textiles. The first modern textile mill became operative in the city in 1858, only about three years after the beginning was made in Mumbai. The progress, however, was slow, and even by 1878 there were only four mills employing only about 800 workers. The growth picked up in the 1890s, and by 1905 there were 32 mills with about 17,000 workers, and by 1918 there were 51 mills employing nearly 40,000 workers. This was a big number, and the prospect of keeping the strike by so many workers peaceful was daunting.

After he assumed the responsibility, Gandhi wanted to find a middle path between the millowners and workers in every respect. To begin with, he decided to introduce the idea of arbitration between the contending parties. But after this was unsuccessful, he decided that a demand for an increase of 35 per cent in the wages would be right as it was placed midway between what the workers demanded, which was 50 per cent increase, and what the millowners wanted to give (20 per cent). Similarly, he did not want that the self-respect of either the workers or the employers be compromised.[1] He also wanted that the interests of both the workers and the employers be protected: 'We shall promote the workers' interests while duly safeguarding [those of] the employers.'[2] He advised the workers to follow the path of non-violence to achieve their aims. Right from the beginning, the struggle was termed as 'Ek Dharmayuddha', the meanings of which unfolded as the struggle proceeded forward. In one of the meetings addressed to the workers, Gandhi told them that 'we must remain firm ... and must not resume work even if we have

---

[1] M. K. Gandhi, *The Collected Works of Mahatma Gandhi*, Vol. 16 (Delhi: Publication Division, 1976), 285.
[2] Ibid., 297.

to die.' It was true that the workers were poor, but 'they possess a wealth superior to money.' It was 'their courage and their fear of God'. He also assured them that they would not be allowed to die of starvation. He was convinced that the demand for a 35 per cent increase was just and fair and it should not be changed from either side.[3] During the course of a prayer discourse at his Ashram, Gandhi made clear that

> it is not only against Government that satyagraha can be employed. It can be employed in any situation, against any person or body.... In Kheda, satyagraha has been going on against the Government and in Ahmedabad against the rich and also against the scriptures on the issue of the untouchables.[4]

He, therefore, drew a parallel between various types of struggles going on in the country in which the satyagraha was being applied. This signified that he was placing this particular struggle in the broader context of nationalist quest. Moreover, he also applied his particular way of conducting a struggle which, as he often said, was tested successfully in South Africa. In a leaflet issued on 27 February 1918, he advised the workers to be truthful, to have courage, to possess a sense of justice, not to be angry with the employers, to remember that there would be suffering, and to have faith in God.[5] He, thus, wanted the workers to be real satyagrahis who would struggle to achieve their aims regardless of consequences through particular means which would be moral, ethical and spiritual. On the same day, in a meeting with the striking workers, he cautioned them not to heed the advice of those who tell them to accept whatever the millowners had agreed to pay as increase, which was 20 per cent. Instead, they should stick to their demand and show firmness. He advised them to rely on the strength of their hands and feet, which would get them work anywhere. Only then could they assert their dignity and standing

---

[3] Ibid., 287.
[4] Ibid., 288.
[5] Ibid., 289–90.

before the employers who should not take them for granted.[6] He further exhorted them not to give in and to stick to their pledge, otherwise their children and the future generation would not think highly of them. So, even if they starved, they should not forsake their vow.[7] In order to sustain the strike, Gandhi advised the workers not to indulge in 'mischief', not to gamble, not to sleep during the day, not to gossip or to idle, and not to go to the mills. Instead, they should spend their time in cleaning their surroundings, repairing their houses and compounds, and the literates among them helping the others by reading books and sharing their knowledge with the illiterates; those who are skilled workers might look for some work for which help from his side as well as from that of the organizers would be offered; those who know only the mill-work should try to learn some subsidiary occupations.[8] Here he also laid out his idea about the desirability of learning and doing any occupation for everyone:

> In India, a person in one occupation thinks it below his dignity to follow any other. Besides, some occupations are considered low and degrading in themselves. Both these ideas are wrong. There is no question of inferiority or superiority among occupations which are essential for man's existence. Nor should we be ashamed of taking up an occupation other than the one we are used to. We believe that weaving cloth, breaking stones, sawing or splitting wood or working on a farm are all necessary and honourable occupations. We hope, therefore, that instead of wasting their time in doing nothing, workers will utilize it in some such useful work.[9]

On the other hand, he also promised, on behalf of his organization, that all help would be provided to the workers for achievement of their goals. Public sympathies would be mobilized; the economic, moral and educational position of the workers would be improved:

---

[6] Ibid., 292.
[7] Ibid., 293.
[8] Ibid., 294–95.
[9] Ibid., 295.

> We shall show the workers how they may improve their economic
> condition; we should strive to raise their moral level; we shall think
> out and teach them ways and means of living in cleanliness and
> we shall work for the intellectual improvement of such of them
> as live in ignorance.

Moreover, he promised that medical help would be provided
for the needy workers.[10] He, however, was never in favour of
providing monetary help as this 'would only spoil them if we
collected public funds and utilized them for feeding them unless
the able-bodied among them were ready to perform bread
labour'.[11]

Meanwhile, Gandhi was also trying to persuade the industrialists to be reasonable and sympathetic to the workers' cause. In
a letter to Ambalal Sarabhai, the president of the Ahmedabad
Millowners' Association, Gandhi puts forward a moral argument:
'If you succeed, the poor, already suppressed, will be suppressed
still more ... and the impression will have been confirmed that
money can subdue everyone.' It was, therefore, imperative for
the employers not to create hurdles in the path of securing justice
for the workers, because the success of the employers would be
failure of humanity. Thus, it was better if they retracted from their
rigid stand: 'your failure lies in your success.... How if Ravana
had succeeded? ...Your efforts are of the nature of *duragraha*.'[12]
Gandhi argued that it was in everybody's interest that workers'
demands were conceded. By doing so, the employers would have
done favour to themselves, because the defeated workers might
turn vindictive. If, however, workers' demands were met, they
'will ever remain grateful ... and there will be increased goodwill
between them and the employers. Thus, the employers' success
lies in that of the workers'.[13] This would be real justice, Gandhi
asserts, in which both sides benefited and nobody suffers. But 'As

---

[10] Ibid., 297–98.
[11] Ibid., 363.
[12] Ibid., 300.
[13] Ibid., 302.

against this way of pure justice, the employers have adopted the Western, or the modern, Satanic notion of justice.'[14]

In a leaflet issued on 3 March, Gandhi elaborated and historicized this idea:

> Pure justice is that which is inspired by fellow-feeling and compassion. We in India call it the Eastern or the ancient way of justice. That way of justice which has no place in it for fellow-feeling or compassion is known as Satanic, Western or modern justice.[15]

The example he gives is that of the servants who served their masters for generations, and were in turn treated as members of the family. He also asserts that 'In those days, India was reputed for a social order free from friction, and this order endured for thousands of years on that basis.'[16] Both these notions were quite ahistorical and failed to see the fundamental contradiction of interests between the master and the servant. However, what is important is the focus of Gandhi's argument which was in tandem with his long-held belief in the basic divergence between the West and the East. Moreover, he thought that the modern India had fallen prey to Western ideas. Thus, 'The employers, in refusing to consider the workers' demands, have accepted this Satanic principle of justice.' He exhorts them to have regard for the Dharma because 'you will never find in ancient India a situation in which the workers starved was regarded as the employers' opportunity'.[17]

He also demanded from the workers that they should act as true satyagrahis. As examples of 'bold and resolute satyagrahis' he mentioned the names of Imam Hussain and Prahlad.[18] He also gave instances of the struggle by Indian workers in South Africa as just struggle.

---

[14] Ibid., 302.
[15] Ibid., 302–303.
[16] Ibid., 303.
[17] Ibid., 304.
[18] Ibid., 308.

On 12 March, the employers resolved to withdraw the lock-out and take back those workers who were willing to accept 20 per cent increase. Seeing the condition of the strikers, it was not unlikely that most of them would have joined back. Now Gandhi insisted the workers should not resume work on less than 35 per cent increase because they would lose their honour. He argued that even the employers would not benefit 'by taking work from workers who are too weak to keep their oath'.[19] He, however, insisted that those willing to join would not be stopped except by persuasion.

Gandhi realized that the workers were facing the condition of starvation for themselves and their families. In such a situation, it might be difficult to hold them back from joining. Some sympathizers offered to help with money and material to prolong the strike. But Gandhi politely refused them by saying that: 'What is the meaning of satyagraha if you help the workers with money to carry it on.... The essence of satyagraha lies in cheerful submission to the suffering that may follow it. The more a satyagrahi suffers, the more thoroughly he is tested.'[20] But with workers' weakening resolve, Gandhi felt that the strikers did not understand his views. In a leaflet on 15 March, he was more explicit and candid about what he expected from the strikers as satyagrahis:

> As the weapon of the rich is money, that of the workers is their labour.... One who does not work is not a worker. A worker who is ashamed of working has no right to eat.... Those who collect funds and, remaining idle, maintain themselves out of them do not deserve to win. Workers are fighting for their pledge.... This struggle is not merely for a 35 per cent increase; it is to show that the workers are prepared to suffer for their rights. We are fighting to uphold our honour.... We must maintain ourselves by our own labour [and not by public funds].[21]

---

[19] Ibid., 327.
[20] Ibid., 332.
[21] Ibid., 333.

He, therefore, expressed the hope that 'every worker will work to maintain himself so that he may be able to keep his oath and remain firm'.[22] By then, however, some of the workers had remarked that while Gandhi and Anusuya Sarabhai are living and eating well, they are demanding from the workers to starve for their vow. Such sarcastic remarks stung Gandhi and he decided to undertake fast to show his commitment, and also make the workers steadfast in their struggle. As he said: 'My pledge is directed to making the mill-hands honour theirs.... And for ten thousand mill-hands to break faith with themselves would spell ruin for the nation.'[23]

Gandhi's fast created quite a stir, and the millowners were forced to meet him and offered to do whatever he wanted. Gandhi was not very happy with this situation because he felt that the employers had given in due to his fast and not due to either in appreciation of the workers' condition or workers' struggle: 'The mill-owners came and told me, "We shall give 35 per cent for your sake".... It would be extremely humiliating to me that they offer you 35 per cent for my sake.'[24] It was because if 'the mill-owners have acted under pressure of my fast.... It is against the principle of justice'[25]. He, therefore, moderated his original demand for 35 per cent increase on the first day, 20 per cent on the second day and 27.5 per cent subsequently until the arbitrator accepted by both the parties gave his judgement. After this, the strike ended. Although Gandhi was not initially satisfied with the fact that the millowners yielded to the pressure created by his fast and were not convinced about the justness of the workers' demands, he later praised the efforts of workers in sustaining the strike with enthusiasm. Initially, he felt that his act of fasting on this issue was 'exceptionally tainted' as it would put undue pressure on the owners. But he justified it on the ground that it created renewed enthusiasm among the workers who were completely

---

[22] Ibid., 334.
[23] Ibid., 342.
[24] Ibid., 343.
[25] Ibid., 346.

transformed as 'Everyone immediately realized that the protect-
ing power of God was as much with us today as it used to be in
the days of yore.' Moreover, 'I preferred the ignominy of having
unworthily compromised by my vow the position and independence of the millowners rather than that it should be said by pos-
terity that 10,000 men had suddenly broken a vow.'[26] Thus, for
him, the 'Ahmedabad strike provided the richest lessons of life.
The power of love was never so effectively demonstrated.... The
existence of God was realized by the mass of men.'[27]

III

A summary of Gandhi's stand on the strike may be given as
follows:

1. Right from the beginning, Gandhi interpreted the strike as a
   moral struggle against injustice. He placed it in comparison
   with broader struggle not only in India but the world over,
   particularly his own experiences in South Africa.
2. He wanted the striking workers to act as satyagrahis who
   would be prepared to suffer for achievement of justice and
   harbour no ill will against the millowners.
3. Moreover, he wanted workers to be able to earn their livelihood through work during the period of the strike and not
   to be dependent on contributions from the sympathizers,
   not only because he thought that such dole would soon
   dry out but also because he felt that any such dependence
   would degrade the workers in the eyes of the employers
   and others.
4. He wanted to maintain a balance between the interests of
   both the parties so that none of them would claim victory
   because he felt such a feeling would create lasting bitterness
   between them.

---

[26] Ibid., 365.
[27] Ibid., 398.

5. Finally, his retrospective assessment of the strike was positive because it ultimately restored faith among the workers and taught them to remain steadfast in face of adversity.

However, there was a partial failure of communication as the ideas which Gandhi wished to convey to the workers as well as to the millowners were not fully carried through. Certain methods of communication employed by Gandhi, such as leaflets, public meetings and dissemination through newspapers, were derived from the earlier and contemporary forms. But certain other methods, such as prayer meetings, intense personal communication and, finally, fasting were quite new. Although these newer channels widened his reach, they also created newer forms of misunderstanding. Moreover, the messages which he tried to convey also had certain novelty so far as the conduct of labour strikes was concerned. The vivid mythological and secular imagery he invoked were not easy to grasp in the mundane and conflict-ridden world of capital–labour relations. Finally, his conception of the satyagrahis was quite new and idiosyncratic and, in a way, it remained so till the end, at least for the majority of people. Thus, certain communication failure was in-built in the polysemic nature of Gandhi's various concepts. It does not mean, however, that it was a total failure. The Ahmedabad labour union remained different from the rest of unions in the country, and the influence of Gandhi's ideas was responsible for this.

5

Multi-verse of Gandhi's Charkha
Spinning Experiences and the Question of Information

Sadan Jha

My language is aphoristic, it lacks precision. It is therefore open to several interpretations.

—Mahatma Gandhi

Introduction

Mahatma Gandhi once talked about 'believing eye'. This phrase was used by him while responding to a criticism of the national education in 1926. He wrote:

A Gujarati correspondent has raised certain questions about national education. Some of them are summarized below:

Since some of the staunchest supporters of non-cooperation have lost faith in it and since the numbers attending national institutions are dwindling, what is the use of holding on to these tottering schools and colleges and wasting good money after bad institutions?

My believing eye detects a flaw in this argument. My faith in non-co-operation remaining as staunch as ever, I can find it possible to reconcile myself to the existing national institutions even though the attendance may be reduced to half a dozen. For the half a dozen will be the makers of swaraj whenever it comes. When virgins are required to perform certain sacred ceremonies, others are not accepted as substitute if no virgin is found. And even one virgin if found is enough to save the situation. So will it be with the planting of the swaraj flag-post? The flags will be unfurled with the unsullied hands of those, be they ever so few, who have remained true to their creed.[1]

In Gandhi's language, believing eye is an embedded eye and quite different from an observer's eye. The embedded qualities in the former case come from its inseparable attachment with the experiences of seeing both an object and an inner belief/faith in the object. To me, Gandhi's believing eyes also take us to the cusp between information and experiences. Mediating in between these two poles, my study looks at the multi-verse of a key Gandhian symbol, the spinning wheel.

I begin with a *maithili* folk saying. It says,

Budhiya'k charakha tanman bhail
Dhiya puta'k man khan bhail

(Old woman's spinning wheel came into action, children are alarmed.)

Here, the body of old woman is placed in opposition to the body of the new generation (children). In fact, at second thought, reading of this couplet seems revealing three and not merely two sets of oppositional locations: old woman and new generation, and these two sites are mediated by the presence of a third body, the site of the spinning wheel. It is the coming up of the spinning wheel into action that puts two different

---

[1] Mahatma Gandhi, 'National education'. In *Young India*, 3 June 1926, *The Collected Works of Mahatma Gandhi* (Delhi: Publication Division), Vol. 30: 519.

generations in opposition to each other. The couplet intends to suggest that the old woman is back to work, do not fiddle with her. Here the space of spinning wheel is central to the environment of the old woman. This wheel defines the activity of the old woman.

Invert these oppositional sets and we come face to face with a different layer of relationship among agencies of this narrative. Two generations are actually communicating/connected to each other through the action of the spinning wheel. It is actually the body of the spinning wheel that allows the gestural dialogue across the generation possible. The body of the spinning wheel is bridging the generational gap.

There must be various other reading possibilities with this couplet. My reading points out merely two sets of interpretations of the spinning wheel as a site, a body. First, the spinning wheel acts as a carrier of certain action and works as a linkage between two bodies/generations/narrative positions. Second, the spinning wheel acts as a contested site in itself—a site where the drama of opposition is performed. A site where both the old woman and children are making their own claims. The old woman through her action as spinning wheel belongs to her space and she enjoys the right to put it in motion. On the other hand, without consider-ing the effect produced by this action (of the wheel), the meaning of the couplet remains incapable of generating any communities of responses. It is the effect that defines the significance of the spinning wheel. Children got alarmed—some kind of order is restored (very mention of the fact that children are alarmed pre-supposes a state of affair where children are playful and in some kind of a situation of orderlessness). Thus, it is the body of the children and their awareness about the active spinning wheel that completes the narrative process; hence, this body owns a legiti-mate say over the body of a spinning wheel. The bodies of (aged) woman, young generation and spinning wheel all participate in the textual celebration of this couplet. However, the contestation goes on.... I try to follow the track....

The spinning wheel is one of the most popular and sacred among Gandhian symbols. 'For me', Mahatma Gandhi once wrote, 'nothing in the political world is more important than the spinning wheel'.[2] The spinning wheel (*charkha*), for Mahatma Gandhi, was not just a tool of political emancipation but it was a metaphor of 'ancient work ethics' and a symbol of economic and social reaction to the British rule. This 'ancient work ethics' and the goal of the 'swaraj' (self-rule) in Gandhian framework had to be mediated in and through the 'daily life'. For him, 'it is in the daily life where dharma and practicality come together', and spinning wheel was the realization of this possibility. Thus, any study of Gandhism needs to bring into focus this metaphor of 'ancient work ethics', this site of 'daily life' and this symbol of social and economic reaction. In the Gandhian discourse, the spinning wheel signifies 'decentralisation against centralised production', 'the sole remedy' for the dwindling handloom industry in particular and India's traditional sector in general, a weapon for stopping the import of foreign goods, the only solution for hidden mass unemployment of the rural population and last but not the least 'a dear forgotten friend of Indian widow'. The significance of the spinning wheel can be seen in Mahatma Gandhi's insistence that 'India as a nation can live and die only for the spinning wheel'.[3]

At one level, through a history of the spinning wheel, I try to explore the centrality of the category of experience and its play with information and knowledge in Gandhian experiments with spinning wheel and swaraj. At another level, I have tried to analyse the ways in which the narratives of this symbol have changed over the time in the last century.

---

[2] Mahatma Gandhi, *The Collected Works of Mahatma Gandhi*, Vol. 19: 454–56.
[3] Ibid.

Locating/Searching a Gandhian Symbol

Those not familiar with the history of the spinning wheel may find it surprising that Mahatma Gandhi, at the time of writing his most famous treaty, *The Hind Swaraj,* had neither seen the spinning wheel nor had any understanding of the difference between the loom and the spinning wheel. Yet, he was quite convinced about the sacred nature of the exercise of weaving, and hence looms were written prefixed with 'ancient' and 'scared' in *The Hind Swaraj.*[4] It was in London in 1909 that Gandhi 'saw' in 'a flash that without the spinning wheel there was no swaraj'.[5] This flash vision convinced him immediately that 'everyone had to spin', thus began the search for a charkha.

The history of the spinning wheel is about the responses to the ruptures caused by colonialism. In India, weaving and spinning were much more than simply an indigenous way of producing textile goods. Spinning was very much a part of everyday lives and activities of women of almost all the sections of society. William Crooke notes that spinning was the only industry in India that is performed by persons of all castes and concerning which there seems to be no caste prejudice.[6] Historians such as C. A. Bayly, B. S. Cohn, Emma Tarlo and others have contextualized the mass appeal of Gandhian Swadeshi and anti-foreign cloth campaign in the social history of cloth, cloth production and in the power of semiotics.[7] Bayly writes that in India, 'society

---

[4] Anthony J. Parel, ed., *Hind Swaraj and Other Writings* (Delhi: Cambridge University Press, 1997), 109.

[5] Ibid.

[6] William Crooke, *Things Indian: Being Discursive Notes on Various Subjects Connected with India* (Delhi: Oriental Books Reprint Cooperation, 1972(1906)), 509.

[7] C. A. Bayly, 'The Origins of Swadeshi (Home Industry): Cloth and Indian Society, 1700–1930', in *Origins of Nationality in South Asia: Patriotism and Ethical Government in the Making of Modern India* (Delhi: Oxford University Press, 1998); Bernard S. Cohn, 'Cloth, Clothes, and Colonialism: India in the Nineteenth Century', in *Colonialism and its Forms of Knowledge* (Princeton, NJ: Princeton University Press, 1996), 106–62; Emma Tarlo, *Clothing Matters: Dress in India* (Delhi: Viking, 1995); Susan

spoke partly in "the idiom of cloth", though idiom is really too weak a word since cloth could actually transform power and transform relationships.' In his view, the disruption of the Indian economic fabric was 'a crisis of legitimacy for the new colonial rulers'.[8] Can we then argue that Gandhi was an astute reader understanding this legitimacy crisis and developing a strategy by placing the spinning wheel in the centre of it and terming it as a symbol for the 'regeneration of a glorious past'? Thus, the economics of Gandhian symbols must be analysed by situating them in the context of the Gandhian notion of Indian life and his vision of India's well-being. Along with this, any reading of this Gandhian symbol of 'regeneration of a glorious past' must incorporate various ways in which this symbol was accepted in the commoners' notion of defiance and in their strategies of resistance to the colonial economy.

Historians have helped us look into the generations who lived through the alleged period of transition and the particularities of the colonial experiences. In this alleged period of transition, the most severe impact of the British rule fell on the small-scale and traditional industries for two primary reasons: technological obsolescence (hand tools competing with modern machinery and losing) and closer economic integration between India and the Britain. According to Tirthankar Roy, hand spinning was 'more or less the only example of a major traditional industry that became extinct due to competition from imported British goods'.[9] William Crooke writes that weaving, 'one of the earlier and up to modern times the most widely spread rural industry is now in a state of decline'.[10] George Grierson in his *Bihar Peasant Life* indicates towards an indirect marker of this decline when he writes that the Musalman weaver or

---

Bean, 'Gandhi and Khadi, The Fabric of Indian Independence', in *Cloth and Human Experience*, ed. Annette B. Weiner and Jane Schneider (Washington: Smithsonian Institution Press, 1980), 355–76.

[8] Bayly, 'The Origins of Swadeshi (Home Industry)', 190.

[9] Roy Tirthankar. *Economic History of India 1857–1947* (Delhi: Oxford University Press, 2000, p. 126).

[10] Crooke, *Things Indian*, 508.

jolha is the proverbial fool of Hindu stories and proverbs.[11] In the examples of proverbs that Grierson sites, a *jolha* is a figure of caricature in a dislocated situation, away from his loom, doing some other task:

karigah char tamaasa jay,
Nahak chot jolaaha khaay

('He left his loom to see the fun, and for no reason got a bruising.'). Another proverb says, *kaua chalal baas ken, jolha chalal ghaas ken* [the weaver went out to cut grass (at sunset), when even the crows were going home].[12]

The power of the Gandhian discourse was the power of his reading of this displacement of Indian traditions by colonialism. Gandhi hardly invented any idea or any symbols. All what he did was a careful selection and reworking of old symbols. This process transformed the nature of even ordinary everyday objects. Objects and metaphors that were closely related to a wide cross-section of Indian people and were part of day-to-day life of the nation very soon acquired different connotations. Gandhi invested new meanings and gave them new vitality and life.

Many a time the spinning wheel acted as an extension of the weaver's loom, which was more than merely the means of livelihood for a major chunk of Indian society. Historian Gyan Pandey writes, 'Even during severely straitened circumstances, many handloom weavers carried on, looms were sometimes "kept up merely in order that the children may not forget how to weave."'[13] In 1942, the magistrate of the Azamgarh district

---

[11] George Grierson also writes that a Muhammdan weaver is *jolha* or *momin* and a Hindu weaver is *tantwa* or *tanti* or in Shahabad *tanto*. Sometimes in Hindi, *jolaha* is used instead of *jolha*. George A. Grierson, *Bihar Peasant Life: Being a Discursive Catalogue of the People of That Province* (Calcutta: Bengal Secretariat Press), 69.

[12] Grierson, *Bihar Peasant Life*, 70.

[13] Gyan Pandey, 'Economic Dislocation in Nineteenth Century Eastern Utter Pradesh: Some Implications of the Decline of Artisanal Industry in Colonial India', in *Rural South Asia: Linkages, Change and Development*, ed. Peter Robb (Delhi: Oxford University Press, 1983), 110.

wrote that the Julahas of Mau could still think of nothing but their looms and their religion.[14]

A Symbol of Hopes and Aspirations

At the popular level, the charkha made a radical difference in terms of the attitude of the common folk regarding their own life and well-being. This difference can be seen on the issue of migration and its social responses in folklore. Citing the example of migration, Gyan Pandey has written that in the pre-colonial period, mass migration was an emergency remedy in the situations of crisis and it was a natural method, a weapon of protest against the tyranny of local landowners. But, in the later decades of the 19th century, the wholesale migration of a community, to escape from oppression and a collective act of protest, had been transformed into an individual act of desperation.[15] The folklore of the Bhojpuri region captures some of the hopes and travails that arose out of this transformation:

> *Poorab ke deshwa men kailee nokaria Te kare*
> *sonwan ke rojigar jania ho.*
>
> (One who gets a job in the East can fill his house with gold.)[16]

This folklore is not just a statement of the shift of occupation (from agriculture or weaving to petty jobs and wage labour), but it is also a narrative of the protest. One can see an element of contrast between this narrative of protest and the following narrative of appeal which has been composed around the text charkha. In one of the Bhojpuri Gramgeet, womenfolk sing,

> *Ab ham katabi charakhaba piya mati jahu bideshwa.*

---

[14] Gyan Pandey, 'Economic Dislocation in Nineteenth Century Eastern Utter Pradesh: Some Implications of the Decline of Artisanal Industry in Colonial India', in *Rural South Asia: Linkages, Change and Development*, ed. Peter Robb (Delhi: Segment Book Distributors, 1983), 89–129.

[15] Pandey, 'Economic Dislocation', 112–13.

[16] Thakur in Pandey, Ibid., 113 (translation in original).

Ham Katabi Charkha sajan tuhu jaab mili ahi se surajabaa, piya mati....[17]

(Now I shall ply charkha, O dear please don't go to alien lands

O dear I shall ply charkha and we shall attain Swaraj...O dear don't go....)

Both the above narratives resist the dislocations caused by colonialism, but in *charkha geet* it has been claimed that the act of spinning can reverse the whole process of dislocation. Thus, while the hidden aspect of the text attacks colonialism and its evil effect in the speech part, the overt text conveys the hopes of a golden future. However, these hopes and promises revealed social conflicts and patterns of a fractured social life.

The reference is too innocent, almost mythical, creating highly non-authoritarian appeals about the power of the spinning wheel. The mythical hope, playfulness associated with the ideal golden future ('Ram rajya') and the rhythmic lyrical optimism coming from the humming of the spinning wheel in this Maithili/Bhojpuri folk song not just widened the field of play for Gandhian politics, but it had a tendency to even politicize the most mundane moments of everyday life (of womenfolk in particular).

From the perspective of organized politics, the khadi movement (which was central to the propagation of the Gandhian ideology of spinning wheel) had clear organizational motives. It supplied the core of Gandhian followers. The extension of the spinning wheel ideology obviously meant the broadening of Gandhi's mass political base and strengthening of his cadre organization.[18] Along with organizational politics, one of the clear messages the spinning wheel conveyed was the removal of unemployment of the Indians in seemingly quite an innocent-looking approach to

---

[17] '*Charkha A. Bhojpuri Gramgeet*', Shiva Kumar Mishra, comp. and ed. *Azadi ki shikhayan* (Delhi: Indian Fertilisers Co-operative Ltd, 1998), 248 (translation mine).

[18] J. P. Kriplani, *The Politics of Charkha* (Bombay: Vora, 1946).

a very complex and integrated economic planning with immense faith over human potential. In its pursuit to develop a sound critique of colonialism, the Gandhian khadi movement responded to the colonial challenge not merely at the level of economics and culture but also by providing alternatives to the colonial science and knowledge system at each and every level.

Spinning the Technology

C. Shambhu Prashad has analysed colonial strategies for replacing the Indian cotton culture with import of American cottonseeds.[19] He writes that the Gandhian khadi movement responded to the colonial challenge by providing alternatives to the colonial science and knowledge system at each and every level. He has shown that the factors responsible for the decline of handicraft can only be identified by posing questions related to a series of administrative measures frustrating and choking the economic activities even at the bottom of the hierarchies. We need to pose questions such as

> how bullocks were taxed; the Charkha taxed, the bow taxed and the loom taxed; how inland custom houses were posted in and around every village, on passing which cotton, on its way to the coast for sale was stopped and like every other produce taxed afresh; how it paid export duty both in raw state, and in every shape of yarn or thread, cloth or handkerchief in which it was possible to manufacture it.

This is how Brown, a planter who spent several years in Madras Presidency, describes the British strategy to replace Indian cotton culture, which was not suitable for their own interests.[20] The import of machine-made yarn into India broke the connection of cotton, the spinning and the weaving. Cotton, which had largely been grown for local use, began to be grown specifically

---

[19] Shambhu C. Prashad, 'Suicide Death and Quality of Indian cotton', *Economic and Political Weekly*, 30 July 1999, PE-12–31.
[20] Ibid., PE-14.

for exports, and this resulted in the decline of numerous textile-producing centres. But Indian cotton, which was certainly better than the American cotton, was in fact not suitable for the machines of Lancashire. Thus, it was systematically propagated as inferior to the American cotton. Studies revealed that the hand-spun fibres had better adhesion and were thereby stronger and finer than machine-made yarn. It required at least four such threads of land-spun British Indian cotton twisted together to make one thread equal to the finest machine-spun cotton in this country (comparing Indian and American cotton). However, the length of staples of Indian cotton was shorter in comparison with American cotton, and so it was not suited for British machinery. It was more prone to injury in Whitney's saw gin, which was seen as an improvement over the roller gin because of the speed of operation. It was on account of saw gin that the longer the staple, the more was the chance that even if it broke in processing, the remaining pieces would still be long enough to engage in the machine. In contrast to this, the superior qualities of Indian cotton—fineness silkiness, softness, durability and absorbency—are enhanced by low speed operations. But now what mattered was the speed and not the fineness. Even the quality of the cotton fibres was dictated by the limitations of the spinning machine.[21]

The inferiority of Indian cotton further pushed the claim for the cultivation of American seeds. Cotton produced by these seeds well suited for export rather than home spinning. In this way, the demand of industrial Europe, systematically promoted by colonial power-knowledge, hegemonized the demand curve of spinning industries at home and finally contributed to the decline of household spinning. Just as Indian varieties were unsuited to modern textile production and caused injury to staples, American varieties were unsuited to indigenous cottage mode of production. The seeds of these varieties were too soft and would get crushed in the spinning wheel. It was thus not possible to conceive of a

---

[21] Ibid.

Swadeshi khadi movement with American cotton. One of the primary objectives of the khadi movement was to revive household spinning by challenging this notion of inferiority of Indian cotton production. For this, the khadi movement had to look at the alternative indigenous crops. In fact, the khadi movement was not only engaged in the dissemination of spinning wheels and replacement of mill yarn by hand-spun khadi cloths, but it was very much concerned about providing alternatives and viable technologies and towards the revival of indigenous cotton culture. The khadi movement, through various columns in Gandhian journals and books, was in fact resisting the hegemony of Western science and technology. The spinning wheel in this way not only symbolized 'the regeneration of glorious past' but also challenged the established axioms of the textile industry in particular and the Western knowledge system in general.

The khadi movement pushed this claim through propagating an indigenous methodology of research. The response of the movement was thus not one of cultural only but very much technological too.[22] Talking about the essence of the scientific method, Gandhi once remarked:

> no science has dropped from the skies in a perfect form. All sciences develop and are built up through experience. Perfection is not an attribute of science. Absolute perfection is not possible either for man or for the science that he creates.[23]

The centrality of experience as the guiding spirit of any scientific experiment is one of the distinguishing features of the Gandhian framework on science and progress, and it is amply clear by even a cursory glance through the manuals and pamphlets a genre produced to disseminate both the ideas and the science of spinning.

---

[22] On how the khadi movement disseminated its ideology with the help of visual aids, see Lisa N. Trivedi, 'Visually Mapping the "Nation": Swadeshi Politics in Nationalist India, 1920–1930', *The Journal of Asian Studies* 62, no. 1 (February 2003): 11–41.

[23] *CWMG*, Vol. 83: 355–56, cited from Shambhu Prasad, ibid., 3732.

Unfortunately, the spinning wheel was very soon appropriated as a symbol of loyalty and an image to reflect true nationalist spirit by Gandhian leaders. It was a mark of identification for Congress leaders. Regional leaders often circulated their photographs in which charkha, Gandhian cap and khadi dress were depicted quite prominently. For Gandhi, the satyagrahis had to wear white khaddar; 'coloured cloths were out at least until Swaraj was attained'. However, at local levels, Gandhi's instructions were received in quite different ways and (as we saw in the chapter on the flag) *geru bastar* (deep saffron colour dress), red or simple coloured cloths were described as the *pahirawa* (uniform) of volunteers.[24] Gradually, there developed a disconnect between the experiential and the ethical. Charkha, the modern notion of politics, pushed earlier practices of politics as well-being. Like the modern scientific knowledge, which uses experience as a passive repository of information to validate or refute truth claims, politicians and policy-makers also began distancing themselves from this amorphous category of people and their experiences. Thus, for them what mattered more was the precision of knowledge that can be applied for the building of a new nation. In other words, progress over people, history over past. We may see this conflict by revisiting the decade of the 1940s.

The Political Assassination of Gandhi and the Narratives of Charkha

Scholars have pointed out that the 1940s witnessed the marginalization of Gandhism in the nationalist discourse. Writing on the politics of the assassination of Gandhi, Ashis Nandi has said, 'Every political assassination is a joint communiqué.'[25] This is

---

[24] Shahid Amin, *Event, Metaphor, Memory: Chauri Chaura 1922–1992* (Delhi: Oxford University Press, 1996), 185.

[25] Quoted by Ashis Nandi, 'Final Encounter: The Politics of the Assassination of Gandhi', in *At the Edge of Psychology* (Delhi: Oxford University Press, 1980), 47–70.

also true in the context of marginalization or political death of Gandhi, which came earlier than his physical death. This political assassination was certainly more cruel because it was authored not by any outsider or unknown but by his own men. It was long lasting too, because it was performed at the level of representation and narratives. On the murder of Mahatma Gandhi, Jawaharlal Nehru said, 'Even in his death there was magnificence and complete artistry. It was from every point a fitting climax to the man and to the life he had lived....'[26] It was long lasting too, because what mattered was merely the death of Gandhi but a systematic and gradual process making the Gandhian language and politics as less practical and less relevant.

Part of the story of this marginalization and gradual but steady decline of the mass appeal for the Gandhian activities was rooted in the historical process of its growth itself, which can be explained by focusing on the institutionalization of Gandhian activities. J. C. Kumarappa, writing in 1948, rightly understood the weakness when he wrote that various sanghs—the All India Spinners Association, the All India Village Industries Association, the Hindustan Talimi Sangh, the Harijan Sevak Sangh and the Gau-Seva Sangh—were 'working in their own spheres without much co-ordination amongst themselves and without laying much emphasis on Gandhian philosophy based on non-violence and truth'.[27]

The conspiracy against the Gandhian model of swaraj, the strategic replacement of Gandhian symbols and the gradual marginalization of Gandhi from the centre stage of politics were all to supplement the metaphorical and political death of Gandhi in the post-1945 period. This hegemonization of the discourse has been scripted in many and varied ways. Partha Chatterjee

---

[26] Cited from Partha Chatterjee, *Nationalist Thought and the Colonial World: A Derivative Discourse?* (Delhi: Oxford University Press, 1986), 156–57.

[27] J. C. Kumarappa, 'Lok Sevak Sangh', 26 February 1948, *Gandhi Seva Sangh Papers*, microfilm reel no. R-5805, Delhi: NMML.

writes, 'The logical, the rational, the scientific, clearly conceived ends etc. triumphed over the indeterminate, over somebody who was more or less of a philosophical anarchist.'[28] In the case of the final design of India's national flag, the charkha was replaced by the Ashoka wheel in the Constituent Assembly.

Thus, while the basic format of the popular Congress flag remained more or less the same, the spinning wheel vanished from the centre space. Speaking on the philosophy behind the semiotics of the national flag, Dr Radhakrishnan said, 'Ashokan wheel represents to us the wheel of law, the wheel of Dharma.'[29] According to him, the perpetually revolving wheel indicates that there is death in stagnation.[30] The spinning wheel that was replaced with this perpetually revolving wheel of ancient history was not merely 'wheel of dharma' or law, an abstract symbol devoid of everyday life. It was a metaphor for the attainment of the swaraj, and swaraj obviously meant much more than the political freedom, but that dream was kept aside by the 'makers' of Independent India. It is very hard to believe that a philosopher

---

[28] Chatterjee, *Nationalist Thought*, 293–98 and 304.

[29] The colour *bhagwa,* or the saffron, for him was the colour of renunciation of disinterestedness. He said, 'our leaders must be indifferent to material gains and dedicate themselves to their work'. Ibid., 745. In one of the popular and iconic patriotic Hindi film songs, *Mere Desh Ki Dharti,* from a patriotic Hindi film *Upkar* (1967), the colours acquire different connotations. The third and last stanzas go: *ye baag hain gautam naanak kaa, khilate hain aman ke phool yahaan/gaandhee, subhaash, taigore, tilak ayese hain chaman ke phool yahaan/rang haraa hari singh nalawe se, rang laal hain laal bahaadoor se/rang banaa basantee bhagatasing rang aman kaa veer jawaahar se* (In this garden of Buddha and Nanak prospers flowers of peace/Gandhi, Subhash, Tagore, Tilak—such are the flowers that blossom here/Colour green from Hari Singh Nalava, red from Lal Bahadur/Colour saffron is drawn from Bhagat Singh, and white from brave Jawaharlal.) See a write up by Prashant Kadam, '(Imagi)nation Without the Subaltern', *The Hindu Magazine*, online edition, 25 January 2009, http://www.hindu.com/mag/2009/01/25/stories/2009012550020200.htm viewed on 26 January 2009. For Prashant, this song is another 'symptom of Brahmanical patriarchal bias'.

[30] Ibid., 746.

like Radhakrishnan would not have anticipated the difference in the philosophical positions of 'motion', 'go forward' and 'the swaraj' or that he would not have anticipated the displacement of the earlier notion of the motto of 'struggle for Swaraj' with that of 'motion', 'change' or, to simply, 'go forward'. The problem becomes a bit more complex in the speech of Jawaharlal Nehru. Moving the resolution for the adoption of the final design of the national flag, he justified the replacement of the charkha with the Ashoka wheel in following words:

> ...In the white, previously there was the Charkha, which sym-bolised *common man in India,* which symbolised their industry, and which came to us from the message which Mahatma Gandhi delivered. Now, this particular Charkha symbol has been slightly varied in this Flag, not taken away at all. Why has it been varied? Normally speaking, the symbol on one side of the flag should be exactly the same as on the other side otherwise, there is a difficulty which goes *against the conventions.* Now the charkha as it appeared previously on this Flag had the wheel on one side and the spindle on the other. If you see the other side of the Flag, the spindle comes the other way and the wheels comes this way. There was this *practical difficulty.* Therefore, after considerable thought, we were convinced that this great symbol which enthused the people should continue in a slightly different form, that the wheel should be there and not the rest of the Charkha, that is, the *spindle and the string which created this confusion.* The essential part of the Charkha should be there, that is the wheel. So the old tradition continues in regard to the Charkha and the wheel (ital-ics are mine).[31]

To me, the operative words are 'common man', 'conventions', 'practical difficulty' and 'confusion'. It was for the sake of 'practical difficulty' and to avoid the 'confusion' that a symbol of common man charkha's wheel was removed from its spindle and strings.[32]

---

[31] Ibid., 739–40.

[32] However, it should be kept in mind that even at this stage when the Ashoka wheel replaced the 'common men' at the level of emblem,

The systematic attempt to put Gandhi into the backyard by the mainstream top leadership of the Congress began soon after 1942. By 1945, when Independence was not a distant affair any more, 'many a time he was the cause of anger and irritation for the people engaged in the negotiation of power (both for country and for themselves)'. In the final years of transfer of power, they found Gandhi's style slightly anachronistic and the mahatma somewhat unmanageable.[33] Mahatma's isolation and agony in this phase was sourced not merely from communal riots but also from the fact that he was helplessly witnessing the privileging of the political freedom over the attainment of swaraj—and thus wanted to dissolve Congress as a political party to be replaced by a Lok Sevak Sangh.[34]

In this mad race for the future authority, the differences widened among Congress leadership also on the social and economic objectives after Independence. Following one such round of discussions in September 1945 in the Congress Working Committee

---

the 'common men' and their sacrifices remained alive at the level of narrative. Moving the resolution of the flag, Nehru told: 'In a sense this Flag was adopted not by a formal resolution, but by popular acclaim and usage, adopted much more by the sacrifice that surrounded it in the past few decades. We are in a sense only ratifying the popular adoption' (ibid., 739).

[33] Sarkar, *Modern India*, 437–54. Nandi writes: 'Finally though to his political heirs he remained a father figure, 'he remained no more young for them. 'In this situation he himself 'now openly yearned for a violent death while preaching Pacifism. As he becomes fond of telling Manuben, his grandniece and constant companion of his last' days, he now only wanted to die bravely; he felt that could turn out to be his final victory' (Nandi, 'Final Encounter', 88–90).

[34] Sumit Sarkar writes, 'On the eve of his murder, he had warned that the country still had to attain social, moral and economic, independence in terms of its 7000,000 villages, that Congress had created a rotten boroughs leading to corruption and ... institutions popular and democratic only in name and that consequently the Congress as a political party should be dissolved and replaced by a Lok Sevak Sang'. Sarkar, *Modern India*, 453.

meeting, Mahatma Gandhi wrote a letter to Nehru with much deliberation, hesitations and hope.[35] Admitting 'sharp difference of opinion', Gandhi wrote to his heir, Nehru:

> I fully stand by the kind of governance which I have described in *Hindi Swaraj* ... My experience has confirmed the truth what I wrote in 1909 ... I am convinced that if India is to attain true freedom, through India the world also, then sooner or later the fact must be recognised that people will have to live in villages, not in towns; in huts, not in places. Crores of people will never be able to live at peace with each other in towns and palaces ...

Gandhi, however, was ready to make amend many of his earlier rigid stances. For example, he candidly confessed, 'My ideal village still exists only in my imagination. Perhaps there will even be railways and also post and telegraph offices. I do not know what things there will be or will not be.' The later part of the letter clearly reveals Gandhi's emotional weakness for Nehru as he reiterated his declaration of Nehru as his heir and also offered few minor incentives to Nehru.

Unfazed, Nehru, however, wrote an extraordinarily firm reply to Gandhi:

> A village, normally speaking, is backward intellectually and culturally and no progress can be made from a backward environment. Narrow minded people are much more likely to be untruthful and violent ... It is many years since I read Hind Swaraj and I have only a vague picture in my mind. But even when I read it twenty or more years ago it seemed to me completely unreal. In your writings and speeches since then I have found much that seemed to me an advance on that old position and an appreciation of modern

---

[35] Mahatma Gandhi, 'Letter to Jawaharlal Nehru', 5th October 1945, *CWMG*, Vol. 81, 319–21. Very rarely we find Gandhi deciding the language of his letter in such an anxious manner as he did in this case, thinking whether to write in English or in Hindusthani. He finally wrote in Hindusthani.

trends. I was, therefore, surprised when you told us that the old picture still remains intact in your mind...[36]

For Nehru, the future nation builder, the speedy attainment of sufficiency of food, clothing, housing, sanitation and so on for the nation was of prime significance. These developments were premised upon the inevitability of modern means of transport, modern developments, heavy industry and, more fundamentally, a technically advanced country in terms of scientific growth.

One can read the removal of charkha with the Ashoka wheel as an extension of this exchange, as a further push to Gandhian swaraj from the centre stage of colonial struggle to the oblivion in the scheme of things visualized by the nation builders of Independent India. The common man vanished from the agenda and the 'magnificent name' of Ashoka acquired that space. Keeping in mind the low literacy rate, I wonder how many of the 'common men' were familiar with the name of Ashoka.[37] The nation established its lineage by placing this historic personality at the centre or, in other words, history replaced the common men, their sufferings and their past experiences. Gandhi had his own critique of history as a mode of rendering the past, and he advocated for an open past in *Hind Swaraj* when he wrote, 'I believe in the saying that a nation is

---

[36] Gopal, *Selected Works of Jawaharlal Nehru* (Delhi: Orient Longman, 1981), Vol. 14, 554–57. It may be noted here that in Gopal's edited volume, Nehru's letter is dated 4 October 1945, and he in the text of the letter refers Gandhi's letter as dated 2 October 1945. Also see M. J. Akbar, *Nehru: The Making of India* (Delhi: Lotus/Roli Books, 1988), 469–70.

[37] Ashoka, a product of the 19th-century intellectual discourse, has been highlighted in order to meet some political demands of the historical narrative. One can see a line running through between Ashoka, Akbar and colonial state. The big states and the myth of centralized bureaucratic administration of Ashoka and Akbar have functioned as a justification for the thesis of 'hydraulic despotism' of pre-colonial oriental states for quite a long time. Along with the image of a stable centralized state, regimes of Ashoka and Akbar also shared a harmonious co-existence of different religious faiths, a dream of post-Independent Indian state.

happy that has no history'.[38] A particular discourse of history triumphed ultimately in the semiotic sphere of the national flag, and he was made to be a failed man on 'practical fronts'.

The removal of the charkha did not go unchallenged outside the Constituent Assembly. One correspondent from Hyderabad wrote, 'Gandhiji is being buried alive.' Referring to some of the speeches of the Constituent Assembly Debate, he further wrote, 'The new wheel or Ashokan chakra has no connection with Gandhi's wheel; wheel is the sign of "non-violent economy" while the new one represents the Sudarshan chakra, which represents violence'.[39] In the beginning, Gandhiji had himself reacted bitterly over the issue of the removal of the spinning wheel from 'the flag'. He wrote, '... I must say that if the Flag of Indian Union will not contain the emblem of the charkha I will refuse to salute that Flag...'.[40] He further wrote, 'if we neglect the charkha ... we will be acting like a man who remembers God in sorrow and forgets him when he showers happiness'.[41] Earlier he had suggested the

---

[38] For Gandhiji's view on the history, see Mahatma Gandhi, *Hind Swaraj*. Also see quite a provocative essay by Sunil Khilnani, 'Gandhi and History', *Seminar* 461, January 1998, 110–15.

[39] Mahatma Gandhi, 'The Tricolour', 3 August 1947, *The Collected Works of Mahatma Gandhi* (Delhi, 1976), Vol. 89: 2.

[40] Gradually, he came to believe that the *chakra* (wheel) of the flag was Ashoka chakra (Ashoka wheel) and had nothing to do with Sudarshan Chakra. He also accepted that popular meaning of the Sudarshan chakra as a symbol of violence was wrong. Gandhi, 'Letter from Professor Radha Kumud Mukherji (31 August 1947)', ibid., 120.

[41] Gandhi, 6 November 1947, ibid., 484. Gandhiji was also worried about the problem of the existing stock of one lakh flags with charkha at the central space. Mahatma Gandhi said, 'The Charkha Sangh has a stock of old tri-colour flags valued at ₹2 lakhs. The Charkha Sangh is an organisation of very poor people. I am its President. The people working in that organization are paid very little. They want to know what they are to do with the flags. There is not much difference between the new and the old except that the old one was a little more elegant. The old flag had the charkha. The new one the wheel but not the spindle and the mal. The new flag does not render the old flag redundant. Even after the king is dead, the kingdom remains and old coins are not discarded for the new ones. When

design of the tricolour with the little Union Jack in the corner of the flag. He said that this would represent our humble gesture towards our own past ruler.[42]

The replacement of charkha with the wheel was also made on the pretext of preparing the country to speak the vocabulary of universalism.[43] Hence, the invocation of heraldic *convention* in Nehru's earlier mentioned speech at the time of moving the resolution. However, more than this heraldic convention, Nehru referred both the history and the future while giving the Ashoka wheel an international dimension. For him, the Ashoka wheel represented an era that was 'essentially an international period of Indian history'. It was not a narrowly national period. It was

---

the new coins are issued old coins do not suffer any depreciation of value. Therefore, so long as there is even old flag in stock at the Gandhi Ashram the two flags will have the same value. People who have old flags should not tear them up and if they want to buy more flags they should buy the same flags from the Gandhi Ashram so that goods worth of ₹2 lakhs are not wasted. Of course in future the Charkha Sangh will make flags only of the new design.' Mahatma Gandhi, 'Prarthana Pravachan', *The Hindu*, 24 July 1947, *Mahatma Gandhi, Collected Works* (Delhi: Publications Division, Ministry of Information and Broadcasting, 1976), Vol. 88: 416.

[42] Ibid., 375.

[43] Following Partha Chatterjee's formulation, Srirupa Roy suggests that the Gandhian moment of manoeuvre enabled the elaboration of an inner realm of spirituality and cultural autonomy in which national distinctiveness, rather than international similarity, was proclaimed. A key feature of this inner realm is its territorial–cultural specificity; that is, the appeal to values and ethics is spatially circumscribed. Thus, although satyagraha was a translatable concept that could travel beyond geopolitical boundaries, like other Gandhian concepts of Ram rajya, village republics, vegetarianism, and, above all the *charkha*, or the spinning wheel, they were seen to resonate most profoundly in India with Indians. In short, for Gandhi, nationalism began at home, and then could travel the world. The Gandhian imaginary, thus, ordered the representations of spatial relations between the inside and the outside in the image of nationalist internationalism rather than internationalist nationalism. This difference had implications well beyond semantics because it posed questions of belonging and membership—the question of who could become an Indian nationalist—very differently (Srirupa Roy. 'A Symbol of Freedom': The Indian Flag and the Transformations of Nationalism, 1906–2002, *The Journal of Asian studies*, 65, no. 3 (August 2006): 508).

a period when India's ambassadors went abroad to far countries and went abroad not in the way of an empire and imperialism but as ambassadors of peace and culture and goodwill. Thus, a symbol from this era was a befitting candidate for a flag which he declared was 'a Flag of freedom not only for ourselves but a symbol of freedom to all people who may see it'. This aspiration transformed a party flag to the national flag and that too as an embodiment of universal values and meanings.[44] In this aspiration, we find the Constituent Assembly as an arena that tried to re-position the flag on several grounds. The basic premise of this repositioning was to simultaneously establish legitimacy by associating the flag with the popular usage, its recent history of sacrifice and patriotism yet also redefine it as a symbol of the sovereign state. People were the source of its authority but it had to be re-ordered to comply with specific logic of the state.

To summarize, the Constituent Assembly debate revolved around three fundamental objectives. The first objective was to create some distance from the party flag and give it territorial connotation without wiping the popular association that people had with the party flag. This was least difficult as the Congress always projected its own party flag as the national flag even in the 1920s when it had not adopted a formal flag or in the 1930s and 1940s when the Congress, in very many ways, successfully planted its flag as the national flag. Looking at the composition of the Constituent Assembly and the manner in which it functioned under the Congress leadership (without Mahatma Gandhi), the road was rather less bumpy. Aditya Nigam has underlined the three great absences that haunted the Constituent Assembly: the Muslim League, the representatives of the Indian states and the father of the nation, Mahatma Gandhi. He has also shown that the assembly largely worked under the leadership

---

[44] Srirupa Roy writes, 'Coincident with the recalibration of global economic and political power after the recent conclusion of II World War, Indian sovereignty was proclaimed at a time when the template of international sovereignty itself was in flux, when it was possible, and even feasible, to envision a radically new way of being in the world' (Roy, " A symbol of Freedom", 513).

with a desire for a modern and homogeneous nation-state. In this environment, members of the minority communities such as Muslims or people holding minority positions (such as P. S. Deshmukh), who wanted to retain Gandhi's *charkha*, were under severe pressure to perform according to the codes of the dominant group.[45]

The second major thread, in my view, was to create necessary condition for this desire for a modern homogeneous nation-state, and this had to be articulated by wiping out any ambiguity. Hence, we have Nehru taking recourse in the logic of 'convention' and in the name of 'practical difficulty' in his advocacy for the removal of *charkha*. At a more deeper level, this had to address the ambiguous nature of the past and make room for the peda-gogic history. In Gandhi's language, the past remained open; it was a realm of experience and hence it was open to very many usages. It is always difficult to control and contain production of meanings in these open realms of past experience. Hence, *charkha* as an emblem of common men's suffering and their past always carried the very many meanings and one of them was a symbol of resistance. A symbol of freedom had to be devoid of its experience of resistance. In Gandhi's scheme of things, *charkha* was never a tool for statecraft. In his doctrine, state and society were not separated from each other. In other words, *swaraj* was premised not in the language of Western science and modernity. Modernity needed precision in its language to define and segregate the whole in parts.[46] Modern statecraft needed categories and constituencies that should not overlap. In *swaraj*, categories of life cannot be

---

[45] For a good discussion on this issue, see Aditya Nigam, 'A Text without Author: Locating the Constituent Assembly as Event', in *Politics and Ethics of the Indian Constitution*, ed. Rajeev Bhargava (Delhi: Oxford University Press, 2008), 119–39.

[46] Zygmunt Bauman writes, 'The typically modern practice, the sub-stance of modern politics, of modern intellect, of modern life is the effort to exterminate ambivalence: an effort to define precisely—and to suppress or eliminate everything that could not or would not be precisely defined.' He further writes that the sovereignty of the modern state is the power to define and to make the definitions stick—everything that self-defines or eludes the power assisted definition is subversive. He quite insightfully

disentangled from each other; hence, from the perspective of modernity, it was a language disorder, an ambivalence that had to be erased or at least reworked. Hence, the wheel was cleaned from its strings and spindle, history from past, freedom from resistance and the singularly identifiable figure of Ashoka from common men with a potential of plural identifications.

The third important feature of the Constituent Assembly debate was the failure of this ordering, this gleaning of singular from the multiplicity of meanings. The Constituent Assembly wanted to establish a singular symbolic authority in the arena of the nation's flag. This singular authority was also defined in non-communal terms; hence, the equation between colours and communities was summarily rejected. Like 1931, in 1947 too, the burden of immediate communal violence was on the shoulders of designers of the flag, and like 1931, they successfully maintained to project the flag's non-communal character. Both these desires remained unfulfilled in very many ways. Outside the sphere of state governance, a different section of the society continued to practice multiple flags. Speaking on behalf of what he proclaimed as the real owners of this country, the 30 million 'adivasis' who have been fighting for freedom for the last six thousand years, Jaipal Singh from Bihar made the following submission in the Constituent Assembly:

Sir, most of the members of this House are inclined to think that flag hoisting is the privilege of the Aryan civilised. Sir, the

---

refers to Paul Ricoeur's formulation of close ties between science and state power and writes:

  ... the practice of science is in its innermost structure no different from that of state politics; both aim at a monopoly over a dominated territory, and both reach their aims through the device of inclusion/exclusion (of science Ricoeur writes that it is 'constituted by the decision to suspend all affective, utilitarian, political aesthetic, and religious considerations and to hold as true only that which answers to the criteria of the scientific method)'.

Zygmunt Bauman, *Modernity and Ambivalence* (Cambridge: Polity Press, 1993), 7–8.

Adibasis had been the first to hoist flags and to fight for their flags. Members who come from the so-called province of Bihar, will support me when I say that, year after year, in the *melas, jatras* and festivals in Chota Nagpur, whenever various tribes with their flags enter the arena, each tribe must come into *jatra* by a definite route by only one route and no other tribe may enter the *mela* by the same route. Each village has its own flag and that flag cannot be copied by any other tribe. If anyone dared challenge that flag, Sir, I can assure you that that particular tribe would shed its last drop of blood in defending the honour of that flag. Hereafter, there will be two Flags, one Flag which has been here for the past six thousand years, and the other will be this National Flag which is the symbol of our freedom as Pandit Jawaharlal Nehru has put it. This National Flag will give a new message to the Adibasis of India that their struggle for freedom for the last six thousand years is at last over, that they will now be as free as any other in this country.

I do not intend to either agree or judge the audacity of Jaipal Singh's claim when he said that the struggle for freedom for the adivasis was finally over. To me, Jaipal Singh's declaration is suggestive as it forecloses the possibility of the flag as a symbol of resistance and at the same time denies its singularity. A number of similar claims along community and religious lines can be shown where the sovereign symbol of the nation continued to function along with other traditional conventional flags. This co-presence of sovereign and the community flag is not illustrated here to question the authority of the former. It only tells us that the process of modern state to eradicate the multiple sites of authority always remains incomplete.

The proliferation of his image, his ideology and his symbols continued even in post metaphorical, political or physical death of Mahatma Gandhi. Neither the Gandhian triumph nor his death was a complete process. It had various slippages.

We know that Gandhian imagery acquired a cult-like status even during his lifetime. Shahid Amin's work, as we saw from our earlier examples, tells us that the Gandhian movement owed a lot to the processes of ritualization.[47] The mythification of the figure of Gandhi acted as the most influential means to engulf the domain of ordinary life in the nationalist movement. In the same manner, it is also true that just as we see the spread of the Gandhian movement in and through these processes, we also see the decline of the Gandhian movement due to inversion of these processes of ritualization. In metaphorical ways, it can be said that Gandhi was murdered at the practical sphere and his corpse was placed for worship in the moral or spiritual sphere. The example from a well-known Hindi novel, *Maila Anchal* of Phanishwar Nath Renu, would not be out of context here.[48]

A character of this novel, Baban Das, was a true Gandhian; he had done great works in the pre-independence period. In his region, Baban Das was recognized as a living legend in the field of community service, social welfare and fight against any kind of immoral activities. But all his correspondences with Gandhi were stolen by Baldeo (a fellow disciple of Baban Das) who used them to project himself as a leader of the region. Baldeo was suitably rewarded with a post in the newly formed government. Baban Das kept fighting the black marketers and the smugglers, and in this fight he was killed by them in the forest one night. His corpse was disposed away but his bag (*jholi*) was found hanging on a banyan tree. One of his murderers even took that away. But the lace (belt) of the bag remained there hanging on the branch of the tree. Very soon the village womenfolk started worshipping it as '*Chetharia pir*'.[49] William Crook writes that this widespread custom is 'probably based on more than one line of thought'. Sometimes it is an offering of respect to the true spirit, at dangerous places such as river-crossings or cannon bridges in

---

[47] Shahid Amin, 'Gandhi as Mahatma: Gorakhpur District, Eastern UP, 1921–2', in *Subaltern Studies II*, ed. Ranjit Guha (New Delhi: Oxford University Press, 1987); Amin, *Event, Metaphor*.

[48] Phanishwar Nath Renu, *Maila Anchal* (Delhi/Patna: Rajkamal, 1954).

[49] *Chetharia pir*: particular trees that people recognize as a ritual space for wish fulfilment; to worship the tree in terms of saint.

the lower Himalayas. Here the offering may be intended to win the support of a kindly tree spirit. In Berar, it is '*Chindiyadeo*' or Lord of tatters. In United Provinces while we have '*chithariya bir*' or 'rag hero', in the Panjab we find '*Lingri Pir*' or 'rag saint'.[50] The belt of the bag acquired ritual status and became an object of worship, a medium of wish fulfilment. On the other hand, we have no dearth of evidence of irreverence when in most innocent ways, Gandhi, his ethics and his philosophy have been derided.

In the post-colonial conditions, in his study on the use of khadi/white in Indian public life, Dipesh Chakrabarty reads the political culture that shapes the meanings of khadi in terms of value systems and zones of engagements 'desired' by 'alternative modernity'. He writes:

> It is the site of the desire for an alternative modernity, a desire made possible by contingencies of British colonial rule, now impossible of realization under the conditions of capitalism and yet circulating insistently within everyday object of Indian public life, the (male) politician's uniform.

The evaporation of Gandhian values from the khadi 'would signify the demise of a deeper structure of desire and would signal India's complete integration into the circuits of global capital'.[51]

A cartoon from 'The Folio' on 'woven art' of a leading Indian newspaper, *The Hindu*, is a case to cite here. In this cartoon,

---

[50] See the section 'godlings of disease', in William Crook, *Religion and Folklore of Northern India* (Delhi: S. Chand, 1925), 138–39. He writes that pilgrims also tie knots in the grass of roadside leading to a shrine, and a common form of making a vow is if you grant me my desire I will tie a knot to you'. At Mathura stood the tree known as *vastra-harana*, clothes' stealing, where Krishna sat bathing in the Jumna, and forced them to appear unclothed before him—a tale which, as it has been suggested, may well be based on a rag tree (a phenomenon we shall return to later in a different context).

[51] See Dipesh Chakrabarty, 'Clothing the Political Man: A Reading of the Use of Khadi/White in Indian Public Life', *Postcolonial Studies* 4, no. 1 (2001): 27–38.

Gandhiji is depicted as plying his spinning wheel and his one eye is open. His figure occupies central space and is flanked by two teenagers. They are scoffing at him. One of them yells, 'hip up old man or just ship out!'[52] These examples do not belong to Gandhian narratives as we conventionally interpret the words- 'Gandhian narrative', yet these all are essential components of the Gandhian discourse. The text of the spinning wheel here ridicules its author, Gandhiji. These are the echoes of Gandhism—echoes full of ambiguities and contradictions, forming the 'poetics of volition'.

Khadi today symbolizes both a dress code for political leaders and the sense of austerity (until very recently, it was only a dress code). However, at a different level, its products such as *matka*, *Bhagalpuri khadi* silk and *kagaji* silk are some of the costliest and delicate varieties of cloths which are ceremonial dress codes for elite sections of the rural, urban and even metropolitan populace. These varieties are used to convey not only an elitist ethno-spiritual image, but also the idea of simplicity (austerity), which always remains dominant in this projection.

This husky image of the symbol, the spinning wheel becomes more explicit in the following example of a kitsch. One of the *fagua* song from Renu's *Maila Anchal* is relevant here[53]:

Jogi ji, tal na tute
Jogi ji teen taal par dholak baaje
Jogi ji taak dhina dhin!
Charkha Kaato, Khaddhar Pahano, rahe hath me jholi
Din dahare karo dakaiti bole suraji boli
Jogi ji sar..ar..ar...ra...![54]

---

[52] 'Woven Art', *The Folio, The Hindu* (20 June 1999), 25, http://www.hinduonnet.com/folio/fo9906/99060240.htm.

[53] Fagua is another name for one of the most popular festivals called Holi. It is a festival of colours when social sexual norms are relaxed to a great length. In the carnival atmosphere, people sing songs and play with colours.

[54] Renu, *Maila Anchal*, 125.

O pure hearted! Don't break the rhythm, O pure hearted! The drum will be on three bits, *jogi ji tak dhina dhin*, spin, wear Khaddar, keep a bag in your hand (like a saint or a beggar, but) carry out robbery in the daylight with a language of swaraj volunteers, *jogi ji sar..ar..ar..ar.*

This is one of the serious threats Gandhism faced in the later stages of the freedom movement. These songs, especially *fagua* songs, do not demand anything in return from its viewers. These songs do not even demand any serious attention. These are sung at moments when the audience appears to be politically unconscious. In fact, political meanings of the text derive its authority from seemingly apolitical context and format of the text. The north Indian '*jogiras*' have their own world,[55] a world still unexplored by social linguists and scholars of popular culture. These *jogiras* or *Holi* couplets are not just examples of life released from the shackles. These *jogiras* are also not just another form of satire, entertaining laughter or mockery when the text of humour turns the existing order and its value system upside down. These *jogiras*, though certainly humour, work at the margins of the texts which they criticize. These *jogiras* work both outside and inside of the text. This dual position then enables them to widen the field of the text, which they attack, and at the same time ridicule the significance of the text. It is at this second point the *jogiras* create their own 'field of play'. Bachtin says, 'Laughter doesn't exclude the exalted.... Laughter builds itself a counter world, as it were, to stand against the official world.'[56]

---

[55] *Jogiras*, as is the case here, are poetic compositions often in the form of couplets. These are attributed to jogi ji a cultural metaphorical figure who can be loosely translated as pure/good-hearted souls. The intended meaning of this figure is, however, often inversed in such compositions.

[56] Bachtin, cited by Peter Claus Zoller and Christina Oesterheld, ed., *Of Clowns and Gods: Brahmans and Babus. Humours in South Asian Literature* (Delhi: Manohar Publishers, 1999), 15; also see Lee Siegal, *Laughter Matters: Comic Tradition in India* (Delhi: Motilal Banarsidass, 1987).

Contrary to the nationalist meaning structure, here charkha, khaddar or politicians bag creates its own image. One can safely argue that the legitimacy and authority of a special critical interpretation of the spinning wheel comes not from the person but from the occasion that produces this text. As Bourdieu writes:

> every critical affirmation contains, on the one hand, a recognition of the value of the work which occasions it ... and on the other hand an affirmation of its own legitimacy. All critics declare not their judgement of the work but also their claim to the right to talk about it and judge it. In short they take part in a struggle for the monopoly of legitimate discourse about the work of art, and consequently in the production of the value of the work of art.[57]

There is, as Bourdieu puts it, 'an interest in disinterestedness'.[58] The spinning wheel has been attacked in this song, precisely due to its association with 'Swaraj', but the spinning wheel has also been claimed as a cover to hide corruption and dacoity. Contrary to the nationalist job, here the spinning wheel, *khaddar* or politicians bag creates its own image. Here, the text 'charkha' is totally devoid of its original meaning and historical purpose assigned to it by the author and the historical context in which it acquired political significance. This is an image of corruption and exploitation of the downtrodden. Along with this kitsch (above-mentioned '*jogira*'), in the same novel, *Maila Anchal*, we observe the glorification of Gandhi and his comrades in '*Batgamni Fagua*' (song for the travellers):

aye re horiya aye phir se aye re!
Gabat Gandhi rag manohar
Charkha chalabe babu Rajendar
Goonjal bhart amhai re, horiya aye phir se.

---

[57] Pierre Bourdieu, *The Field of Cultural Production* (Cambridge: Polity Press, 1993), 19.
[58] Ibid.

(Holi has come again!

Gandhi sings manohar (*lit.* charming) raga, Rajendra (Prashad, another Congress leader and the first president of India) ply the spinning wheel, reverberates the sound of mango forest across the India,

Holi has come again!)[59]

When put together these two songs, we get contradictory images pointing to the change in the nature of audience. In kitsch (in the *jogira*), the self-image of the text is quite overt and comes from outside. But in various narratives of the spinning wheel (i.e. *Batgamni fagua* or in earlier-mentioned songs and couplets), the presence of the spinning wheel legitimizes the Gandhian ideology and work as a rhetoric. It has been incorporated in these songs as an ornament, enhancing the power of these songs. This ornamentation also betrays the Gandhian cause, the very role assigned to the spinning wheel by Gandhi himself.

---

[59] Renu, *Maila Anchal*, 126.

6

Gandhi
Journalist, Communicator and Satyagrahi

Keval J. Kumar

Mahatma Gandhi was a 'mass communicator' par excellence. The hundred volumes of the *Collected Works of Mahatma Gandhi*, each volume comprising around 500 pages, and put together by the Publications Division from 1956 to 1994 are witness to the prolific journalist and mass communicator that he was. These volumes include in chronological order not just the four books[1] that he wrote but also the numerous journalistic pieces, speeches and interviews as well as the thousands of letters he addressed to all and sundry. As he himself once remarked, 'I am not made for academic writings; action is my domain.'[2]

During India's freedom movement, the press in English and some Indian languages was well developed, though its

---

[1] Mahatma Gandhi. *The Story of My Experiments With Truth* (Navajivan Press, 1940); *Satyagraha in South Africa* (Madras: S. Ganesan, 1938); *Hind Swaraj or Home Rule* (Ahmedabad: Navjivan Press, 1938); *Key to Health* (Ahmedabad: Navjivan Press, 1948).

[2] Quoted in B. R. Nanda. *In Search of Gandhi: Essays and Reflections* (New Delhi: Oxford University Press, 2002), 254.

impact was restricted to the literate in large urban centres. In 1924–1925 for instance, there were hardly 18.6 million literates, and the population undergoing instruction less than four per cent of the entire population of 320 million inhabitants. Scarcely three per cent were enrolled in the primary and less than 0.6 per cent in the secondary schools.[3] The total railway mileage at the time was 3,800 miles, but large areas of the country still had no railways at all. (By comparison, England had over 50,000 miles.[4]) The total mileage of metalled and unmetalled roads maintained by public authority was only about 216,000.[5] The post and telegraph facilities too were meagre and undeveloped.

How was it then that Mohandas Karamchand Gandhi, an obscure lawyer before he set out for South Africa, rose to be the only national leader of the freedom movement to be accepted, by the masses of India? His appeal was nationwide, cutting across region, caste, religion and socio-economic status. He was hailed the Mahatma not only by the *bhadralok* of Bengal, the Brahmins of Madras and Maharashtra and his fellow Gujaratis but by the illiterate, the backward classes, the untouchables, and by Muslims, Christians, Parsees and tribals in almost every region of the land. As early as March 1921, a CID report on a mass meeting held in an Uttar Pradesh village provides evidence of his mass appeal. Never before, says the report, has any political leader in his own lifetime stirred the masses to their very depths throughout the country and received the homage of so many people, Hindus and Muslims alike. His influence is certainly phenomenal and quite unprecedented.[6] In July the same year, the *Bengali* commented:

---

[3] *India in 1924–1925* (Government of India Central Publication Branch, 1925).

[4] Ibid.

[5] Ibid.

[6] Judith Brown. *Gandhi's Rise to Power (1915–1925)* (London: Cambridge University Press, 1972), 345.

Being present at the various meetings held in Calcutta on June 30 we have been struck with two things. First, that a new spirit has taken hold of the lower class people and secondly, the majority of the people in India have accepted Gandhi as leader.... What a leadership! Such a leadership in politics has never seen before.[7]

Gandhi did, indeed, exercise a charismatic appeal to the lowest levels of Indian society right from the early 1920s. The idea that he was divine took deep root in the country as 'miracle stories' about him were spread, *pujas* (prayers) began to be held in his honour and his 'darshan' came to be sought everywhere. The lower-class people reacted to him with a mixture of religious adulation and millenary anticipation. Time and again local reports showed that Gandhi's appeal depended on a popular belief that if he came to power, all distress and hardship would end,[8] the Ramraj he spoke of.

For his political leadership, however, Gandhi depended upon the strength and loyalty of 'sub-contractors' who held the reins of power in local society and could act as brokers between the centre and the periphery.[9] They consisted of men educated in the vernacular or English, small-town lawyers, traders, money-lenders, village officials, village priests and *ulema*, prosperous cultivators, men typified by the Marwaris of Calcutta and Bihar, and the Patidars of Gujarat. They formed an efficient network of propaganda and command,[10] and it was their support throughout the non-cooperation movement that was critical for Gandhi's status as a national leader. It was this influential group that helped Gandhi give a mass and popular base to the Congress Party—a party of the Western-educated elite to begin with.

---

[7] Quoted in Brown, ibid., 346.
[8] Ibid.
[9] Ibid., 346.
[10] Ibid., 343.

Mass-based Organization for Effective Communication

With his experience of rejuvenating the Natal Indian Congress in South Africa, Gandhi recognized the imperative need for a strong mass-based organization for effective communication with the masses. One of the secrets of Gandhi's remarkable success in communicating with the vast majority of the rural masses was that he used—and helped develop—the communication facilities of the Congress Party. Without the party, Gandhi's message would not have been transmitted so successfully.[11] He set about transforming an elite and passive debating body which met once a year into a mass political organization, manned by full-time political workers and capable of mobilizing public opinion and bringing it to bear on governmental policy and administration.[12] He also made its structure and procedure more rational, professional and dramatic,[13] through his revision of its constitution in 1920.

'I have attempted', wrote Gandhi to N. C. Kelkar on 2 July 1920, 'to give the Congress a representative character such as would make its demands irresistible'.[14] Thus, Gandhi succeeded in introducing regular procedures for the selection of delegates and the president by creating an orderly, graduated structure of party organizations with fixed jurisdictions, rights and responsibilities.[15]

The structured core, however, of Gandhi's democratization of the Congress Party lay in the proliferation of units capable

---

[11] Kusum J. Singh and Bertram M. Gross. 'The Village Communicator'. *Seminar*, 235, 12–13.

[12] Lloyd I. Rudolph and Susanne H. Rudolph. *The Modernity of Tradition* (Chicago, IL: University of Chicago, 1967), 232. The Rudolphs' essay on Gandhi has been reissued under the title *Gandhi: The Traditional Roots of Charisma* (Chicago, IL: University of Chicago, 1983).

[13] Ibid.

[14] M. K. Gandhi. *Collected Works*, 28: 3.

[15] Lloyd I. Rudolph and Sussanne H. Rudolph. *The Modernity of Tradition* (Chicago, IL: University of Chicago, 1967), 238.

of attracting and channelling a mass membership base.[16] The Subjects Committee, Annual Session, Provincial Congress Committees (PCCs) and District Committees (DCCs) were already in existence, but they were geared to a limited membership. To give the organization a mass membership base, Gandhi wanted 'the delegates to be elected through the choice of millions', and anyone paying the fee of four annas (a quarter of a rupee) and signing the Congress creed could become a member. Further, he re-divided India so far as the Congress was concerned into provinces on a linguistic basis, creating 21 PCCs, each corresponding to a linguistic region. The pre-1920 PCCs, on the other hand, coincided with the administrative boundaries of British India which cut across those of language, with the result that English literacy was a prerequisite of participation.[17]

The reconstitution of the PCCs and the mass orientation of the Congress necessitated and indeed encouraged the use of Hindi and the regional languages, and dethroned the value of English, the language of the rulers and of the Western-educated elite. This gave a new sense of self-esteem to the people, and a medium of communication that led to a more active participation by ever greater numbers. More importantly, the use of Hindi-Hindustani (which soon came to be accepted as the national language) and the regional languages brought the masses into a movement that was (prior to Gandhi) largely urban, elitist and narrow in its interests.

From his experience in the reorganization of the Natal Congress in South Africa, the Gujarat Sabha and of service societies, Gandhi had come to recognize the power of a common language, especially the mother tongue, to weld a people together, to raise their self-esteem and to ensure dynamic participation. The same power he imbued the Congress with. It was the deft stroke of a mass communicator at work. He saw language as a

---

[16] Ibid.
[17] Ibid.

powerful means of achieving national unity,[18] not the suppression of regional languages by Hindi but the addition of Hindi to the former so as to enable provinces to establish a living contact with one another.[19] The Hindustani he advocated as the national language was neither the Sanskritized Hindi nor the Persianized Urdu but a happy combination of both. It would also freely admit words wherever necessary from the different regional languages, as also assimilate words from foreign languages, provided they can mix well and easily with our national language. Thus, our national language must develop into a rich and powerful instrument capable of expressing the whole gamut of human thoughts and feelings.[20]

He insisted on the use of the mother tongue (and not Hindi) in education, especially at the primary and secondary stages, for that is the language one is nourished on and sustained by. 'I must cling to my mother tongue as to my mother's milk', said Gandhi, 'in spite of its shortcomings. It alone can give me the life-giving milk'.[21]

As a mass communicator, Gandhi understood the intimate attachment of people to their own languages and dialects, and the most effective appeal was one couched in the listener's own dialect. According to Lord Bhiku Parekh, Gandhi

> developed a language of discourse that allowed him to speak to each group in its own idioms and also left him enough room to escape when the idioms conflicted. His speeches at the time of the Vaikom Satyagraha are a brilliant example of how he placated both the orthodox Brahmins and the impatient untouchables.[22]

---

[18] Ibid.

[19] Ibid., 239.

[20] M. K. Gandhi. *Thoughts on National Language* (Ahmedabad: Navjivan Press, 1956), 55.

[21] Ibid., 30.

[22] Lord Bhiku Parekh. 'Foreword" to Usha Thakkar and Jayashree Mehta. *Understanding Gandhi: Gandhians in Conversation with Fred J. Blum*, 2011, xiii–xiv. See also Bhiku Parekh. *Colonialism, Tradition and*

No Gift of Tongues

Gandhi was no polyglot like Vinobha Bhave, the gift of tongues was not his possession. The only languages he was fluent in were Gujarati (his mother tongue), Hindustani and English. The Gujaratis took him to their hearts immediately on his return from South Africa; even there in the beginning, his most ardent admirers and followers were the 'Arabs', Muslims of Western India. Indeed, he would have been satisfied with serving his own linguistic community as he wrote to Pranjivan Mehta, a friend, in October 1911: 'Please do not think that I shall incur the sin of falling into the delusion that I should serve the entire world. I well realize that my work can only be in India and that in Gujarat, rather in Kathiawar.'[23]

Fluency in spoken and written Hindustani helped Gandhi reach almost the entire country. His own estimate was that out of a population of 350 million only about 38 million comprising the Madras Presidency could not follow a Hindustani speaker. He excluded the Muslim population for it was common knowledge that a majority of Muslims of Madras Presidency understood Hindustani,[24] which he called 'the daughter language of the motherland'.[25]

Gandhi's mastery over the nuances of spoken and written English provided him easy access to the educated elite in India and Britain, and indeed to an international audience. He hailed English as a world language, useful as it was for the acquisition of knowledge and for international intercourse, but sought to weaken the spell it had cast on the educated in India. 'It had led,' he wrote in *Harijan*, 'to the impoverishment of Indian languages, and a break between the millions and the English-educated few

---

Reform: An Analysis of Gandhi's Political Discourse (New Delhi: SAGE, 1999). Revised Edition.

[23] Gandhi. *Collected Works*, 2, 166.

[24] *Young India*, 21 January 1920.

[25] *Young India*, 15 December 1927.

who happen to be the natural leaders for the simple reason that they are the only educated class.'[26]

Gandhi's Techniques of Communication

The kind of communication Gandhi succeeded in developing during his leadership of the freedom movement was fundamentally people-based and two-way. In such a communication system not only the dominant elites but also various strata and sections of the poor communicate among themselves and send their messages effectively to the upper strata of society.[27] Gandhi's reorganization of the Congress Party into a grassroots-based set up with units and sub-units linked by a system of 'sub-contractors' or 'soldiers' ensured that local issues were not brushed aside by the chain of command. Champaran, Kheda, Ahmedabad and Vykom were the models followed. Socio-economic issues were accorded prime importance, and they were sorted out through the technique of satyagraha.

Essentially, then, Gandhi developed, what Kusum J. Singh terms, the 'mass line' approach. The 'mass line', she explains, 'is a leadership concept which renounces elitism by leaders'. It is based upon the non-elite idea that even the poorest, most oppressed and most downtrodden people of a country—including those who are illiterate—possess many kinds of knowledge, judgement and wisdom from which highly educated leaders, managers, technicians and theoreticians may develop a trained incapacity which can be rectified only by a modest, humble and truly non-arrogant effort to learn from ordinary people. Gandhi practised non-elitism every day and it was this practice that established the close link between himself and his associates on the one hand, and on the other hand, with hundreds of millions of illiterate peasants. It was through this practice that the Indian liberation movement achieved mass communication with only the most limited use of

---

[26] Gandhi. *Collected Works*, 99.

[27] Singh and Gross. 'The Village Communicator', 12–13.

elite media and with no help whatsoever from the mass media. Gandhi created a low-cost mass communication system with high mass participation.[28]

It was through this approach/practice that he could make ordinary people feel that he appreciated and cared about their particular problems, however local or insignificant these might have seemed in the rarefied atmosphere of Congress debates. His *padyatras*, for instance, took him to places where ordinary people lived, and whose concerns he came to know at first hand. So, far from reaching down with political ideas like the Home Rulers, Gandhi started at the bottom with issues at stake in local society.

Padyatras

The many *padyatras* he undertook across the length and breadth of the land (beginning with an extensive one-year trek at the bidding of Gopal Krishna Gokhale, his political mentor) provided him intimate knowledge of the lives of the masses. No other leader had reached out to so many millions scattered in far-flung and inaccessible villages. Wherever he went he was received as a messiah, and his 'darshan' was sought as though he were a saint and a god. His identification with the masses and their concerns was never in doubt or held to be a mask put on for effect.[29]

The *padyatra* as a technique of mass communication suited the Indian tradition and the primitive development of modern communication systems in the country. The saints and sages took their message to the masses in similar treks across the land. That

---

[28] Ibid. See also Kusum J. Singh. Gandhi, Mao and the Masses. Unpub. Doctoral Thesis, University of Pennsylvania.

[29] Cf. Peter Gonsalves. *Clothing for Liberation: A Communication Analysis of Gandhi's Swadeshi Movement* (New Delhi: SAGE Publications, 2010), pp. 93ff, for an analysis of 'Gandhi as Performance Manager of a Nation' where it is argued that there was a symmetry between his public performance and his private life.

is how Gandhi came to be looked upon as a saint and not as a politician. He himself drew no distinction between religion and politics, though the British and the educated class in India insisted that he was 'a saint who strayed into politics.'

The *padyatra* succeeded as no other technique did in putting the leader and the masses in close communion, in helping them to reach out to each other, and in total identification with each other. It was, in sum, interpersonal communication at its best. The physical appearance of a leader had, of course, a magnetic effect (as in cooling communal flare-ups in Noakhali and elsewhere), but Gandhi also made it a point to interact with groups of people in their own language.

This bare-bodied man in a loincloth, thus, symbolized for the masses a charismatic figure who was one with them in their hunger and deprivation. Added to this was his frugal diet, his vegetarianism, the frequent fasts he undertook to purify himself and others, his celibacy and his *tapasya* (penitential penance). All these practices turned him into a 'Mahatma' in the eyes of the common people, though this was a title he himself frowned upon.

Symbols, Slogans and Gestures

Gandhi set great store by symbols, slogans and gestures, especially those with a strong religious flavour. Even the terms he found most efficacious in his attempts to catch the imagination of the masses were those with powerful religious connotations (such as satyagraha, sarvodaya, swaraj, Ramraj). But unlike the intellectual religious reformers such as Raja Ram Mohan Roy and Swami Vivekananda, Gandhi's religious thought and practice belonged to folk tradition and popular religion. Hence *bhajans*, hymns and prayer meetings were vital to his methods of communication. He was perhaps influenced by Lokmanya Tilak who revived the Shivaji and Ganesh cults in order to whip up patriotic fervour in the Bombay Presidency during the freedom movement.

Gandhi drew on mythology in his religious thinking, enlisting an imagination that was singularly in tune with the ethos of the masses whose spokesman he was. He found in the mythological world of the common man a storehouse of symbols to which *new* meaning could be given.[30] The symbols he chose to drive home his messages were thus readily intelligible to the masses.

He saw the cow, for instance, as a symbol of exploited creatures, of gentleness, a poem of pity. So cow protection was a symbol of caring for one's own, a tending of links with nature which gives of her bounty only if she is served by man.[31]

Likewise, spinning on the *charkha* apart from being sound economic sense as an occupation for peasants in between crops becomes a symbol for a common activity which can link men of all castes, a sacrificial act in the sense that it means giving up of time, indeed a husbanding of time in the interest of bringing men together.[32] Gandhi also saw the spinning wheel as a symbol of non-violence.

For the freedom movement, however, the *charkha* signified the spirit of independence from colonial values represented by imported textiles. The Swadeshi movement which Gandhi launched with the symbolic burning of foreign clothes swept the entire country and gave rise to a greater self-esteem and pride in things Indian. And the wearing of *khadi* became the hallmark of the freedom fighter and the nationalistic spirit. It signified simplicity and the purity of life.

The gesture that most strikingly communicated the fearlessness of Gandhi to the world was the 200-mile Dandi March and the making of salt in utter defiance of the Salt Act. Indians throughout the country participated, and though the majority of participants were Hindus, Muslims too did take part.

---

[30] Margaret Chatterjee. *Gandhi's Religious Thought* (New Delhi: Macmillan, 1983), 7.

[31] Ibid., 3.

[32] Ibid.

An unexpected element of the protest was the participation of thousands of women—many being of good family and high educational attainments.[33]

Prayer Meetings

Prayer meetings were an integral part of Gandhi's practices in mass communication. They were frequently interfaith gatherings, beginning with Gandhi requesting all present to shut their eyes in order to 'turn the gaze inward'. The gatherings often ran into thousands, most joining in for *darshan* or to pray with a man of god. Congregational prayer, Gandhi felt (influenced perhaps by his association with Quakers in South Africa), generated power, unity and peace. However, he preferred *mantric* prayer to petitionary or supplicatory prayer.[34] The repetition of 'Rama Naam', the name of god, for instance, had *mantric* power for him, especially when it was recited along with others. He considered this type of prayer democratic, for even the most illiterate village could participate in it as much as a pundit. But he eschewed image-worship and the performance of rituals.

Hymns and bhajans were a regular feature of Gandhi's prayer meetings whether in the ashrams or in public. He saw hymns and *bhajans* as aids to focusing the vision on god, as a means of remaining constantly attuned with truth.[35] These hymns, he once remarked, are like any army that stops the mind from going out to eat grass (food of an army) and makes it drink only nectar (the drink of gods).[36] The hymns were generally those that formed part of the folk tradition as transmitted by the saint-bards of medieval

---

[33] Joan V. Broadbent. *Conquest of Violence: The Gandhian Philosophy of Conflict* (Oxford University Press, 1959), 90. For a fuller account, see Thomas Weber. *On the Salt March: The Historiography of Mahatma Gandhi's March to Dandi* (New Delhi: Rupa Publications, 2009).

[34] Chatterjee. *Gandhi's Religious Thought*, 109.

[35] Ibid., 28.

[36] Ibid., 28.

India, such as Surdas, Tukaram and Narsinh Mehta. According to Mahadev Desai, Gandhi's favourite hymn was Narsinh Mehta's 'The True Vaishnavite' which begins: He is a real Vaishnavite, who feels the sufferings of others as his own suffering.[37] When Christians were present at the prayer meetings, Christian hymns such as Cardinal Newman's 'Lead Kindly Light' were sung.

Few Muslims took part in these prayer meetings. Those who did happen to participate in them raised objections to the Hindu orientation of the prayers. Gandhi's practice was to pass on to the post-prayer speech which centred on events of the day.[38] This speech or 'prayer-address' which concluded the prayer session was an occasion for Gandhi to make known his views on political and social happenings, and to plead for tolerance, non-violence and truth. His discourse was amazingly full of rich metaphors and parables which had deep resonances for those who heard him, which had deep roots not only in scripture but also in the folk tradition transmitted by the saint-bards of medieval India.[39]

Sucheta Kripalani, who attended several such prayer meetings, told Fred J. Blum in an interview:

His prayers were a kind of synthetic, where he took bits from all religions. Anything good in any religion was acceptable to him. And he tried to make it a general prayer where people of all faiths could join. When the people were gathered he would come with two or three people who are his close associates and sit on the dais and the prayers will start. He would have a Muslim prayer, then a Buddhist prayer, then recitation from Gita and a hymn ... it took about half an hour or so, maybe a little more time. Gita recitation sometimes took more time.[40]

---

[37] Mahadev Desai. *Day to Day with Gandhi*, I, 132. Quoted in Chatterjee. *Gandhi's Religious Thought*, 271.

[38] Chatterjee. *Gandhi's Religious Thought*, 128.

[39] Ibid., 13.

[40] See Fred J. Blum's Interview with Sucheta Kripalani, in Thakkar and Mehta. *Understanding Gandhi*, 467.

Public Meetings

As at the prayer meetings, in satyagraha meetings too, Gandhi insisted on respect for different views and beliefs. He disallowed speeches that sought to arouse violent feelings of anger and hate. His own addresses were marked by a Biblical simplicity. G. N. Dhawan noted:

> He utterly lacks the dramatic pageantry, hypnotic mannerisms of delivery and semi-historic shouting and shrieking which characterized Hitler's demagogic performances. All the same his simple utterances make an irresistible impact.[41]

In *Seven Months with Mahatmaji*, Krishnadas described a speech of Gandhi in English thus:

> I know not whether to call it a speech or an inspired utterance pregnant with celestial force ... every single word came from the innermost depth of his heart and acted like a charm. Hence the mere sounds of his words pierced and entered the hearts of his hearers. As he went on talking in solemn strain it seemed as though he was causing a hypnotic spell over the audience, and irresistibly drawing all hearts to himself. I noticed that as he spoke there was no emotion in his eyes, nor was there the slightest movement of his limbs.[42]

Krishnadas was not the only one to be carried away by Gandhi's eloquence. Lord Reading, the Viceroy, who met Gandhi in May 1921, was similarly moved:

> My first impression on seeing him ushered into my room was that there was nothing to arrest attention in his appearance and that I should have passed him by in the street without a second look at him. When he talks the impression is different. He is direct and expresses himself well in excellent English with a fine appreciation

---

[41] G. N. Dhawan. *The Political Philosophy of Gandhi* (Bombay: Popular Book Depot, 1946), 175.

[42] Krishnadas. *Seven Months with Mahatmaji*, Vol. 1. 91. Quoted in Dhawan, ibid., 115.

of the value of the words he uses. There is no hesitation about him and there is a ring of sincerity in all that he utters, save when discussing some political questions. His religious views are, I believe, genuinely held and he is convinced to a point almost bordering on fanaticism that non-violence and love will give India its independence and enable it to withstand the British government. His religious and moral views are admirable.[43]

Traditional Terms in a New Garb

The ace communicator that he was, Gandhi invariably made it a point to speak in traditional terms familiar to his audience. Yet he often invested these terms with new meanings. 'I use the old words, giving them a new meaning', he wrote.[44]

For instance, he expanded the meaning of the traditional Hindu utopia, Ramraj, to make it acceptable to Muslims and Christians. 'It is a convenient and expressive phrase,' he observed,

> the meaning of which no alternative can so fully express to millions. When I visit the Frontier Province or address predominantly Muslim audiences, I would express my meaning to them by calling it *Khuda Raj*, while to a Christian audience I would describe it as the 'kingdom of God on earth.'[45]

He also lent this religious term a secular interpretation. 'What is Ramraj?', he asked, 'It can be religiously translated,' he stated,

> as 'the kingdom of God on earth; politically translated, it is perfect democracy in which inequalities based on possession and non-possession, colour, race or creed or sex vanish. In it land and state belong to the people, justice is prompt, perfect and cheap, and therefore, there is freedom of worship, speech and the press—all this because of the reign of the self-imposed law of moral restraint. Such a state must be based on Truth and Non-Violence, and must

---

[43] Quoted in Brown. *Gandhi's Rise to Power,* 328.
[44] *Harijan,* 16 October 1939.
[45] *Harijan,* 18 August 1946.

consist of prosperous, happy and self-contained villages and village communities.'[46]

In the same manner, Gandhi translated 'Jaya, Jaya' in a verse from the ashram hymnal as 'Thy will be done' or 'Thy Kingdom Come' for Mirabehn.[47]

'Swaraj' was yet another term he reinterpreted to give it a wider meaning. Almost synonymous with Ramraj, he defined it as 'complete freedom of opinion and action without interference with another's right to equal freedom of opinion and action.'[48] It also meant self-rule and self-restraint. 'My notion of "purna swaraj"', he explained, 'is not isolated independence but healthy and dignified independence.'

Satyagraha was the term he himself coined to describe his strategy of non-violent resistance first in South Africa and then in India. He distinguished it from passive resistance. 'Satyagraha,' said Gandhi,

> is pure soul force. Truth is the very substance of the soul. That is why this force is called Satyagraha. The soul is informed with knowledge. In it burns the flame of love. If someone gives us pain through ignorance we shall win him through love. 'Non-violence is the supreme dharma' is the proof of this love.

In a similar manner, Gandhi reinterpreted traditional expressions such as *dharma, ahimsa, brahmacharya* and *sarvodaya* so as to make them meaningful to contemporary Indians.

Gandhi: The Journalist

Gandhi's literary output is astounding. On a rough count, during the 50 years of his public life, he ground out some 10 million

---

[46] *Harijan*, 1 June 1947.
[47] Chatterjee. *Gandhi's Religious Thought*, 128.
[48] *Young India*, 27 September 1921.

words. These consist chiefly of his profuse journalistic writings, reports of his speeches and conversations, letters and memoranda, and other fragments, besides the four books that he wrote. The books themselves (except for that early and exotic *Hind Swaraj*) were written as serials. So, the Gandhian corpus is a vast scatter of outwardly ephemeral writings, none of them longer than an average piece of journalism.[49] He wrote as he himself put it 'as the spirit moves me at the time of writing'. His aim was not to be consistent with 'my previous statements but to be consistent with truth as it may present itself at a given moment'.[50]

Besides, he believed that an exponent of satyagraha should make the reasons for his actions transparently clear so that they should not be open to misinterpretation.[51] Hence the detailed self-examination in his *Autobiography*, diaries and the columns of the press (his own and that of others) and the meticulous instructions given to fellow satyagrahis during every effort at fighting social, economic and political repression. Hence also the mound of papers and correspondence he kept, knowing that these would probably be made public (on the rare occasions when he wanted some exchange to be private he had the letters destroyed).[52] In fact, Gandhi was one of the most public of men, and lived his life in full view of friends and followers. Even his so-called 'sex experiments' in order to test his chastity (which his biographers Arthur Koestler, Erik Erikson and Louis Fischer and others make so much of) were not secret. In Ramakrishna Bajaj's words: 'Gandhi did not assume a persona when dealing with the world. There was no distinction between the public and private image … his life was an open book.'[53]

---

[49] T. K. Mahadevan. *Gandhi My Refrain: Controversial Essays (1950–1972)* (Bombay: Popular Prakashan, 1973), 147.

[50] Ibid., 147.

[51] Brown. *Gandhi's Rise to Power*, xv.

[52] Ibid.

[53] Ramakrishna Bajaj. 'Gandhi's Techniques of Communication'. *Service for Communicators* (November 1983).

He took up journalism, not for its sake but

merely as an aid to what I have conceived to be my mission in life. My mission is to teach by example and present under severe restraints the use of the matchless weapon of *satyagraha* which is a direct corollary of non-violence.

So he wrote 'with disciplined simplicity, seeking only to make himself understood.'[54] His choice of words and phrases is kept to the bare minimum. He uses small words, short sentences and simple grammar. A content analysis of a sample of his writings reveals that the average number of syllables per word amounts to 1.49, out of a total average of 729.41 words per article; the number of different words used in an article (with an average of 729 words) is 314.39. There is an almost perfect correlation between the number of words and the number of different words … a clear indicator to say that despite the fact that simple words were used, the vocabulary of the author was in no way limited.[55]

To educate the Indians of South Africa on satyagraha, he started the weekly *Indian Opinion,* published in four languages: Hindi, Tamil, Gujarati and English. On his return to India, he edited *Young India, Navjivan* (Gujarati) and *Harijan* (in English, Urdu and Hindi). He wrote much of the matter himself, using the journals as political weapons rather than as commercial enterprises. Through them he issued instructions about his tactics, and propagated his views on subjects close to his heart.[56]

---

[54] Sunil Sharma (ed.). *Journalist Gandhi: Selected Writings of Gandhi* (Bombay: Gandhi Book Centre, 1960). Quoted in Gonsalves. *Clothing for Liberation, 9.*

[55] Ibid., 33, citing Ralin de Souza's study, 'Gandhian Style of Journalism'. Dissertation for the Master's Degree submitted to Salesian University, Rome, 2007.

[56] For a study of Gandhi as journalist, see Anju Choudhary and Carter R. Bryan. *Summer* 1974. 'Mahatma Gandhi: Journalist and Freedom Propagandist'. *Journalism Quarterly,* 51(2): 286–91. See also S.N. Bhattacharya. *Gandhi the Journalist* (Bombay: Asia Publishing House, 1965); Babani Bhattacharya. *Gandhi the Writer* (New Delhi: National Book Trust, 1969).

During satyagraha campaigns, Gandhi spared no effort at publicizing the issue at stake not only through his own journals or in statements to the press but also through distribution of leaflets and copies of satyagraha pledges at mass meetings, and observation of fasts as a discipline to fit one to offer civil disobedience. Besides, Gandhi and his 'sub-contractors' or 'soldiers' would sign petitions, appeals and also tour districts to preach satyagraha.

To publicize the Champaran campaign, for instance, Gandhi distributed to the press copies of his statement in court; and copies of his telegram to his ashram announcing that he was allowed to investigate were freely distributed in Ahmedabad. The Bombay police even called the Champaran episode 'a revival of his old "passive resistance" game with improved methods in the publicity department'.[57] Again, in the Kheda Satyagraha, Gandhi did his utmost to capture public sympathy by writing to friends, speaking in Bombay and courting the press as he had refused to do, with letters to editors and numerous public statements.[58] Similar strategies of publicity were employed in the satyagraha campaigns in Vykom, Bardoli, Ahmedabad and against the Rowlatt Bills and the Salt Act.[59]

During the anti-war satyagraha (1940–1941), Gandhi feared government suppression of the press. He, therefore, advised extensive use of 'walking newspapers'. 'Let everyone', he advised in *Harijan* (10 November 1940), 'become his own walking newspaper and carry the good news from mouth to mouth ... the idea here is of my telling my neighbor what I have authentically heard. This no government can overtake or suppress. It is the cheapest newspaper yet devised, and it defies the wit of the government, however clever it might be.'[60]

He also made a plea for 'small handwritten unregistered newspapers' in the event of press restrictions. Those who receive

---

[57] Brown. *Gandhi's Rise to Power*, 75.
[58] Ibid., 101.
[59] See Bondurant. *Conquest of Violence*, 45–102.
[60] *Harijan*, 10 November 1940.

the first copy, he advised, (should) recopy it until the process of multiplication covers the whole country. Besides, one copy passes from hand to hand and serves a surprisingly large number. These handwritten sheets make a deep impression of sincerity, eagerness to suffer and defy consequences, and exert a far greater influence upon public opinion than regular newspapers.[61]

Radio and Cinema

Gandhi had no access whatsoever to radio, rigidly controlled as it was by the British government. He made what was possibly his only broadcast over radio on 12 November 1947, less than three months before an assassin's bullet felled him. In that year, All India Radio had only nine stations.[62]

The cinema was a more popular medium. It was in the hands of private studios and filmmakers but censorship forbade references to national leaders. Topical films on the freedom movement were banned outright from 1930 to 1937. Yet, during these years as many as 17 films on Gandhi were shot and Gandhian symbols were subtly introduced in feature films.[63]

Gandhi, however, almost despised the medium, as the following incident suggests: On the occasion of the silver jubilee (in 1939) of the Indian film industry, a Bombay trade paper (of which there 68 at the time, half of them in English) asked him for a message. This was the note it received from his secretary:

As a rule Gandhi gives messages only on rare occasions—and these only for causes whose virtue is ever undoubtful. As for the cinema

---

[61] Quoted in Dhawan. *Political Philosophy of Gandhi*, 177.

[62] See *Akash Bharati: National Broadcasting Trust*, Report of the Working Group on Autonomy for Akashwani and Doordarshan, Vol. II, New Delhi: Information and Broadcasting Ministry, 1978, A2–17.

[63] Erik Barnouw and S. Krishnawamy. *Indian Film* (New Delhi: Oxford University Press, 1980), 117.

industry, he has the least interest in it and one may not expect a word of appreciation from him.[64]

Satyagraha: A Life of Service

The most powerful means of communication to Gandhi was, however, one's life lived according to the principles of truth and non-violence. 'Those who believe in the simple truths I have laid down', said Gandhi, 'can propagate them only by living them.'[65] Indeed, ideally speaking, satyagraha or soul force transcends all media, for it is self-propagated. Truth and non-violence, the language of the soul, can best be represented by life itself, not by mere words, spoken or written, or even symbols. As he reminded Christian missionaries once:

> The moment there is a spiritual expression in life, the surroundings will readily respond. There is no desire to speak when one lives the truth. There is thus no truer or other evangelism than life.[66]

But this life must be lived in the spirit of direct personal service to the people, and of suffering, for service involves suffering. In the words of Gandhi, 'the silent and undemonstrative action of truth and love produces far more permanent and abiding results than speeches or such other showy performances'.[67] And again, 'non-violent action does mean much silent work and little speech or writing'.[68]

The 'silent work' he had in mind was what he termed 'constructive service'. It is quite solid, substantial work, he explained, direct personal service of the masses, suffering for them, organizing them, educating them in the ways of non-violence and thus

---

[64] Ibid., 117.
[65] *Harijan*, 28 March 1936.
[66] *Harijan*, 12 December 1936.
[67] *Young India*, 8 August 1929.
[68] *Harijan*, 10 June 1939.

bringing about a peaceful atmosphere of solemn determination. Constructive work is thus collective, purificatory effort through service.[69]

It was, in sum, a 15-point programme enjoined on all his followers, and was intended to mobilize people's power 'from the very bottom upward' so that they could effectively control and influence the government's decisions and actions. Gandhi set up many organizations to implement this 'constructive' programme which sought to promote communal harmony, basic education, village sanitation, Hindustani as the national language, cottage industries, swadeshi as a religious discipline, and to eradicate untouchability and the drinking habit. He urged satyagrahis to 'work for the masses, through them and in their midst, not as their patrons but as their servants'.[70] For he looked upon the construction programme as 'the permanent part of the non-violent effort', as 'the embodiment of the active principle of ahimsa and the construction of *purna swaraj*'.[71] It represented a life in the service of the masses, and there was no more effective a 'technique' of communicating with them.

---

[69] Dhawan. *Political Philosophy of Gandhi*, 179.
[70] *Young India*, III, 69.
[71] Dhawan. *Political Philosophy of Gandhi*, 178.

Revisiting the Mahatma in the Media Age

7

Munna and Gandhi
Rethinking Gandhi, 'Gandhigiri' and Popular Hindi Cinema

Arunabha Ghosh and Partha Ray

To say that Gandhi has been omnipresent in Indian ethos, including Indian cinema, is perhaps stating the obvious without being necessarily informative or analytical. With the coming of age of the consumerist culture in the wake of globalization, popular Hindi cinema—at first grudgingly and later admiringly referred to as Bollywood—lost little time to stake its claim on the national icon. *Lage Raho Munnabhai*, a film made in 2006, cashing in on Gandhi and his ideas created a wave in the cultural life of the nation that generated a flurry of commentaries on the subject.[1] The present chapter delves into the nature of the link between the branding of the ideas of Gandhi and popular culture.

---

[1] Ganesh, S. 'Lage Raho Munnabhai: History as Farce'. *Economic and Political Weekly* 41, no. 41 (2006): 4317–19; Ghosh, Arunabha, and Tapan Babu. 'Lage Raho Munna Bhai'. *Unravelling Brand Gandhigiri, Economic and Political Weekly* 41, no. 51 (2006): 5225–27.

The keys that link Munna, the small-time goon with a golden heart, to the Mahatma are his courage and 'jadu ki jhappi', the magical embrace of compassion. Lest we forget: the singular contribution of Gandhi to the psyche of a nation in bondage was to lift the pall of fear. No one was better suited than Jawaharlal Nehru to analyse the effect:

> So suddenly, as it were, that black pall of fear was lifted from the people's shoulders.... It was a psychological change, almost as if some expert in psychoanalytical method had probed deep into the patient's past, found out the origin of his complexes, exposed them to his view, and thus rid him of that burden.[2]

If this was true of Gandhi as the political man, the messiah of the mass, then it is no less true of the essential man because fearlessness is consequential to being truthful. What is unique, therefore, of the Gandhian ethical scheme is the uprooting of fear. 'Abhay' or fearlessness comes from the courage to face truth. Since the real adversary resides within, it is a constant and continuous battle with the self. In both the *Munnabhai* movies, the protagonist undergoes this process to overcome the fear of the revelation of truth. His success is the success of the Gandhi in the goon.

The rest of this chapter is organized as follows. While the first section gives the storyline of the film *Lage Raho Munnabhai* (*LRMB*), issues relating to the emergence of *LRMB* as a cult film are dealt with in the second section, and its unique selling propositions as a film related to Gandhi are taken up in the third section. The fourth section specifically looks into the question 'Why Gandhi', and *LRMB*'s brand of *Gandhism* is discussed in the fifth section. While the historical context is dealt with in the sixth section, the seventh section, instead of presenting any linear set of concluding observations (which would have perhaps been misleading), speculates on the intimate links between Gandhi, Munna and popular culture.

---

[2] Nehru, Jawaharlal. 1946, 1994 editions. *Discovery of India*. New Delhi: Oxford University Press, 299.

Munna Bhai for the Uninitiated

He first appeared in *Munnabhai MBBS* in 2003. And it was there right from the beginning. Only we did not notice it. Munnabhai was a Gandhi acolyte even in *Munnabhai MBBS (MBM)*, only he did not realize it then. Not that he realized his pre-existing affinity with Gandhi in *Lage Raho Munnabhai (LRMB)* either because these are two different and unconnected films; just that the protagonist Munna and his Man Friday Circuit are common in the two films. Murli Prasad Sharma, nicknamed Munna Bhai, is a *bhai* or goon—a minor don in Mumbai. Pretending to be a doctor and running a sham charitable hospital named after his father, Munna's real identity is on the verge of being exposed when his parents arrive. His father meets his old friend Dr Asthana, and they decide to marry Munna to Dr Asthana's daughter, Dr Suman. It is at this point that the Munna chooses to reveal the truth to Suman, though it brings on Dr Asthana's insults on Munna's parents who, heartbroken, leave for their village. To redeem himself and to avenge the humiliation suffered by him and his family, Munna tries by hook—and mostly by crook—to get a degree in medicine with help from his right-hand man Circuit. His methods are hardly Gandhian and are too coercive to justify the means. While Munnabhai's skills as a doctor are abysmal, he transforms those around him with the *jadu ki jhappi* ('magical hug')—a method of comfort imbibed from his mother. The compassion that he shows towards the hapless patients tugs at a chord of the heart. Despite the school's emphasis on mechanical, Cartesian, impersonal, often bureaucratic relationships between doctors and patients, Munna, the do-gooder, turns all conventions and disciplines on the head and does what his inherent goodness prompts him to do. Under the hilarity is a subversiveness that threatens the world of the dean, Dr Asthana. If Munna had adopted unfair means to get admission and score high marks, he displays his inner mahatma (great soul) by infusing a soulless system with love and sympathy to the extent of curing and bringing back Anand, from an almost vegetative existence, to life. But, then, Munna is a conscientious being; he quits college unable to stop a young man from dying. With his banishment, hope, compassion, love and happiness also disappear from the institution.

The ending is what makes a popular cinema popular. Dr Asthana realizes his folly, Munna marries Dr Suman, the Medical College under Rustam Pavri's management begins to put to practice Munna's radical methods of treatment. Munna and Suman open a hospital in Munna's home village, and with the birth of their children, Munna actually becomes MBBS 'Miya Biwi Bachhon Samet' (husband and wife with children). Munna's parents reconcile with him. His sidekick Circuit marries and has a son nicknamed 'Short Circuit'. At the conclusion, we find Anand, having regained normalcy, narrating the story to children.

If *Munnabhai MBBS* (2003), written by Vidhu Vinod Chopra and Rajkumar Hirani, the producer and the director of the film, respectively, was a resounding commercial success, what followed as *Lage Raho Munnabhai* (2006) three years later added a dimension to the culturalscape of the nation with the latent 'Gandhigiri' of *MBM* becoming patent in *LRMB*. *Lage Raho Munna Bhai* (*LRMB*) is not the run of the mill sequel to the earlier avatar. Since it was made more than a decade ago in 2006, a quick recap is in order. *LRMB*, produced by Vidhu Vinod Chopra, directed by Rajkumar Hirani and scripted jointly by the duo together with Dr Abhijat Joshi, is simple, racy, witty and uproariously funny, where Munna Bhai is not an MBBS doctor anymore but his original self that is, a local goon. He is soft-hearted, an ingénu of sorts who falls in love with the voice of the radio-jockey Jahnavi and, in his desperate bid to meet her, participates in a dial-in quiz on Mahatma Gandhi's birthday. Munna obviously is out of his depth on Gandhi or Gandhism but he has other means at his disposal, lethal but funny. He forces five experts on Gandhi at gunpoint to prompt the answers to the quiz, wins the contest, meets Jahnavi and undergoes some transformation. Munna fights land sharks bent on grabbing the Second Innings Home that Jahnavi runs for the aged by employing his own brand of 'satyagraha'. The goon as a satyagrahi is a unique feature that adds to the hilarity of the film. That is not all. He also works at a radio programme, propagating his own brand of Gandhian ideology. As it happens in formulaic films, Munna on disclosing his identity falls out with Jahnavi but finally wins her back as he wins back her cherished old people's home. Munna is a *bhai*, a goon. Yet when he comes in contact with Gandhi (in fact, he begins hallucinating him), he interprets Gandhi in his own way and finally wins applying Gandhian techniques of non-violence in contemporary times. The adaptation of the *mahatma*, the saint, by a goon is a thinly veiled morality tale for the contemporary audience. We are reminded of the ancient tale of the robber Ratnakar who recites the name of Rama and becomes the saint Valmiki, the author-creator of the epic Ramayana. Munna creates his imagined Gandhi and moulds himself in that image.

In hindsight, we have arrived at the insight. Gandhi is inextricably linked with the protagonist; Munna and Gandhi are inseparable.

LRMB: A Cult Film?

Any doubt about the popularity of a Gandhi-inspired commercial film was laid to rest as *LRMB* turned out to be a blockbuster at the box office. While the production budget was $2,700,000, the domestic box office collection was $2,217,561 and international box office yielded $29,300,000; the film grossed $3,15,17,561 worldwide. No wonder *LRMB* acquired a cult status.[3] But popularity is not the only criterion for a film to become a cult object as Umberto Eco sees it. 'It must', Eco holds,

> provide a completely furnished world so that its fans can quote characters and episodes as if they were aspects of the fans' private

---

[3] https://www.the-numbers.com/movie/Lage-Raho-Munna-Bhai#tab=box-office (accessed 30 September 2020).

sectarian world.... I think that in order to transform a work into a cult object one must be able to break, dislocate, unhinge it so that one can remember only parts of it, irrespective of their original relationship with the whole.[4]

The disconnects of the parts with the whole are numerous in *LRMB* but that is beside the point for our purpose. What is interesting is that the larger iconic figure of the Mahatma is superimposed on the iconic figure of Munnabhai from his earlier avatar, and without delving deep into the socio-economic and political thoughts of Gandhi, this Bollywood movie manages to repackage and market moralism for its audience who lap it all up. In a cheeky reference to Gandhi being called 'bhai' in South Africa, an audacious link is established between the Mahatma and Munna. But again their moralscapes are poles apart. For Munna the end justifies the means, and he has no qualms in using muscle power to get things done. For the Mahatma, however, the dichotomy between the means and the end is inconceivable. The hallucinatory figure of Gandhi that Munna meets himself says that he is not a spirit (*atma*) but a consciousness (*chetna*). It takes just a small step from consciousness to conscience. It is the route that Munna takes in his lecture to the elder citizens (prompted by Gandhi himself) where he abjures the statist project of commemoration of Gandhi through statues, images, naming of public works and projects and finally when he urges everyone to preserve the Mahatma's name in one's heart, it touches an emotional chord in the public. That the institutionalized image of Mahatma Gandhi has been rendered hollow in today's context is brought out by an unquiet conscience. The country's development narrative is also rejected outright by Munna: electrical connections without power, roads with more potholes than macadam, schools without teachers, a corrupt bureaucracy that drives people to desperation—in short, an independent India that Gandhi did not envisage. It is as far as this political statement that the film will go. A step ahead and there is every chance of

---

[4] Eco, Umberto. 1986. *Trends in Hyper Reality*. London: Picador.

being mired in Gandhi's socio-economic thoughts—a complete no-no for today's consumer economy-driven India.

What's New?

That Gandhi could be merged with a goon or *bhai* is a unique proposition that is introduced deftly with humour in *LRMB*. Lal, in his survey on Hindi language movies made on or relating to Gandhi, has shown that documentaries were being made on the Mahatma even in the 1930s. But post independence, Hindi cinema had started to depict Gandhi in a different light. He writes:

> The second phase of Indian cinema's engagement with Gandhi can be dated to the second half of the 1950s and the early 1960s. The documentaries of the 1920s to the 1940s cast Gandhi as a predominantly political figure, but the filmmakers working in the aftermath of independence took Gandhi's place in the political life of India as a settled fact.[5]

They, thus, focused on the teachings of Gandhi against the social reality emerging in a post-colonial society. They were now primarily motivated by 'Gandhi's social teachings and his insistence that reform of self had a fundamental relationship to reform of society'. He cites as examples such films as V. Shantaram's *Do Aankhen Barah Haath* ('Two Eyes, Twelve Hands', 1957) and B. R. Chopra's *Naya Daur* ('New Era', 1957), which he convincingly argues, are based on the Gandhian principles—the first where convicts in a prison are transformed into moral beings, and the second which illustrates the Gandhian concept of the village pitted against a soulless and mechanized industrial society. If these were obliquely Gandhian films, Bimal Roy's *Sujata* (1959) was not. Its subject being untouchability, reference to Gandhi was only natural. Then there was a lull. Apart from Gandhi being

---

[5] Lal, Vinay. 2008. 'Moving Images of Gandhi'. Available at http://www.vinaylal.com/ESSAYS(Gandhi)/mov9.pdf.

present in portraits hanging from the walls of the courts or police stations, Hindi films no more followed the Gandhian thought in any significant way. Lal's observation is succinct and perceptive:

> Whatever moral presence Gandhi may have exercised, the genera-
> tion that had shepherded India's fortunes after independence was
> beginning to disappear by the early to mid-1960s, and Gandhi is
> scarcely present in popular Hindi cinema of the 1960s through
> the mid-1980s.

Then came Richard Attenborough's *Gandhi* in 1982. A hagi-ographic film, it got worldwide accolade but failed to impress the Indian middle class, which had largely moved away from the abstemious and non-ostentatious life style of the earlier genera-tion. As Pavan Kumar Verma[6] has demonstrated, the rising Indian middle class was steadily inclining towards a more consumerist worldview. Even if we ignore the disenchantment of the middle class with Gandhian ideals, the fact remains that the film was far from the popular genre and generated hardly any response from the otherwise imitative Hindi film industry. However, filmmak-ers, specially the more serious ones, had not entirely abandoned Gandhi. Shyam Benegal's *The Making of the Mahatma* (1996) brought Gandhi back to film studies, but here the emphasis was, undoubtedly, on a lesser-known period of his beginnings in South Africa. This biopic, though more nuanced, could serve as an imag-ined prequel to Attenborough's *Gandhi*. Kamal Hasan's *Hey Ram* (2000) was a departure though. It showed Gandhi from the point of view of the Hindu ideologues, but what is more important is that Gandhi is an individual in this film with his idiosyncrasies and his charming fallibility.

Consider this. Three films of completely different lineage were made in three successive years: Jahnu Barua's *Maine Gandhi Ko Nahi Mara* in 2005, *Lage Raho Munnabhai* in 2006 and Feroz Abbas Khan's *Gandhi, My Father* (2007). While the last

---

[6] Verma, Pavan K. 1998. *The Great Indian Middle Class*. New Delhi: Penguin Books India.

is another biopic centring on the poignant relationship between Mohandas and his oldest son, Harilal, the first amongst the three is a complex version of the national shame at having abandoned Gandhi. Jahnu Barua's *Maine Gandhi Ko Nahi Mara* is a complex, layered, psychologically plausible film that revolves around a deep-rooted guilt caused by a childhood trauma of the protagonist. A red colour-filled balloon hits the cutout of Gandhi with which the boy is playing, as a consequence of which he is punished by his father for killing Gandhi. The splashing of the cutout in red coincides with the breaking news of Gandhi's assassination that eats into the boy throughout his life until he becomes severely paranoid after retirement, causing a collapse in his immediate world. It is a parable of the guilt of the nation in erasing Gandhi's value system. Barua's film was obviously not made with an eye on the box office. This is where *LRMB* brings something new to the table. The film is successful because it has no confusion about its target audience and its branding. Its orientation is unabashedly mass-market based. Munnabhai also protests against the relegation of the Gandhian value system in contemporary India, but his approach stems out of popular perceptions about Gandhi. Unlike Barua's protagonist, Munnabhai does not shoulder the guilt himself; his appeal, equally moral, is to the collective amnesia of the nation. To Munnabhai and his ilk, Gandhi represents the image that is printed on currency notes. For them, 2 October is a 'dry day'; the name of his children are Indira Gandhi and Rajiv Gandhi; he is the one who had effectively spiked ('wat laga di' in street or *tapori* lingo) the British; to walk along his path is to take a walk along M G Road for three kilometres every day. In looking at Gandhi through the eyes of the metropolitan underbelly, the makers of *LRMB* have taken the route of popculture to pop up a non-statist view of Gandhi. As noted earlier, *LRMB* is not a sequel to *Munnabhai MBBS*. Apart from the two central characters, namely, Munna and Circuit, there are no commonality between the two films. With the goon meeting the mahatma, *LRMB* gave birth to a brand Munna along with brand 'Gandhigiri', the on-screen icon merging with the real-life national icon. This is something unique in the world of Hindi cinema.

Why Gandhi?

This is a simple yet tricky question. Why Gandhi should be brought back to the public consciousness through popular cinema in the new millennium where consumerism and the concommittant violence have become the norm is not an issue that could be easily resolved. There may be numerous causes but the one that can be readily brought into the realm of fruitful conjecture is the growing disquiet in public consciousness—expressed or not—about the effects of a globalized world where the value system is breaking down at a pace colateral to the growth in material prosperity in general. *LRMB* presents a Gandhi who is accessible, witty and understanding to the point of being a common man with an uncommon commitment to truth and *ahimsa*, the two most important values that are part of the national myth but lost in translation by today's politically and economically dominant class. Who is Munna's Gandhi? Munna's Gandhi perhaps is not someone distant and historical but someone with whom the contemporary masses can relate—more in the nature of the conscience personified (called the 'bibek') of traditional Bengali folk theatre, '*jatra*'.

The choice of the vehicle is significant. Gandhi is a figure whom all pay lip service to but seldom follow. If Attenborough had iconized Gandhi, *LRMB* does the same more effectively because the treatment of the subject is not concentrated on Gandhi the historical figure but on an inspirational image who becomes an icon for Munna, the large-hearted goon. While there are attempts to see Gandhi of *LRMB* in the historical perspective,[7] such an attempt tends to miss the point that the Gandhi of *LRMB* is not so much a historical figure as he is an icon of popular culture. In fact, the irrelevance of the Gandhian ideology is hinted and

---

[7] Ganesh. 'Lage Raho Munnabhai'.

just so when Munna visits the Gandhi library that has not seen a footfall in years. He is the most welcome reader, worthy of being treated to tea. The irony is inescapable. A 'bhai', a don, whatever be his compulsion, is the sole consumer of the vast literature on Gandhi! Munna reads on—relentlessly and indefatigably. And voila Gandhi appears to him, speaks to him and assures him of his advice whenever sought with true ardour.

Admittedly, Gandhi as a subject is fit to be 'reinvented', and the process has been going on long after his political relevance has been lost not only on the contemporary world but also on the nation of which he is the undisputed spiritual 'father'. It has been observed:

> Gandhi erected no monument to himself, except the masterwork of ambiguity which is the *Autobiography*. He was not carried on the shoulders of any definite ideology, not even nationalism. He can therefore be continuously reinvented according to the needs and fashions of the times, and this reinvention has been going on incessantly…. The future certainly holds other Gandhis in store.[8]

LRMB attempts at another reinvention of Gandhi, albeit through the mediation of a character who is otherwise farthest from the Gandhian ideal. Gandhi could be reinvented, and so he was reinvented to project his ideas through the popular medium of cinema to create a DIY (do it yourself) version of Gandhism termed 'Gandhigiri' in *LRMB*.

LRMB's Brand of Gandhism

'Gandhigiri', as practised by Munna the goon, spawned a number of similar protests across the country during the first few years of the release of the film, cutting across the rural–urban divide. The fad has faded, but any non-violent protest shaming the authorities to action is still referred to as 'Gandhigiri'. The term

---

[8] Markovits, Claude. 2003. *The Un-Gandhian Gandhi: The Life and Afterlife of the Mahatma*. New Delhi: Permanent Black.

had entered the vocabulary of a large number of Indians and is still current. At least two websites, inspired by 'Gandhigiri', were created: www.gandhigiri.org and www.gandhigiri.co.in. While the former is now ostensibly a forum for leveraging the Right to Information Act to fight corruption, the latter is perhaps extinct. Be that as it may, the 'Gandhigiri' that the film espouses is not entirely a comic creation. According to Abhijat Joshi, a co-author of the story of the film, 'It was important for us to dispel the myth about Gandhi being a sedate, ascetic person. We wanted to show his other side—witty, humorous, light-hearted and creative'.[9] This aspect of Gandhi is not the usual one depicting his persona, because to most Indians he is a revered figure intrinsic to the idea of independent India. Ashish Nandy's essay 'Gandhi after Gandhi' distinguishes between four Gandhis,[10] of which the first is the Gandhi of the Indian state and Indian nationalism, the second Gandhi is that of the Gandhians, who according to Nandy, keeps away from politics. The third is the Gandhi of the 'ragamuffins, eccentrics and the unpredictable' and 'is more hostile to Coca-Cola than to Scotch whisky and considers the local versions of Coca-Cola more dangerous than imported ones'. Finally, the fourth Gandhi walks the mean streets of the world threatening the status quo and pompous bullies in every area of life. *LRMB*'s Gandhigiri is perhaps closer to the fourth variety of Gandhi that Nandy postulates. But let us not forget that it is not Gandhi who does 'Gandhigiri', it is Munnabhai who promotes the brand 'Gandhigiri' and acts as its brand ambassador.

Subscribing to a prototype is one of the stratagems of popular cultural texts for easy connectivity with the audience already geared to the image or the idea. It has been rightly pointed out that 'a stylised figure representing the streets of Mumbai, the *tapori* has primarily been a cinematic invention. He stands at the intersection of morality and evil, between the legal and the illegal,

---

[9] Joshi, Abhijat. 26 September 2006. 'How Gandhigiri Found a Place in Munnabhai'. Available at www.rediff.com///movies/2006/sep/26joshi.htm.

[10] Nandy, A. 2005. 'Mahatma Gandhi—Gandhi after Gandhi'. *The Little Magazine*. Available at http://www.littlemag.com.

between the world of work and those without work'.[11] Munna
epitomizes the typical '*tapori*', and his connectivity to the audience is immediate. The *tapori* (the local friendly goon) lingo that
Munna employs is extremely accessible to the common Mumbai
slum dweller and therefore brilliant as a healing strategy. It is the
language that Munna and his associates use that, linguistically
speaking, sets them apart from the rest of the characters and
thereby adds another dimension to the Munnabhai brand.

> Using the popular 'Bambayya' language as his weapon
> against an unequal world, the *tapori* creates a space through
> insubordination—of sub cultural practices that endow him with
> a certain dignity in the cinematic city. The *tapori* represents the
> hybrid culture of Mumbai's multilingual and regional diversity; it
> is he who uses a speech that creates the possibility of transcending
> various other identities.

One cannot but agree with Mazumdar in this respect.

> It is this language that sets the agenda of discourse in and on
> popular culture. Language plays a crucial role in beefing up the
> brand. In a remarkable manoeuvre of communication skill, the
> street-smart Mumbai tapori lingo, peppered with slangs, is used
> to create instant communication with the audience, especially
> GenNext. This is especially true in case of *LRMB*. Thus Gandhigiri
> stands for Gandhism ('Gandhivad')—a coinage that has proved
> potent enough to warrant a condemnation by the Indian National
> Congress (*The Telegraph*, 10 October 2006). Change of hearts
> is termed as 'chemical locha'. In fact so potent and catchy is the
> medium of communication that Bapu himself cannot but use it,
> albeit in jest, to pick Munna's brain.[12]

Not only Bapu. Contrary to the claim that 'the subaltern classes
find the bourgeois setting of Hindi cinema attractive in the
same way as Hollywood appears alluring to the Indian middle

---

[11] Mazumdar, Ranjani. 'Figure of the 'Tapori' Language, Gesture
and Cinematic City'. *Economic and Political Weekly* 36, no. 52 (2001):
4972–80.

[12] Ghosh and Babu, 'Lage Raho Munna Bhai'.

class',[13] the effect of such a film as *LRMB* has set a trend among the sophisticated middle class to talk *'tapori'* to the best of their ability. It may be trendy to imitate the stylized *'bhai'* in manners and language, but it is better to cautiously desist from crossing the boundary to the world of the subaltern.

Figuring Out Brand Gandhigiri

In 1838, William Llyod Garrison and his friends founded the 'Non-Resistance Society' in Boston to fight slavery by non-violent means. In 1849, Henry David Thoreau wrote 'Resistance to Civil Government' which was republished in 1866 as 'Civil Disobedience' and later under the title 'On the Duty of Civil Disobedience'. The second half of the 19th century witnessed non-violent struggles by the Quakers of England and America. However much as we admire the image of Gandhi as an apostle of non-violence, it would serve us better to remember the perspective and not usurp the foundational role for him. Gandhi himself acknowledged his debt to Thoreau and Tolstoy. Accepting the fact that Gandhi is not original in his preaching of non-violence, distinction can be made between the concepts of 'non-resistance', 'non-violence' and 'pacifism' prevalent in the Western world in various points of time and Gandhi's idea of *'ahimsa'* and 'satyagraha' which have come to be loosely translated as non-violence. The concept has stuck in popular belief with Gandhian thought.

> *But I say unto you, that ye resist not evil:*
> *but whosoever shall smite thee on the right*
> *cheek, turn to him the other also*[14]

Although Gandhi himself endorsed St Mathew's gospel in *The New Testament* (Ch V, verse 39) as it conformed to his idea

---

[13] Deshpande, Anirudh. 'Indian Cinema and the Bourgeois Nation State'. *Economic and Political Weekly* 42, no. 50 (2007): 95–101.

[14] Matthew 5: 39 (Bible, King James' Version).

of passive resistance, Munna remains unconvinced of this technique. So he reverts to his core competence; sometimes bashing up the villainous realtor Lucky Singh's security guard, sometimes dangling the recalcitrant son of Atmaram upside down from his 12th-floor office until he joins the birthday celebration of his father abandoned in an old-age home and makes him happy. Popular culture can be subversive and Gandhian non-violence is not spared either.

But then is it simply a subversion of the Gandhian non-violence or is it an interpretation of the qualified support that Gandhi lends to violence in one of his seminal works, *Hind Swaraj*.[15] Dwelling here on the ethics of non-violence, Gandhi takes a pragmatic view. According to him, there was no way of completely avoiding unintentional violence that comes with everyday life. But he was not totally averse to intentional violence, of course in a limited way, if it was directed at preventing greater harm. Limited violence again was also sanctioned by him as a means of self-defence. The Mahatma envisaged satyagraha as a weapon for the strong but it does not mean that every human being was expected to conform to his idea of a practitioner of satyagraha. 'The world is not entirely governed by logic. Life itself involves some kind of violence and we have to choose the path of least violence.' So wrote Gandhi in *Harijan*.[16] Or, consider these words he wrote in *Young India*: 'My creed of nonviolence is an extremely active force. It has no room for cowardice or even weakness. There is hope for a violent man to be some day non-violent, but there is none for a coward.'[17] Munna in *LRMB* abjures violence to a great extent to follow Gandhism in his own idiosyncratic manner, terming it Gandhigiri. It would not be impertinent, therefore, to suggest that Gandhi himself had left a leeway for a creative writer to exploit his approval of violence however conditional and qualified that might have been.

---

[15] Gandhi, M. K. 1909. In *Hind Swaraj and Other Writings*, edited by A. J. Parel. Cambridge: Cambridge University Press, reprint 1997.

[16] *Harijan*, 28 September 1934, 259.

[17] *Young India*, 16 June 1927, 196.

Truth had been a life-long quest for Gandhi. To arrive at truth one needs courage to face it. Gandhi termed it 'abhay', fearlessness. Therefore, uprooting of fear is central to the Gandhian ethical scheme. In *LRMB*, Gandhi manages to instil that moral courage in Munna to confront his fear and come to terms with truth. Goaded by Bapu, Munna asks Circuit for forgiveness and even reveals to Jahnavi his actual identity after a long spell of self-doubt and dithering. Once he does that, his fear of Lucky Singh's threat to expose him vanishes. Munna is no more subject to Lucky's blackmailing. Overcoming fear is one lesson that Munna imparts successfully through his radio programme. In a kind of chain reaction, Victor, saved from committing suicide by Munna, confesses blowing up money in the stock market to his father; Victor in turn saves Simran, Lucky's daughter, from the same fate; Simran overcomes her fear of her father to reveal the truth about the timing of her birth to her prospective father-in-law. Reverting to non-Gandhian methods once more, Munna, in a climactic scene, rips the myth of astrological certainty shattering the fear of superstition. But Munna's brand of 'Gandhigiri', as propagated by him through the radio programme, is followed by others as well: a person smilingly mops up the spittle strewn around his door by a boorish neighbour; a retired teacher offers everything on his person, including his clothes, as bribe to the clerk for getting his pension papers. 'Gandhigiri' attains its height when Munna exhorts the listeners of his radio programme to send flowers with a 'get well soon' card attached to bring the unscrupulous realtor Lucky Singh back to his senses. Thus satyagraha, the ethico-political tool that Gandhi had used to shake up an imperial power, is now an instrument to nail erring individuals. Whether it is friendly persuasion of the quakerist kind or a method of psychological coercion is open to debate. What is really interesting, perhaps, is that the contours of 'Gandhigiri' and coercive methods of a goon, known as 'Dadagiri' in Mumbai parlance, get blurred; they perhaps permeate each other. It is not 'Gandhigiri' over 'dadagiri' as S. Ganesh suggests. It is a trivialization no doubt—but a trivialization necessitated by a decidedly debased contemporaneity. A link having been established between the *bhai*s separated by almost a century, it is no wonder that Gandhigiri and *dadagiri* become implicitly interchangeable. Gandhi, the man, was once the message. In the India of post-liberalization, brand Gandhigiri is the message.

Gandhi, Munna and Popular Culture

Considering the plurality of the term 'culture', it would be futile to concentrate on a simple or single definition. Suffice to say that culture is the expression of identity of a people or society, and it is a set of skills that facilitates negotiation between the members of the society. A subset of the collective identity is artistic expression that includes music, art, literature, performing arts and so on, which in common parlance and understanding is referred to as culture.[18] Speaking of culture one cannot ignore the ambivalence that exists between culture and *homo oeconomicus*. Culture in some sense, being endogenous to economic development, poses a challenge in determining a causal connection between the two.[19] Apparently at odds with each other, the cultural identity and the economic aspirations of a society are in effect inextricably linked because together they constitute the well-being of a society, enriching the quality of life. Moving on to 'popular culture' it, simply put, is what people like. This is where the distinction between 'high' and 'low' culture gets blurred. The foremost reason for such blurring of distinction is that 'popular culture' is necessarily a phenomenon of the post-industrial world where universal suffrage, technological innovations and the principle of consumption are primarily

---

[18] Woolcock, Michal, Vijayendra Rao, and Sabina Alkire. 'Culture and Development Economics: Theory, Evidence, Implications'. *Romanian Journal of Political Science* 2, no. 2 (2002): 39–62.

[19] Tabellini, Guido. 2005. *Culture and Institutions: Economic Development in the Regions of Europe*, Working Paper, Innocenzo Gasparini Institute for Economic Research, June.

dependent on the *vox populi* and on the mass market. Although it is true that existing in layered epochs India exhibits diverse traditions of social and cultural practices, the fact, however, cannot be ignored that post-liberalization of the economy since the 1990s has brought about unprecedented changes especially in communication and information technologies. This has, in its turn, resulted in the burgeoning of the service sector. All these factors have phenomenally increased the role played by the entertainment industries and the media in the formation of opinions and ideas and the functioning of the society in general.

It has been argued that with the spread of the communication technologies and the emergence of a culture of consumption, the products of contemporary culture now shape many social practices in India. And cinema emerging out of Bollywood—as the Hindi film industry was disparagingly referred to earlier—has become one of the potent arbiters of cultural consumption.[20] Cinema has overtaken the popular Indian imagination to such a degree that it is impossible to embark upon a discourse on culture without any reference to films or filmmaking in India. It is an obvious paradox that a technology-driven art form of the 20th century has carried forward and propagated ideas that are not always in consonance with modernity. One reason for this, as Dipankar Gupta has argued, is a misconception about modernity.[21] It depends less on technological advances than on equitous societal relations where the primacy of individuality is not sacrificed at the altar of privileges. If a precondition of modernity—to quote Zygmunt Bauman—is to live 'in a state of permanent war against tradition',[22] it must be said that, confident in the new millennium about its own identity and status, Bollywood has shown,

[20] Sen, Biswarup. 2006. *Of the People: Essays on Indian Popular Culture*. New Delhi: Chronicle Books.

[21] Gupta, Dipankar. 2000. 'India's Unmodern Modernity'. In *India, Another Millennium*, edited by Romila Thapar. New Delhi: Penguin Books India.

[22] Bauman, Zygmunt. 1997. *Postmodernity and its Discontents*. Cambridge, UK: Polity Press.

and is showing, remarkable maturity to question and even play around with the handed-down notions of tradition and culture. *LRMB* is a supreme example of this chutzpah. Gandhi, hitherto the sacred symbol of the nation, has been reduced to a couple of dicta that can be followed by one and all. The audaciousness of popular culture boggles the mind.

That a man like Gandhi, Einstein had said, had ever walked the earth would astound the generations to come. The generations to follow the film *LRMB* might wonder how such greatness could be tossed up and turned around for mass consumption.

8

Reading Gandhi with/in Popular Cinema
A Pedagogue's Perspective

Dev Nath Pathak*

In a classroom with students of 11th standard in a school, when a schoolteacher refers to Gandhi and his ideals, in a sermonizing tone, the blank faces of students hardly screen the repulsion of their minds. This is not hard to find that inspiration for valuelessness stems from the quaint preaching in the period/class on value education in schools.[1] Not very remote is the sight in

---

* The author teaches sociology at South Asian University, and edits the journal, Society and Culture in South Asia.

[1] For a debate along this line, see the volume of the *Journal of Value Education*, January–July 2005, Especially, the article titled 'An Approach to value orientation of Teacher Education' by C. Seshadri, refuses to treat value education as an exclusive and distinguishable kind of education; the process of education in general ought to be capable of inculcating values; the question of value education, teaching and learning of the same, leads to the question of value orientation in teacher education. Besides, there has been another line of thinking in educational discourse in India, which relates values (of/in) education to the experiences and practices of the learners. For example, Krishna Kumar would argue in 'Crafts at School' (*Seminar*, No. 570, February 2007: http://www.india-seminar.com/2007/570.htm) that children learn about the ideals of Gandhi much by actively engaging with

the classroom where undergraduate students are taught about the historically iconic characters. Teachers as well as students are vulnerable to sides—for or against—in a manner of school debates, while discussing these larger-than-life characters from the pages of history. Teaching, thereby, amounts to propaganda and rabble-rousing. The prerequisite anarchy, meaningfully cultivated for engaging with the ideas and characters of historical significance, does not reflect in either curriculum or pedagogic practices. No wonder, then, Gandhi is not discussed beyond, the mystique halo of a Mahatma, of postcard value utilized for textbook presentations. Or, on the other extreme, Gandhi is yet another character to evoke utmost hatred and wonder conditioning the minds of learners. Treading this extreme, teachers as well as students succumb to debunking anything called Gandhi(an). Often, this line of engagement with Gandhi also invokes other historically significant personalities. B. R. Ambedkar becomes, thereby, an easy ploy to beat Gandhi, in the theatre of teaching and learning. As a corollary, engagement with Gandhi, in schools and colleges, is merely for serving the official requirement, as it were. Also, this leads to usage of Gandhian ideas, signs and symbols, for mouthing politically correct platitudes. Else, who cares what Gandhi was and what were his ideas, unless it is packaged with the business efficiency to taste palatable for the new middle class.[2] What does the above instance indicate: a pedagogic inertia, a syllabic problem, a skewed relation between syllabus and pedagogy, an institutional error in designing and teaching and

---

them in concrete way rather than by reading about them and listening to teachers on the same. This is further affirmed in the compilation of essays by Krishna Kumar in 'Pedagogue's Romance (OUP). My comment on value education is in the light of the mentioned discourse.

[2] This is the broad outline of the general view students in schools (XIth and XIIth standards) and colleges would offer. I am using this as a point of departure for this chapter. By the repackaging of Gandhi, to make it palatable for the new middle class, I mean the acceptance of *Lage Raho Munna Bhai* (Rajkumar Hirani 2006), which did fairly good business and offered a new perspective on engaging with Gandhian ideas in cinematic narrative. In a recent feature, an expert on Indian cinema, Dwyer, regrets an abysmal cinematic representation of Gandhi. Speaking of LRMB, she says:

so on? Instead of finding the fault, the present discourse in the following pages is interested in developing an analytical understanding about the gap between the productions of knowledge in the two spaces. These are popular Hindi cinema and undergraduate students' academia as two distinct domains of production of knowledge about Gandhi. While the socio-cinematic domain would not react if it is dubbed as 'merely common sense' by the social scientists, the academic production and exchanges of knowledge would stake higher claim in validity. The two social domains, without an imperative bridge, assume the significance of rivals in the market of knowledge. Who wins? Of course, the victor is the fluid socio-cinematic construction of Gandhi rather than its academic counterpart that appears a rigid reification of the same.

It is not impossible to note the plethora of cinematic representations of Gandhi and his ideas in the kaleidoscope of Hindi cinema. These representations, overt as well as covert, suggest of socio-cinematic common sense on/about Gandhi. Unlike the academic discourse on the theory and actions of Gandhi, the socio-cinematic commonsense entails a fluidity and spontaneity. By virtue of being a kind of commonsense, it also reflects the ontological character through the mix of locality, context, agency and emotion. To make sense of the socio-cinematic commonsense on/about Gandhi, the present discourse charts a discursive journey from popular cinema to pedagogy. In simple terms, the attempt is to understand the trajectory of perceptions of and engagement with Gandhi in popular Hindi cinema.[3] The

---

It is not the historical Gandhi, a challenging and difficult figure who urges us to abandon consumerism, but a Gandhi of India's new middle classes. This is not a political Gandhi but a Gandhi who is an inner conscience and moral guide, as well as a Fairy Godmother who will help us to realise today's dreams.

[3] I am using the term popular as a prefix to cinema in the sense Ashis Nandy uses, as an expression in the triad of folk, classical and popular. It is intended to express the ordinary/common forms pointing towards the popular notions of the ordinary masses. See Pinney, Christopher. 1995.

cinematic engagement with Gandhi could be traced back to Gandhi's discourse on cinema as a medium.[4] However, that is not the concern here. Nor is it to do with the Gandhian advocacy of the visual campaigning during the freedom struggle. In a restricted sense, the focus here is to understand people's pulse pertaining to Gandhian ideas, through the acceptance or rejection of some of the films in Bollywood, post-Gandhi (Attenborough 1982). Acceptance or rejection of a cinematic explanation, as expressed by the business success at the box-office, is an arbitrary indicator of the people's interest. However, it is also considerable that cinema is not only defined by people (audience).[5] It is rather the other way round that has ruled the commonsense. After all, every parent has voiced this anxiety at some stage to his/her child that watching cinema may spoil. Nevertheless, in spite of the risk in judging people's perception on the basis of people's acceptance or rejection indicated in the business success or failure of the cinematic flick, this chapter attempts to build the trajectory of notions, ideas, perceptions and an anticipated engagement people have with the Gandhi and his ideas. In the backdrop of this trajectory of perceptions of and engagement with Gandhi, as emerging from the select Hindi cinema, I seek to debate the case of an interdisciplinary course/paper titled 'Reading Gandhi' (IDC). The critical reading of the structure, nature and scope of the IDC paves way to reflect upon the pedagogical issues involved with, the paper in question in particular, and the practice of teaching and learning about Gandhi in general. In a deliberate

---

'Hindi Cinema and Half-Forgotten Dialectics: An Interview with Ashis Nandy'. *Visual Anthropology Review* 11(2):7–16. I am not spending on the formalism, however, due to the paucity of space and thematic concentration of the chapter.

[4] It is well known that Gandhi was not very appreciative of the medium of cinema. However, it would be hasty to draw a Gandhian intolerance to modern technology determining Gandhian disdain of cinema. As in a recent interview, Rachel Dwyer would attempt to argue.

[5] I am using the term 'people' to locate this discussion in the discursive framework of a democracy wherein audiences do form the constitutional category of 'we, the people'.

manner, I avoid to get into discussing Gandhi, his philosophy and actions, and references to the humbling enormity of scholarship on Gandhi.[6] Nevertheless, the influence of the discourse on Gandhi could seep in the present chapter, almost inadvertently. Agreeing with Mandelbaum, 'It is not easy to see Gandhi in a fresh view, without influence of one or another of the notions that have become common'.[7]

To put simply, the primary interest of this chapter is rather to discuss the ways of understanding Mohan Das Karamchand Gandhi, with or without the epithet of *Mahatma*, in historical as well as biographical context of not only Gandhi but also the teacher and the taught. The present discourse thereby unfolds at two levels of irony. First, Gandhi was agnostic about the usage of modern media. Khwaja Ahmad Abbas,[8] a filmmaker, engaged with Gandhi in a bid to convince him of the validity of cinema as a medium.[9] To this, Gandhi remained sceptical until the end. However, Gandhi never shied away from posing in front of camera, which generated visuals for circulation in print media. Peter Ruhe,[10] in a visually stunning work *Gandhi: A Photo Biography*, uses images from the photo works of Gandhi's foremost biographer Vithal Bhai Jhaveri and Mahatma Gandhi's great nephew Kanu Gandhi. As Ruhe mentions, M. K. Gandhi consented to be photographed by Kanu on three conditions, that the freedom movement will not fund the photography, that

---

[6] Mandelbaum, in an attempt to develop the life history of Gandhi within the framework of social anthropology, grapples with the huge compendium of work on Gandhi from all sides, academic as well as non-academic: Mandelbaum, David G. 1973. 'The Study of Life History: Gandhi'. *Current Anthropology* 14(3): 177–206.

[7] Mandelbaum, 'The Study of Life History', 182.

[8] Khawaja Ahmad Abbas is a filmmaker who is popularly known for his films like *Saat Hindustani* (*Seven Indians*, 1969) and *Do Boond Paani* (*Two Drops of Water*, 1972). Both the films won national awards.

[9] Gupta, Akhil. 1983. 'Attenborough's Truth: The Politics of Gandhi'. *The Threepenny Review* 15: 22–23.

[10] Ruhe, Peter. 2004. *Gandhi: A Photo Biography*. London: Phaidon Press.

Kanu will not use flash while photographing and that Gandhi will never pose for the photographs. Similarly, despite Gandhi's agnosticism towards cinema as a medium, he remained an intriguing object of communication through popular cinema. This level of irony reveals a significant meaning for the present discourse. For, it is at this level of irony Gandhi is available as a fluid object susceptible for all kinds of cinematic (mediated) casting. The availability of Gandhi as a fluid object, owed to the ambivalent relation between Gandhi and visual media, adds to the complexity of socio-cinematic common sense. The post-independent India is, furthermore, rife with a variety of visual representations on Gandhi, such as postal stamp, currency, signposts, statues and, of course, the presence of the economic enterprise of the Khadi Bhandar (business of homespun).[11] I restrict the analytical exercise in this chapter to cinema and thereof representation of Gandhi for heuristic convenience.

On the second level of irony, Gandhi appears as a source of lesson in the prescribed literatures in various courses offered to undergraduate students. These prescribed literatures present Gandhi and his values/ideals in an arguably absolute manner. Each piece of literature would propose the validity claim of indubitable understanding of Gandhi, leaving little room for the critical-intellectual engagement of learners and teachers. This occasions a second level of irony. For, Gandhi himself was not in favour of indubitable claim of absolute understanding.[12] The second level of irony leads us to comprehend the phenomenal scholarship on Gandhi, dubbing one man and his ideas in diverse ways. Ironically enough, each way of presentation of Gandhi appears indubitably absolute. For example, it is a postmodern

---

[11] See the work by Trivedi on the symbolism of Gandhi in historical context vis-à-vis discourse on the cultural history of Khadi. Trivedi, Lisa N. 2007. *Clothing Gandhi's Nation: Homespun and Modern India.* Bloomington: Indiana University Press.

[12] Bilgrami, Akeel. 2003. 'Gandhi, The Philosopher'. *Economic and Political Weekly* 38(39):4159–69; Bilgrami, Akeel. 2006. 'Gandhi, Newton and the Enlightenment'. *Social Scientist* 34(5 and 6):17–35.

Gandhi for Ruloph and Rudolph (2006),[13] while for T. N. Madan it is a Gandhi with 'altruistic individualism'.[14] The list of casting Gandhi in one or other category would be nearly inexorable. The purpose is not to recount the list. It is much rather to comprehend the significance of the multiplicity of perception, which goes into the construction of social common sense. At this level, the present discourse gears to ask whether the multiple analytical imagination of Gandhi in academic writings could afford to have the contribution from an oral context in which teachers and students operate.

These two levels of irony, mentioned above, occasion a point of departure for the present discourse. The following is a synoptic survey of the representation of Gandhi in popular Hindi cinema. The focus is to denote the construction of cinematic contribution to the construction of social commonsense. The possible mapping of the myriad representations of Gandhi in popular Hindi cinema ought to be around the turning point given by Attenborough's Gandhi. It is not only for the analytical convenience, but also for the logical reason that a full-fledged biopic on Gandhi before Attenborough's was not available. Second, this section is not meant to claim any historical judgement. It is rather to make the point clear that Gandhi is well represented in cinema and there is a commonsense arising from these cinematic representations, rendering Gandhi arguably omnipresent in cinematic production. Needless to say, the common sense is heterogeneous.[15] The

---

[13] Lloyd I. Rudolph and Susanne Hoeber Rudolph. *Postmodern Gandhi and Other essays: Gandhi in the World and at Home* (Chicago, IL: University Press, 2006).

[14] Madan, T N. 2002. 'Gandhi's Altruistic Individualism'. *The Hindu*. http://www.hindu.com/thehindu/2002/10/02/stories/2002100200031000. htm.

[15] The debate on the nature and scope of common sense is fairly established and popular in social sciences. Especially in sociology, where distinction of the sociological (and hence scientific) is primarily made with reference to common sense, there are divergent views, corresponding with positivistic (functionalist, Marxist, structuralist) and non-positivistic (phenomenological, ethno-methodological and whole omnibus of the post-modern). I am interested in drawing the attention to the potential heterogeneity of the common sense, in the manner in which Deshpande elucidates it. See Deshpande, Satish. 2003. *Contemporary India: A Sociological View*. Delhi:

socio-cinematic common sense is a marker of national subjectivities affirmed by cinematic representation of Gandhi.

Zooming in on Gandhi: Socio-cinematic Commonsense

It is broadly at three levels that Gandhi appears in Hindi cinema: as a personality in historical and biographical contexts, as an absolute inspiration in the background of diverse cinematic narratives, and as an idea at a mundane level of everyday life. While Gandhi in biographical and historical contexts has been dominant attraction in cinema, the other two levels of cinematic engagement with Gandhi are relatively humble. It was about almost five decades before the Attenborough's *Gandhi* (1982) dazzled the audience all over the world that Gandhian inspiration defined the cinematic engagement with the concern for social reforms in India. Criticizing the traditional caste ethos, in 1936, came *Achhut Kanya* (the *Untouchable Girl*), directed by Franz Osten, starring Ashok Kumar (as a Brahmin boy) and Devika Rani (as the daughter of an untouchable railway guard). Without making much explicit reference to Gandhi, the narrative spin of the film does remind of the dominant epochal influence of the decade of 1930s. The male protagonist voices the Gandhian ethos and vision of independent India. The vision of *Hind Swaraj*, without the caste-based discrimination, and engagement with tools of modernity, such as railway, dominate the narrative twists in the film. Also, in 1940, Mehboob Khan directed a film titled *Aurat* (the *Woman*) along the Gandhian discourse on the theme of the feminine and their power. It was remade into the famous *Mother*

Penguin. Also, the intent is to underscore national subjectivity stemming from and affirmed by the cinematic representation of Gandhi. For the correlation between national subjectivities and cinema, see Nandy, Ashis (Ed.). 1998. *The Secret Politics of Our Desires: Innocence, Culpability and Indian Popular Cinema*. London: Palgrave Macmillan. Nandi presents a psychoanalytical reading of the popular cinema to comprehend the political import of the same and its bearing upon the formation of national identity (subjectivity).

India (1957), starring Nargis as the central protagonist who fights her way to dignified social existence through innumerable odds stemming from the traditional social structure. Interesting to note that Mehboob Khan's *Mother India* was an apparent repartee to Catherine Mayo's *Mother India* (1927), which M. K. Gandhi polemically called a *Drain-inspector's report*. Yet another film discussing Gandhi as an absolute inspiration, such as *Jagriti* (*Awakening*, 1954, directed by Satyen Bose), foregrounds the interactive relationship between students and the teacher (essayed by Abhi Bhattacharya). The film discloses the impact and inspiration of Gandhi in a song sequence[16] directly eulogizing the role of Gandhi in the freedom struggle. In a manner of recurrence of the theme of *Achhut Kanya*, yet distinct in presentation and impact, Bimol Roy's *Sujata* (1959) expressed the engagement with the Gandhian idea. The subtext of *Sujata* offers a combination of Gandhi's battle against untouchability and the Buddhist tale of Chandalika.[17] In a panoramic scene, with the dominant vision behind nation building in the post-independent India, the protagonists Adheer (Sunil Dutt) and Sujata (Nutan) exchange their dialogues at the bank of a river (unspecified, but hint is of the Ganga). Adheer recounts the story of Chandalika, subsequently after the theatrical performance of the same story in a college, especially for Sujata.

---

[16] *De Di Hame Azadi Bina Khadag Bina Dhal Sabarmati Ke Sant Tune Kar Diya Kamal* (you got us liberation, without any fight or fuss, the saint of Sabarmati! You got us miracle) was the lyric written by a Hindi poet, Pradeep, and sung by Asha Bhosle on the musical note of Hemant Kumar. Another little less-known song, directly related to Gandhi, rendered musically and vocally by S. D. Burman is *Gun Dham Humare Gandhi Ji, Subh Naam Humare Gandhi Ji* (Gandhiji our attributes and our soul; Gandhiji our auspicious name). The song reveals the importance of Gandhiji, his dedication to the land of this country and the struggle. Gandhi appears in line of great souls, with divine halo, in this melodious non-filmy song by Burman.

[17] Chandalika was also the title of the play written by Rabindranath Tagore, which builds upon the tale of Chandalika, who was a born untouchable. Once Anand, the Buddhist monk, came across Chandalika and sought for water from her. On this, she refused, stating her untouchability. Anand taught her the Buddhist lesson of liberation subsequently.

To this, Sujata says: this is the story of olden times, not relevant now.

Adheer gently argues: Sujata! There is a noble man of this (Buddha) kind even in our times (Mahatma Gandhi), who has consecrated his life to eradicate the sin of untouchability. Have you heard of the story of the untouchable girl Laxmi who was adopted by Gandhi and brought to his ashram at Ahmedabad? All the patrons and donors of the ashram were furious on the decision of the Mahatma. The financial support began to dwindle. Yet Mahatma remained firm in his decision ... what is a religion if it becomes a pretext to perpetuate the sin of untouchability!

Sujata is overwhelmed by the emotional impact of the story recounted by Adheer and her eyes are moist. In the subsequent scene, with the song of the boatman in the backdrop, Adheer expresses her love for Sujata. The film ends with Sujata being accepted by the upper caste family and her being married to Adheer.

It is not only the lofty mention of Gandhi in the Hindi cinema of the kind in the *Sujata*. Arguably, in the pre-Attenborough's Gandhi period, Hindi cinema engaged with Gandhian ideas in a variety of genres of narratives. The genre of patriotic films is full of imageries of Gandhi and other nationalist leaders. From *Shaheed* (1948, directed by Ramesh Saigal, starring Dilip Kumar and Kamini Kaushal) to *Shaheed* (1965, directed by S. Ram Sharma, starring Manoj Kumar as Bhagat Singh), there are a plethora of arguments on/about, for as well as against, Gandhi. In fact, stretching the realm of analysis, Hindi cinema also began to raise critical questions on the notion of 'experiment with truth'. In an exemplary cinematic take, Rishikesh Mukherjee's *Satyakam* (1969), starring Dharmendra as the protagonist named *Satyapriya* (one who loves truth), presents the tension. It offers psychoanalytical subtexts on the character depicting his near obsession with truth. Satyapriya, a civil engineer by profession, working on the governmental projects, underlines the contradiction between the Gandhian and Nehruvian ideals, arguably. While the Gandhian

Satyapriya suffers, the Nehruvian vision of secular and scientific India worshipping in the temples of modernity such as dams scores over. The friend of Saytapriya, essayed by actor Sanjeev Kumar, has no such steadfastness towards truth, and hence he is more successful by performing his own duties without indulging in a moral confrontation with the corrupt officials. On the other hand, Satyapriya copes with the ordeal in the post-independent India, which was far from the Gandhian ideal of *Hind Swaraj*. The film hints at the dim possibility of a truthful existence in an India post-Gandhi. The pain of the protagonist becomes the pain of the masses that, arguably, had faith in the promises of Mahatma.

The state of India, around the same time when *Satyakam* was public, was deliberating upon the possibility of making a biopic on Gandhi,[18] upon the failure of a consensus, also allegedly a Nehruvian unwillingness, on casting Gandhi in the celluloid seemed remote. It was around this time that Attenborough approached Pundit Nehru with the idea of making the film, which was largely inspired by Louis Fischer's book *The Life*

---

[18] 'First idea for a biographical film on the life of Mahatma Gandhi was floated in June 1953, five years after his death. But even the Congress Government headed by his most trusted lieutenant, Pandit Jawaharlal Nehru did not find it commercially viable to give a financial backing. Nehru told the Rajya Sabha, the Upper House of Indian Parliament, in December 1963 that

the production of a film on the life of Gandhiji was too difficult a proposition for a Government department to take up. The Government was not fit to do this and they had not got competent people to it. This was an unfortunate confession and it reflected also dilemma of the Congress leadership to take a position regarding Mahatma. British film maker Mark Robson made a very dramatic film called Nine Hours to Rama, which was released in 1963 all over the West, but was not allowed to be exhibited in India. The film was an intense dramatic and fictional recreation of the nine hours spent by assassin Nathuram Godse before his murder of Mahatma Gandhi.

Quoted from http://www.essaypride.com/essays.php?free_essay= 6285006&title=Mahatma-Gandhi-And-Indian-Cinema (referred to on 7 May 2011 and 12 April 2012).

of Mahatma Gandhi, only to receive a lukewarm response.[19] However, Attenborough did make Gandhi, after the approval of the script by Indira Gandhi, with financial and moral support of the government of India.[20] In spite of the logical criticism of the representation of Gandhi, by Attenborough, for alleged distortion of the historical facts and an apparent hagiographical presentation, it was indeed a film that caught with the people's lore. By implementing some of the typical devices of melodrama, *Gandhi* almost brought about the same impact on the audience that a reader of the Fanishwar Nath Renu's *Maila Anchal* (the soiled border)[21] could feel about the people of rural India during the freedom struggle. Also, another significant development post Attenborough's Gandhi was that a trend of making biopic started. Shyam Benegal directed the 53-episode tele series for Doordarshan *Bharat Ek Khoj* (*India: A Discovery*), based on Jawaharlal Nehru's *Discovery of India*, in 1988. The star cast for the serial had many actors who were cast in Attenborough's

---

[19] Rachel Dwyer, quoted by Suroor, opines

… in 1962, Attenborough got a call from a British Indian Gandhian Motilal Kothari inviting him to discuss the idea for a film on Gandhi and sent him Louis Fischer's book *The Life of Mahatma Gandhi*. When a year later, he met Nehru in New Delhi to seek his approval for the project, Nehru's only advice to him was: 'Whatever you do, do not deify him—that is what we have done in India—and he was too great a man to be deified.'

See Suroor, Hasan. 2010. 'Why Is Gandhiji "Missing" from Hindi Cinema?' *The Hindu* 7. http://www.hindu.com/2010/12/07/stories/2010 120754421100.htm (accessed on 12 April 2012).

[20] Gupta, 'Attenborough's Truth'.

[21] *Maila Anchal* is one of the celebrated works of Fanishwar Nath Renu in vernacular fiction (originally in Hindi, now available in English translation too), which details the rural life in a remote village of Purina district in North Bihar during the freedom struggle. The messages of Gandhi, which would reach the people as gospel of god rather than just a news report, move the masses, remote from the heartland of politics. The novel also presents a love story between a widow and a doctor against the background of the freedom struggle.

Gandhi too, including Roshan Seth, who had become popular for essaying the character of Pundit Nehru. Gandhi was present in the biopic on Sardar Vallabhbhai Patel as well. In 1993, Ketan Mehta directed *Sardar: The Iron Man of India*, starring Paresh Rawal as Sardar Patel and Annu Kapur as Gandhi, earned rave reviews. The film showed transformation of young Patel who ridicules Gandhi into the Gandhian-Satyagrahi Sardar who eventually launches himself on to the nation-building project. As a leap forward from Attenborough's, in a more microscopic vision, Gandhi appears in Benegal's *Making of Mahatma*, with Rajit Kapur as Gandhi and Pallavi Joshi as Kasturba. It presents a more detailed version of Gandhian experimentation and actions in South Africa than what we see in Attenborough's. Also, the biopic on other national heroes than Gandhi, which began to appear afterwards, casts various lights on the latter. It is no longer Gandhi appearing as undisputed central character. Instead, it is Gandhi in debate with others. So, in 1998 (censored and released in 2000), Jabbar Patel's *Dr Babasaheb Ambedkar* comes with a punching debate between Gandhi (essayed by Mohan Gokhale) and Dr Ambedkar (essayed by Mammooty). Gandhi, as a debater, makes another appearance in *The Legend of Bhagat Singh* (directed by Rajkumar Santoshi, 2002). It is here that the storyteller takes liberty of confronting Gandhi with some peculiarly troubling historical question: why did Gandhi sign the Irvin Pact!

From above details, in a somewhat chronological manner, it is obvious that Hindi popular cinema graduated from putting Gandhi as an absolute source of inspiration to zooming in on Gandhi in historical and biographical contexts. Many facets of Gandhi emerged in this cinematic tryst with Gandhi. He is a poser, a communicator, a debater, an ideologue, a propagandist, a conscience-keeper and a historical culprit. Much of it could also be attributed to the cinematic construction and reconstruction. However, the significance of the constructed imageries is undeniable.

In addition to the two levels on which Gandhi's appearance in popular Hindi cinema, there is the third significant level auguring a futuristic trend. It is engaging with Gandhi at mundane everyday scale. Gandhi is not merely a serious moral thinker who dabbled into ethical politics. Gandhi is also someone who could be part of a joke, a father who could listen to his anguished son, a moral figure whose death or insult could be a retired professor's guilt. In the 21st century, the first in the chronological order was Jahnu Barua's *Maine Gandhi ko Nahi Mara (I Did Not Kill Gandhi,* 2005), which locates Gandhi away from the textbook pages of history, in the realm of the biography of a retired professor, Uttam Chaudhury (Anupam Kher). Reminding a viewer of the everyday engagement with Gandhian ideas in post-independent India in Rishikesh Mukherjee's *Satyakam,* Barua tells an ordinary man's engagement with the image of Gandhi on the plane of psychology. Also, the film, which was not successful in doing business, warrants a sociological imagination in connecting the biography of the professor with the history of *India after Gandhi.*[22] In a popular manner, which almost characterizes Hindi cinema, *Lage Raho Munna Bhai* (Rajkumar Hirani, 2006) succeeded in dislocating/relocating Gandhi in the most unusual domain. It is the domain wherein Gandhi becomes a philosopher friend (enacted by Dilip Prabhavalkar) to a street-smart goon, Munna (enacted by Sanjay Dutt). Beyond good and bad of society, Gandhian spirit finds alliance, via the tickling humour, to convey that Gandhi sans history, class and boundaries. In spite of the allegations of packaging Gandhi for the middle-class consumers, it cannot be denied that the film gave an impetus to people's thought process on Gandhi by articulating that Gandhi could be instrumental in shaping personal lives. Needless to mention, the idea of 'personalized Gandhi' has gained currency of late in

---

[22] I am using the title of the book by Ramchandra Guha to indicate the possibility of enlarging the historiography which could entail the lives of not only the spectacular figures, but also unsung ordinary people of India who may have a qualitatively different engagement with Gandhi and his ideas in their everyday life situations. That is what is lacking in Guha's biographical approaches in otherwise commendable history of post-independent India. Guha, Ramchandra. 2007. *India After Gandhi: The History of the World's Largest Democracy.* Delhi: MacMillan.

the cinematic imagination pertaining to Gandhi. An ontological shift in the cinematic perspective enriches the narratives around the persona of Gandhi and breaks away from the preoccupation of periodical drama. History is thereby recast in the experiential–existential domain of the protagonists and characters in the cinematic narratives. For example, the history of Gandhi from the perspective of the protagonists, such as Munna Bhai and Professor Uttam Singh, is selective in tune with the personal experiences and existence. Even for the viewer of these cinematic tales, history appears in more personalized tenor than it could be the case while watching Attenborough's Gandhi. History is, thus, not the result of the craft of the historians; through the cinematic reconstruction, history is within the experiential craft of ordinary individual protagonists on as well as off the screen. No matter how detrimental this is to the conventional historiography and thereof scientific-evidence-seeking tendency, the experiential paradigm in history vis-à-vis cinematic reconstruction offers a chance to rethink historiography too.

On this note, it could be mentioned that *Gandhi, My father*, by Feroz Abbas Khan, in 2007, offered a perspective on Gandhi originated to his deviant son Harilal Gandhi. Based on the biography of Harilal Gandhi by Chandulal Bhagubhai Dalal titled *Harilal Gandhi: A Life*, the film unfolds the historicity of Gandhi through the prism of personal experiences of his son. Harilal, a relatively ordinary individual with ordinary aspirations and capability, undergoes his share of agonies while Gandhi rose to the prominence as Mahatma. The tension between the father of nation and his son also reveals the conflict of priorities in the context of freedom struggle and shaping of the Indian psyche. The narrative complicates the character of Gandhi in the light of the biographic twists in the life of Harilal and enjoins upon the reader/viewer the need to rethink history.

Apart from the aforementioned three levels of cinematic representation of Gandhi in Hindi cinema, there is a little benign thread of representation, which ought to be mentioned in passing. It alludes to the appearance of Gandhi as a spiritual spectre often concertized by his statue or photograph. Gandhi appeared as spiritual spectre in the decade of the 1980s, which was arguably a critical time for Hindi cinema as quality cinema work was on the back-burner, and the divide between commercial and art cinema further exacerbated the same. A framed photograph with the beatified smile of Bapu (fond title for Gandhi) hanging on the wall in the background, behind the characters who would deliver somewhat related dialogue, would be in the focus. It could also be to denote the irony of modern India as the character would indulge in an unethical practice and the camera will focus on the photograph of Bapu. This kind of intermittent references to Gandhi, in no matter how trivial and passing manner, is suggestive of the Bollywood's unstinted association with the image of Gandhi. A scene of rape, a situation to display corrupt behaviour of politician or police, a scenario of unethical practices of journalists, doctors, lawyers and judges, a sampling of the decline in the moral values inside family or in the world outside were emphasized with a glimpse of the image of Gandhi. As a reminder either to the guilty that this is the land of Gandhi or to highlight the ironical failure of institutions, Gandhi remained a visual refrain in even those cinematic narratives which were remotely related to Gandhi.

To surmise, it could be argued that the three levels of the cinematic representation of Gandhi in Hindi cinema amount to the construction of socio-cinematic commonsense of a complex kind. The socio-cinematic commonsense paints Gandhi in multiple colours at once, for those who are aware of the narrative thrusts of the Hindi cinema. Gandhi thereby was, and hitherto is, a lofty ideal, a historical icon who embodied immense values, an inspiration for the educated as well as uneducated in the post-independent India. He was also a communicator, a debater, a satyagrahi, a spiritual leader, a moralist, an ideologue and so on so forth. Gandhi appears as a historical icon in the most dominant fashion, and he is not only eulogized but also subject to critical dialogue with his compatriots such as Ambedkar, Patel and Bhagat Singh. Most importantly, Gandhi becomes an object to relate to for ordinary citizens of post-independent India, whereby the magic of mundane transforms

Gandhi from the textbook material to the everyday material. In the ontological framework, while Gandhi could inspire guilt as well as ethical strength, there is also a possibility that the complexity of the Gandhi as a persona is revealed. Notion of history, historiography, biography, nation and its tryst with modernity, possible negotiations between contradictory ideals in the present context and so on surface in the cinematic panorama that reveals Gandhi in diverse ways. In the light of the forgone discourse on cinema and Gandhi, it is not difficult to figure out the complexity of socio-cinematic common sense about/on Gandhi that emerges as a consequence of cinematic engagement with Gandhi. The above discourse establishes that in the forgone five decades, Hindi cinema has generated, on the one hand, complex common sense and, on the other, it has rendered Mohan Das Gandhi as a fluid matter to be recast in all possible contexts rather than only as a historical icon.

Thus, in this light, it is imperative to ask as to what sense an undergraduate course, as part of bachelor in art, political science (honours) programme, which aims at reading Gandhi as a text, makes. Whether there is an intellectually adequate room to entertain students' and teachers' socio-cinematic common sense or not as well as whether there is a possible orientation in the academic attempt to 'read' Gandhi without excluding the popular readings owed to cinema is a question that the next section grapples with. In sum, the subsequent attempt is to explore the possibility of students' and teachers' engagement with the multiple meanings of/about/on Gandhi emerging from the (socio-cinematic) context rather than just (academically prescribed) text.

Content and Discontent of *Reading Gandhi*

The course titled *Reading Gandhi* was introduced as an interdisciplinary concurrent course for students from across the disciplines in social science by the department of political science in the undergraduate colleges of the University of Delhi. The academic council of the University of Delhi, following a report from the BA Honours restructuring committee set up by the vice chancellor (in 2004), came up with the circular that the restructured BA Honours will include concurrent courses of interdisciplinary nature (instead of the hitherto-used subsidiary courses) from 2005. These concurrent courses, also known as IDC (interdisciplinary courses), will be aimed at diversifying students' interest in disciplinary themes and balance the overspecialization in the discipline in which student has opted to pursue a BA Honours. Each department of the university had to design and propose a concurrent course. Reading Gandhi was one, which came from the department of political science of the University of Delhi, and was used in the departments of political science in the colleges.[23] Recently, it has been elevated to the stature of compulsory course for the undergraduate students of political science, vide the circular from the university administration (dated 30 January 2012, letter number No. C1/R/2011). The key objective of the course, according to the description on the course syllabus, is:

> The course seeks to meet two essential objectives: one, to acquaint the students with the art of reading texts, to enable students to grasp its conceptual and argumentative structure and to help them acquire the skills to locate the texts in a broader intellectual and social historical context. Second, it aims to acquaint the students with the social and political thought of Gandhi.[24]

---

[23] This is based on the personal communication with the university officials (who were too reticent or perhaps ignorant to deliver a clear account of the starting of the IDCs in the undergraduate colleges), students and diverse commercial websites (not at all the university website).

[24] Unfortunately, the course syllabus is not on the website of the University of Delhi, until it was checked last on 13 April 2012. However, the university website mentions the name of the course in different documents (see www.du.ac.in), and in the section on syllabus and courses for the undergraduate, the course title does not appear at all (see http://www.du.ac.in/fileadmin/DU/students/Pdf/admissions/2011/semsys_2011-12/14711_BA_H_PoliticalSc.pdf, now the URL is dysfunctional). Besides, the syllabus for the course is available on sale in the Xerox shops in the north campus of the University of Delhi. It is also available on the commercial websites such as http://www.indiastudychannel.com/resources/22833-University-Delhi-B-A-H-Restruc-Syllabus.aspx, now the URL is dysfunctional, or on a personal blog of a user by the name of open learner on http://polscience-du.blogspot.com. I mention this in the footnote to mark two points: one that the course is right from

From the objectives behind the concurrent course in general and *Reading Gandhi* in particular, some of the leading ideas emerge. First of all, in generic sense, the university intended to abide by the epistemological shift and restructure the Bachelors in Art programme in order to give premium to the contextual learning of students. This indicates the principled willingness to make the learning process adequately ontological and thereby include students' myriad faculty as well as a priori knowledge. Of course, it demands the interdisciplinarity or orientation and hence the courses seem to have maintained the awareness of the demand. Second, at the level of particularity, the course like Reading Gandhi does hint at the need to maintain the bridge between text and context. Hence, the art of reading a text and the context in which Gandhi operated assume prominent significance. However, what is nearly relegated is the ontological temperament of the course in true sense. The structure of the course leaves no room for the pedagogic innovation and engagement with what has been termed socio-cinematic common sense in the foregone section.

The essential components in the structure of course are fourfold. First is the discussion on the art if reading the text, which invites the teachers and students to refer to the texts of Terence Ball and Quentin Skinner. The section leads to the reduction of art of reading a text into a technique of the same by replacing the anarchy of art with the stricture of technique. It instils in learners that text has to be read in only suggested ways, and there is a possibility of error if any innovation is done in the reading of the text. Besides, it also engenders the scientific prejudices, which hermeneutic philosophy highlighted,[25] that a proper technical reading of the text could be prejudice free. The casualty of

the beginning vulnerable to commercial encashment and second that the University of Delhi is least organized in offering and popularizing the course.

[25] I have in my mind Gadamer criticizing science for making a prejudiced claim that science can be prejudice free. See Mueller-Vollmer, Kurt. 1986. *The Hermeneutic Reader: Texts of the German Tradition from the Enlightenment to the Present*. Oxford: Basil Blackwell.

'open reading' occurs in this section in spite of the lofty intent to establish the significance of locating a text of a thinker (in this case, of Gandhi) in his own context. No wonder, then, the second section is a closed reading of Gandhi's *Hind Swaraj*, as if the closeness were an intellectual virtue of an axiomatic kind. Even if the significance of closed reading is accepted, there is a crying need to have an open reading as well. The first and second sections forecloses the possibility of an open reading much as a closed one of the text of Gandhi. The closeness of reading a text is also fairly literal in the syllabus. Hence, the need to locate Gandhi and his text in the larger framework of intellectual tradition of India never figures. It never occurs that Gandhi was talking, writing and enacting his ideas in a background dotted with textual tradition vis-à-vis the scriptures such as *The Geeta* and the Upanishads. It also seldom figures that Gandhi is also bringing about a fusion between the 'other Europe' (of Leo Tolstoy and Ruskin Bond) and the Indic tradition (with the notion of *Sanatan Dharma*). The emphasis on reading Gandhi as text, no matter how much of intellectual preparedness to locate the text in the historical context of Gandhi, obscures the world view of Gandhi. With this, as a disjunction, the third section unfolds a celebration of understanding of the Gandhi by Bhiku Parekh and David Hardiman, respectively. Never does it reflect that there could be myriad kinds of Gandhi(s) of the learners as well as the teachers, pertaining to a priori understanding students and teachers have as social actors. The fourth section is a random sampling of subthemes pertaining to Gandhi's writings and thereof key themes such as nationalism, communal unity, question of women and untouchability. This section establishes for sure that the whole course is nothing but an easy way to get maximum marks in the examination. The non-related way in which these subthemes appear, and also the disjuncture between the discourse on reading the text vis-à-vis the debate on text or/ and context, and understanding of Gandhi's writing by a chosen couple such as Parekh and Hardiman, reveals the fractured structure of the course.

No wonder, then, the course teachers as well as students resort to some of the bestseller textbooks available in the market. Most of them are by the title *Reading Gandhi*, as if a strategy to avoid any confusion in the mind of the buyer. Each textbook religiously caters notes to the book users, adhering to the syllabus of the course. The most popular textbooks are by Surjit Kaur Jolly (2006), Kusum Lata Chadda (2008), B. N. Roy (2009), Ram Chandra Pradhan (2010), and the latest is Anil Dutta Mishra (2012).[26] A critical survey of these textbooks suggests a few moot points of seminal importance. First, the syllabus of the course makes it possible to be rendered easily into an examination guide-like textbook-based course. The textbooks and the syllabus both indicate the little need and importance of the pedagogical intervention except peddling the syllabus like a passive vehicle of the prescribed texts. Second, there is an evident discrepancy between the context of the learner and the syllabus along with the textbooks. The commonsense, owing to cinema and society, which everybody is presumably carrying in and out of classroom, is seldom touched upon. The nature and scope of the course does not occasion any such reference to the a priori knowledge of the learners on the subject and related themes.

The aforementioned observations were nearly vindicated in the workshop organized by the Institute of Lifelong Learning in collaboration with the Developing Countries Research Centre and

---

[26] Students (as well as teachers) keep a copy of one of these books, more often than not. Each of the textbooks deals with the themes and texts prescribed in the syllabus. The textbooks present materials for developing notes. The textbooks help frame good answers to the questions for the final semester examination and score well. Students (in personal communication) have also expressed the same views. These books are Jolly, Surjit Kaur. Ed. 2006. *Reading Gandhi*. Delhi: Concept Publishing; Kusum Lata Chadda. 2008. *Reading Gandhi*. Delhi: Kanishka Publishers; B. N. Roy. 2009. *Reading Gandhi*. Delhi: Authors Press; Ram Chandra Pradhan. 2010. *Reading and Reappraising Gandhi*. Delhi: Macmillan India; Anil Dutta Mishra. 2012. *Reading Gandhi*. Delhi: Pearson Education.

It is noticed that all the college libraries in the University of Delhi have catalogued six to seven copies of the textbooks from the mentioned list.

Kirori Mal College (University of Delhi), on 26 and 27 August 2011. The workshop was titled 'Reading Gandhi for College Teachers', and the objective of which was expressed in the following words:

> Reading Gandhi is a concurrent course taught to B.A. Honours students in Delhi University. It is also taught in lieu of the qualifying course. The course itself was designed as an exercise in how to read a text, and understanding the different ways in which Gandhi and his thought have been interpreted across disciplines. Though we need wider feedback on how this course is taught and received, on the whole there is felt need to strengthen the interpretative aspect of the course as compared to the rendering of a straight narrative of Gandhi's thought and ideas. The proposed workshop will foreground this particular issue through discussions and presentations over two days.[27]

Even if we do not heed the consequences of the workshop and the opinion of the irate teachers who did not find much coming from the workshop, there is a point to be noted in the very execution of the same. There is an exceeding realization that everything is not very well with the structural design and execution of the course. There is recognition that the purpose of the course is nearly defeated. Yet, the recent circular from the administrative office announces to make Reading Gandhi as a compulsory paper in the BA political science (Honours) programme, without any restructuring of the syllabus. Hence, the situation draws a parallel

---

[27] The URL for this reference was See http://www.du.ac.in/fileadmin/DU/ Events0482011_ILLL_reading_gandhi.pdf, which is no longer available. In a personal communication, some of the teachers who participated in the workshop and who have been teaching this course for many years opined: 'It was a workshop by seasoned political scientists for themselves where all they can do is to reprimand the young teachers for their own follies in designing the syllabus. It was a workshop to get captive audience for the aging political scientists who have run out of anything new to say or do; it was form no angle a workshop of the teachers of this course who have first-hand experience of teaching it, for their experience mattered little.'

between teaching a course on Gandhi and teaching values in value education period in the schools.

Inconclusive Conclusion

In this kind of discourse, it is hard to be really conclusive. For, the situation is not a matter of the remote past; it very much pertains to the present; it is susceptible to dynamic changes. However, what I have attempted to do here is to show that there happens to be an uncreative discrepancy between socio-cinematic under-standing and the academic proposition on Gandhi, which could be detrimental to the basic objective of a course like Reading Gandhi. There is little chance for teachers and students to realize themselves in the lectures on Gandhi, which could be in princi-ple about self-realization. The two domains of production of commonsense, popular cinema and (undergraduate) academics, yield two sets of images and ideas about/on a historical icon like Gandhi. In larger analysis, cinematic attempts seem to be more versatile and engaging than the academic attempts. Both domains have evident commercial consequences. But, then, the ideas from the cinematic mills are more layered than those from the academic mills. In an ideal sense, the domain of academic production and circulation of knowledge ought to be critically engaging with the same of the non-academic such as cinema. However, as it were, academic is predisposed to dismiss the commonsense altogether with the prejudices that cinematic is illogical. A youthful engage-ment with the ideas of M. K. Gandhi is, indeed, a casualty.

9

The Rhizomatic Constructions of Gandhi on Web 2.0

Gopalan Ravindran

Introduction

Recent times saw many controversial encounters of Gandhi, in his virtual and rhizomatic self, on what is emerging as the most participatory, discursive and user-generated plane of the Internet, the Web 2.0. Among the prominent ones was a hate group, 'I Hate Gandhi' on Facebook, which was eventually shut down, due to protests and legal action under the IT Act 2000.[1] Those who hate Gandhi are otherwise alive and kicking in other parts of Web 2.0 such as YouTube and blogs. Gandhi on Web 2.0 also evokes strong likes in equal measure. *Gandhitopia* (www.gandhitopia. org) is one of the several sites on Web 2.0 which strives for the promotion of Gandhi's name in a concerted manner. However, what is striking about the presence of Gandhi on Web 2.0 is not the likes and dislikes Gandhi evokes in almost equal measure, but the presence of Gandhi as a rhizomatic site where not only the

---

[1] 'Facebook Bans Online Hate Group on Mahatma Gandhi', *DNA*, 2011.

binary notions of Gandhi, but also the most discursive notions of Gandhi come into play. In this respect, more than Gandhi, the legendary person, what makes the legendary person a rhizomatic subject, which allows multiplicitous encounters of Web 2.0 users, is the rhizome that is Web 2.0. Gandhi on Web 2.0 is accessible to Indians and non-Indians in ways that smack of expressions of adulation, mockery, hatred, inspiration, motivation, peace and love. Gandhi on Web 2.0 is on the verge of reconstitution of unprecedented measure in comparison with the transformation of Gandhi in our non-Web 2.0 encounters. The non-Web 2.0 encounters of Gandhi are mostly enacted by the interfaces between our everyday life contexts and conventional media, and it is fairly certain that these contexts are not rhizomes of the same order as Web 2.0. They cannot harbour and nurture the expressions of adulation, mockery, hatred, inspiration, motivation, peace and love towards Gandhi in one plane. Even if they secretly wish to clamour for one, they would incur the wrath of the disciplinary forces. Hence, Web 2.0 provides a new plane of enchantment and disenchantment for those who seek to rethink Gandhi's life and ideals in their own ways *albeit* drawing on their native contexts of histories and experiences. Web 2.0 has also effectively pushed Gandhi's aura beyond the shores of India and the former British Empire to the larger world where Italians are as enamoured of Gandhi as Indians and certain groups of blacks of South Africa are as hateful of Gandhi as certain groups of Dalits of India. In between these shades of extremes, Gandhi is also providing ample scope for others who seek to rethink Hitler through/with Gandhi and Gandhi through/with Hitler. There are also conformists who do not wish to go beyond the conventional picture of Gandhi as the Mahatma and as the father of the nation. There are also critics of Gandhi on Web 2.0 who seek to mimic native critics of Gandhi in India who do not wish to give up the prisms developed by Bhabasaheb Ambedkar and E. V. Ramasamy Periyar in their powerful critiques of Gandhi. In sum, Gandhi as a rhizomatic subject on Web 2.0 warrants a closer scrutiny with the theoretical support of Deleuze and Guattari's concept of rhizome, a concept that is as enigmatic, relevant and purposeful as Gandhi.[2]

Understanding Web 2.0

Web 2.0 is what Web 1.0 failed to muster—participatory and discursive modes of communication. The rise and rise of Web 2.0, ever since the term was coined by O'Reilly in 2001,[3] attests to the dramatic transformation of the innovative Internet business models, user-generated categories of Internet content, participatory modes of content creation, 'bestial archaeology'[4] of delivery networks and group communication functions that are mimicking social communication. While Web 1.0 was largely HTML-based and seen as non-participatory and anti-UGC (user-generated content), Web 2.0 profited greatly by the development of non-HTML-based technologies and Internet business models that sought to leverage UGC. The dismantling of the non-participatory and uni-directional modes of content creation and dissemination by the wildly multi-directional and endlessly participatory modes of content creation serves as the basic premise and attraction of Web 2.0. There are also a range of reasons not related to Internet or its technologies which have contributed to the success of Web 2.0.

The foremost among these are to be located in the new age of capitalism wherein the most noteworthy sources of capital and the labour are not to be sourced from the natural planes of staple

---

[2] Deleuze, Gilles and Felix Guattari. 1987. *A Thousand Plateaus: Capitalism and Schizophrenia*. Minnesota, MN: University of Minnesota Press, 7–13.

[3] O'Reilly, T. 2005. 'What is Web 2.0: Design Patterns and Business Models for the Next Generation of Software', http://oreilly.com/web2/archive/what-is-web-20.html. Retrieved 23 January 2011.

[4] Parikka, Jussi. 2010a. 'Insect Media Is Out'. http://www.networkpolitics.org/blogs/jussiparikka/09/january/2011/insect-media-out Retrieved 23 January 2011.

industries and markets, but in the minds of entrepreneurs such as Mark Zuckerberg (the founder of Facebook), who could give birth to massively global entities like Facebook, without worrying about the need to source conventional capital, physical raw materials for production and the need to advertise, market and sell the physical products. In these entities, the capital is largely intellectual and partly drawn from the venture capital funds. The raw materials are the templates of the sites and the application modules created and nurtured by the developers' communities that are hooked to new Web 2.0 platforms solely for the reasons of the popularity and size of such platforms. The other important raw material, the content, simply flows like water in a perennial waterfall because of the burgeoning number of users and the content they generate with their activities. The likes of Zuckerberg also do not worry about hiring and paying labour. For them, the labours come calling when they inadvertently register themselves as users of sites like Facebook. The 500 million users of Facebook ought to be seen as the new-age labour aiding the work of new-age capitalists such as Mark Zuckerberg. They are the new-age labour that works 24 hours without asking questions about pay rise, working conditions and so on, all the while churning out voluminous and attractive blocks of content for others and themselves to see. They are also largely invisible to each other, except in their groups. They are what Ritzer and Jurgenson termed the 'prosumers,' the new class in the present age of capitalism which performs both production and consumption functions.[5]

One of the interesting theoretical prisms through which Web 2.0 can be projected and understood in radically different ways is the theory of 'insect media' proposed by Jussi Parikka. According to Parikka,[6] the Web 2.0 owes everything to the models perfected by the insects in their worlds. In Parikka's logic, the other name for Web 2.0 is 'insect media.' In other words, books on

---

[5] Ritzer, George and Nathan Jurgenson. 2010. 'Production, Consumption, Prosumption: The Nature of Capitalism in the Age of the Digital "Prosumer"'. *Journal of Consumer Culture* 10: 13–36.

[6] Parikka, Jussi. 2010b. *Insect Media: An Archaeology of Animals and Technology*. Minnesota, MN: University of Minnesota Press.

entomology could teach us a lot about network cultures that humans think they invented and perfected. Says Parikka:

> Insect Media is not so directly related to contemporary network culture, but works on that topic through a detour. It asks the question: why is our digital network culture so enthusiastic about insects, and related animal metaphors and models? ... In terms of social media culture, the notions of swarms, hive minds and collective intelligence in distributed networks have been harnessed as part of the business discourse of the 21st century. Even if originating as part of the 1990s cyberenthusiasm for the Internet, they gained another chance during the recent years of Web 2.0 when finally the amateur spirit at the core of the Internet project was discoverd as a possible revenue stream. As analyzed by many network theorists including Terranova, the harnessing of free labour as part of the Web 2.0 logic was part and parcel of this neobiologism of networks.[7]

In Jussi Parikka's logic, someone like Marc Zuckerberg's success depends to a great extent on his emulation of the insects that are non-human and non-rational. The new-age capitalism is the other name for humans capitalizing on the insect worlds of webs, swarms, hives and so on in spawning the Web 2.0 media. In this context, the moot questions is: How to relate to the widely held notion of Web 2.0 as social media networks that are tailor-made for human beings by human beings, if such strong notions of 'insect media' are going to govern our understanding of Web 2.0? Is Jussi Parikka throwing us off guard? Not exactly. He is only making us more aware of the less exotic nature (read bestial nature) of the digital network cultures in their sources of inspiration. This is not very different from the earlier waves of emulation of the other non-human living beings in nature such as birds (as a source of inspiration for building planes) and sea animals (for building ships and submarines). One of the implications of working through the prism of 'insect media' is coming to terms with the real level of sociability the so-called social media make possible. The Web 2.0 hides more than it reveals as digitally refined networks that connect people across cultures and continents. According to Parikka:

---

[7] Parikka, 'Insect Media Is Out'.

At the core of the mathematically refined, technologically pol-
ished and scientifically based cultures of network communication
lies something very stupid. The insect is a good figure to think
technological cultures through 'affect' and milieu-bound nature
of our cognitive and perceptual capacities. We are not insects,
but a lot of the stuff we do is mindless, or at least automated.
Network culture and its politics is not always a politics of reflection and decision-making, but of relating, automating, affective
labour, and much lower level modes of sociability, relating and
being in the world.[8]

We need to mark as significant what Parikka mentions as 'much
lower level modes of sociability, relating and being in the world'[9]
as the arbiter when we seek to see Web 2.0 as social media.

On the other hand, if one moves away from the notion
of 'insect media', one encounters the promotion of Web 2.0
platforms as social media networks by mainstream media and
users. This seems a bit outstretched in logic if one subscribes
to the truth that all media are social and they cannot be aso-
cial. All media are social institutions as well as the sources
of the social products they engender. Tagging the likes of
Facebook, Myspace, Orkut and Twitter as social media smacks
of an attempt to misread the real location of these new media
platforms. The tag of social media constricts and distorts the
expanding canvas of the participatory communication modes
enabled by Web 2.0 media in the spheres of interpersonal communication, group communication, political communication,
advocacy communication, development communication and
international communication.

Even though the notion of Web 2.0 platforms as social media
networks is fraught with many downsides, there is also enormous
scope to see them as sources of tremendous socio-political implications. The widespread influence of Facebook and Twitter in
changing the course of events in disparate contexts, such as the

---

[8] Ibid.
[9] Ibid.

hounding of Wikileaks, the recent political crisis in Tunisia, the tapes involving Nira Radia and her friends in media and politics in India and the mobilization of student public opinion against the government's moves for fee hike in the UK, attests to the power of the Web 2.0. In Tunisia, the Web 2.0 tools were part of political communication as well as group/interpersonal communication networks. In the case of Radia tapes, the same characteristics were self-evident. In the case of the Wikileaks, the Web 2.0 tools were part of all the spheres of communication mentioned above. In the case of the UK fee hike protests, the role of Web 2.0 as a group and advocacy communication tool was prominent.

Notwithstanding the above, there is still considerable scope to deal with the likes of Facebook and Twitter as examples of media which have discernible social influences. According to Canadian political economist, Daniel Drache, the age of Facebook is the age wherein 'we are living without curtains'.[10] Daniel Drache's metaphorical indictment of Facebook and its people goes beyond the simplistic understanding of the role of Web 2.0 as social media or participatory media. 'Living without curtains' evokes a notion of the new age of modernity wherein another sphere of public space is taking shape even as the conventional notions of privacy and etiquette in public spaces are being dramatically remapped to the point of being junked. 'Living without curtains' represents a dramatic shift in the expression of the self in this age of modernity wherein the semantic gap between the virtual and the real is fading fast even as the physical gap between the virtual and the real holds on as before. This is to say that 'living without curtains' has been made a possibility in the virtual realms of Facebook even as we might not dare to 'live without curtains' in our bedrooms in the physical world. This dualism between two divergent modes of social engagement by a Web 2.0 platform like Facebook is what makes it problematic as a social institution, not

---

[10] Drache, Daniel. 1 November 2010. 'Revisiting the Information Revolution and Web 2.0: Who Is on First, Habermas or Foucault?' *Media and Society Seminar Series Lecture*, Department of Journalism and Communication, University of Madras.

in the conventional negative connotation of the word 'problematic', but in the deeply convoluted manner in which the social influences of Web 2.0 are touching the lives of Web 2.0 users in the process of giving shape to a new age of modernity.

The above reading of Web 2.0 seeks to reach three conclusions: (a) The Web 2.0 personifies something more than the Internet or the associated technological developments—it signifies the birth of a new age of capitalism. (b) Web 2.0 networks are successful emulations of the models of networks perfected by insects. Web 2.0 networks are nothing but 'insect media'. (c) The Web 2.0 platforms are not to be misread as simplistic entities as social media—they represent our entry into a new age of modernity where 'living without curtains' is as much a reality (in the virtual world that is masquerading as real) as an impossibility (in the physical world).

There is a need to move beyond the notions of 'insect media,' 'prosumers' and 'non-html' of Web 2.0 if one cares to map the discursive and rhizomatic constructions of Mahatma Gandhi made possible by Web 2.0 channels such as YouTube. There is a need to see Web 2.0 as the larger umbrella 'assemblage' or 'rhizome'. There is a need to see YouTube as a large umbrella assemblage. There is also a need to see the groups of videos on a topic or personality (in our case Mahatma Gandhi's teachings and personality) as major 'assemblages' and 'rhizomes'. More importantly, there is a need to see the individual video on any topic or personality as the minor 'assemblage' or 'rhizome'. This chapter examines the rhizomatic constructions of Mahatma Gandhi on one of the important constituents of contemporary Web 2.0, YouTube.

Understanding Gandhi on Web 2.0 with Deleuze and Guattari

In *A Thousand Plateaus*, Deleuze and Guattari explain the six principles of rhizome. These six principles are about 'connection, heterogeneity, multiplicity, rupture, cartography and decalcomania'.[11] According to Deleuze and Guattari,

> any point of a rhizome can be connected to anything other, and must be. ...A rhizome ceaselessly establishes connections between semiotic chains, organizations of power, and circumstances relative to the arts, sciences, and social struggles. A semiotic chain is like a tuber agglomerating very diverse acts, not only linguistic, but also perceptive, mimetic, gestural, and cognitive ...
>
> ... An assemblage is precisely this increase in the dimensions of a multiplicity that necessarily changes in nature as it expands its connections. There are no points or positions in a rhizome, such as those found in a structure, tree, or root. There are only lines. ... Multiplicities are defined by the outside: by the abstract line, the line of flight or de-territorialization according to which they change in nature and connect with other multiplicities. The plane of consistency (grid) is the outside of all multiplicities. The line of flight marks: the reality of a finite number of dimensions that the multiplicity effectively fills; the impossibility of a supplementary dimension, unless the multiplicity is transformed by the line of flight; the possibility and necessity of flattening all of the multiplicities on a single plane of consistency or exteriority, regardless of their number of dimensions.[12]

The lines of flight in a rhizomatic structure are as significant as the 'lines of segmentarity', which are governed by the old rules of territorialization and stratification. It is only when the rhizomatic structure encounters ruptures one sees the transformation of the lines of segmentarity into the lines of flight. As Deleuze and Guattari say:

> A rhizome may be broken, shattered at a given spot, but it will start up again on one of its old lines, or on new lines. You can never get rid of ants because they form an animal rhizome that can rebound time and again after most of it has been destroyed. Every rhizome contains lines of segmentarity according to which

---

[11] Deleuze and Guattari, *A Thousand Plateaus.*
[12] Ibid.

it is stratified, territorialized, organized, signified, attributed, etc., as well as lines of deterritorialization down which it constantly flees. There is a rupture in the rhizome whenever segmentary lines explode into a line of flight, but the line of flight is part of a rhizome. These lines always tie back to one another ...[13]

According to Ravindran:

As rhizomatic networks are depended on connections that are in a flux because of either the lack of fixed points or moving points or even moving connections, they could be seen as similar in structure to the networks of Web 2.0. Web 2.0 personifies a site where flows are able to flow in directions not pre-determined. Here, as in any rhizomatic network, flows and their constituting connections make the rhizomatic network as dynamic as possible.[14]

In Deleuze and Guattari's[15] scheme of things, there are two axes that constitute an assemblage or rhizome—the vertical axis of a molar line and the horizontal axis of a molecular line. The molar line starts as the site of territorialization or segmental line and ends as the line of flight or site of deterritorialization. This progression is defined by the principle of rupture. The segmental lines of the rhizome encounter rupture and then take the line of flight. The horizontal axis of molecular line is about the micro changes the rhizome encounters without causing the line of flight. This is where the building blocks of the assemblage which Deleuze pointed out, such as the perception image, action image and affection image, reside. In the language of his cinema books,[16] this could be read as the form of content and form of expression.

---

[13] Ibid.
[14] Ravindran, Gopalan, 2007. 'The Rhizomatic Flows of Transnational Tamil Cinema in Asia and Web 2.0'. *Philippine Sociological Review* 55:65–78.
[15] Deleuze and Guattari, *A Thousand Plateaus*.
[16] Deleuze, Gilles. 2005. *Cinema 1: The Movement-Image*. London: Continuum.

This chapter examines the rhizomatic constructions of Mahatma Gandhi on Web 2.0 on the basis of two groups of YouTube videos featuring Gandhi. These videos can be grouped into categories such as unaltered archival videos, altered archival videos, animated videos and staged videos. These videos can also be grouped on the basis of their molecular lines as those that seek to play the role of enchantment and disenchantment (form of expression and content) in relation to their subject of expression and content, Mahatma Gandhi. The two groups of YouTube videos chosen for this study deal with the themes 'One World' and the 'Power of One'. These videos have been chosen as they are having significant level of viewership and popularity, as indicated by their number of views. These videos have been chosen to apply gainfully the notions of Deleuze and Guattari in understanding the planes of molar and molecular lines of assemblages. More importantly, these videos have been chosen for their thematic unity and the possibilities they afford in mapping the rhizomatic constructions of Mahatma Gandhi on Web 2.0.

Surprisingly, for reasons yet to be studied, a good number of videos on Mahatma Gandhi have an Italian connection in terms of their origin, language and so on. These videos seek to play the role of enchantment, whereas the videos with the African connection seek to play the role of disenchantment with Mahatma Gandhi. There is also a category where Gandhi is juxtaposed with Hitler to bring out the aspects of material subjectivity between their ideologies and personalities. This chapter chose for its analysis the following terms of reference: (a) Web 2.0 as the super umbrella assemblage, (b) YouTube as the umbrella assemblage, (c) the growing groups of Mahatma Gandhi videos on YouTube as assemblages and (d) the individual videos as sub-assemblages. While we require a large time frame study to understand the umbrella assemblages, it is within the scope of the present chapter to attempt an examination of two of the groups of videos on YouTube which focus on the themes (a) 'One World' and (b) 'The Power of One'. Among the YouTube videos on Mahatma Gandhi, these two groups of videos have large viewership and variants. Variants are the mutating categories of the original upload. Viewership is indicated by the number of views indicated at the right-hand bottom corner of the video player in YouTube.

The 'One World' video has several variants, including the one pointing to the Italian connection. But the one that has garnered the largest number of views (256,817) is the one that was uploaded as 'Mahatma Gandhi—One World' by Ibrahim Lee. This version runs for 6:07 and was uploaded in 2009. The largest views for any Mahatma Gandhi video is registered for 'Eyewitness: Mahatma Gandhi Assassination' (657,814) which was uploaded in 2008 by msjaitly in a 3:16 duration version. The famous vision of Mahatma Gandhi of the 'One World' surfaces in his eloquent speech at the Conference of the Inter-Asian Relations at New Delhi on 2 April 1947. In its most substantive part, Gandhi remarked:

> If you want to give a message again to the West, it must be a message of 'Love', it must be a message of 'Truth'. There must be a conquest (clapping), please, please, please. That will interfere with my speech, and that will interfere with your understanding also. I want to capture your hearts and don't want to receive your claps. Let your hearts clap in unison with what I'm saying, and I think, I shall have finished my work. Therefore, I want you to go away with the thought that Asia has to conquer the West. Then, the question that a friend asked yesterday, 'Did I believe in one world?' Of course, I believe in one world. And how can I possibly do otherwise, when I become an inheritor of the message of love that these great un-conquerable teachers left for us? You can redeliver that message now, in this age of democracy, in the age of awakening of the poorest of the poor, you can redeliver ...

Interestingly, the 'One World' videos only relate to the famous speech of Mahatma Gandhi ephemerally, only in the titles, and not in the aural and visual dimensions of the videos which deal with Mahatma Gandhi's speech on the locations of spirituality, truth and love. However, there appears to be an abiding faith in the 'One World' notion of Mahatma Gandhi, if not as an explicit form of content, but as an explicit form of expression, thereby pointing to the molecular line of the assemblage. The 'One World' tag appears as a label in all the individual videos of this naturally evolving group, even though they have enormous differences in terms of their molecular lines of assemblages. While positing a group location for the 'One World' assemblage, this chapter is particularly interested in the manner in which the molar and molecular lines move from their points of axes. While the videos which use archival footage in modified/unmodified forms have rather static molar lines in so far as their focus on the 'One World' name tag is concerned, there are significant variations in the molecular lines of assemblages, partly because of their states of modification/non-modification of their archival states. However, if taken as a whole, we find significant changes in both molar and molecular lines of the videos of the group 'One World'.

This chapter makes a closer examination of three videos in the group. Besides the 'One World' video uploaded by Ibrahim Lee, this chapter examines two videos, one a commercial one by Italia Telecom and the other a variant of the Italia Telecom commercial. These two videos appear to perform the functions expected of the two axes of the molar line—segmentary and line-of-flight functions. The Italia Telecom video is also titled 'One World'. It has a relatively large viewership (149,612). It was uploaded by Franzelandreas with a duration of 0:51 on 9 February 2008. This opens with a figure of Mahatma Gandhi walking towards a house-like structure with his walking stick. This can be read as the Deleuzian perception image which provides us both the totality of the objective world and the subject's (Mahatma Gandhi himself) subtracted view. Thereafter, Gandhi emerges from the camera plane as another perception image, followed by a series of action and affection images where Mahatma Gandhi propounds something as revolutionary as his vision of 'One World.' At this point, one can observe the close-ups and long shots of a large group of

Italians gazing at the towering figure of Gandhi in a giant screen in a public square and the small screen of their mobiles. Gandhi is also watched avidly by African tribals in their laptops and a lonesome elderly person even as a young couple sitting on a street bench are made to relate to the message of love and truth. As the commercial rolls towards its end, we find subtitles wherein Gandhi's words, in his 2 April 1947 speech on the theme 'One World,' stage a powerful comeback, albeit in a discursive and fragmentary manner, before the logo of Italia Telecom and the sales pitch of the commercial allows the staging of the line of flight to the 'One World' notion of an Italian telecom company, which probably wants to treat the World as One Market, a notion that is a point of rupture for the group videos which start with the molar line of 'One World'.

The variant of this video is also instructive to understand the nature of Mahatma Gandhi videos as an assemblage where the possibilities of connections, heterogeneity, multiplicities and ruptures are real. This variant is titled 'Hitler vs Gandhi Telecom'. It has a duration of 1:12 and was uploaded by *hibbzzzz* in 2009. It has generated views by 33,971. This video of 'One World' is more than a variant of the Italia Telecom commercial, in that it acts as the site where the assemblage forges rhizomatic connections, heterogeneity, multiplicities and ruptures in a manner that propels the rhizomatic construction of Mahatma Gandhi as a discursive process where the subversive rupture caused by the Italia Telecom commercial is subverted further by the presence of Hitler as the subject/signifier and Mahatma Gandhi as the absent subject/empty signifier. Hitler roars along with his guns and the same people who populated the original Italia Telecom commercial are made to do the same narrative functions they performed with Gandhi. This displaced presence of the people other than the lead person (Hitler) proves that this rhizomatic construction of Gandhi can happen even without Gandhi and, in a shocking manner with the presence of Hitler, who held a completely antithetical notion of 'One World'. This video is also unique because it does not have a substantive segmentary axis, but a quite substantive and explosive line of flight even before the segmentary line was in place. These two later videos could be read as two similar and yet divergent points of rupture in the rhizome, that is Mahatma Gandhi 'One World' group videos.

On the other hand, 'The Power of One' group videos look fairly simplistic to work with as the words were not from Mahatma Gandhi and the videos do not have a primary molar location in Mahatma Gandhi's teachings and ideals. Yet, 'The Power of One' represents itself as worthy as the 'One World' group video as the assemblage with all the characteristics of a Deleuzean and Guattarean rhizome. As an assemblage, any rhizome needs to connect anything with anything in 'any space whatevers'. While the 'One World' video group adheres to this norm in connecting the verbal/textual version of the speech of Mahatma Gandhi in 1947 on his vision of 'One World', with an abridged version of a randomly selected speech of Mahatma Gandhi on the subject of spirituality under the tag 'One World', which in turn is connected through the ruptures of the molar line of 'One World' in the Italia Telecom commercial and its variant with Hitler as the proponent of a different notion of 'One World'. The 'Power of One' group of videos also provides similar connections, but on a larger and complex scale, even though at the surface these videos look spartan in their use of Mahatma Gandhi. The leading member of 'The Power of One' group of videos is titled 'The Power of ONE'. This was uploaded in 2009 by Albertgr. This video has attracted 233,080 views. In this video, Mahatma Gandhi appears as a blurry momentary figure which seeks to point his finger towards us as if to underscore 'The Power of One'. Gandhi as the person who personified the meaning of 'The Power of One' is co-located in this video by other personalities such as Mother Theresa.

The words 'The Power of One' first appear as a title of a famous novel set in South Africa by Bryce Carteney in 1989. In 1995, these words appear as the title of a pop ballad in the album of an Australian singer, Merril. Later, these words were immortalized in the song by Donna Summers for a *Pokémon* movie in 2000. These were the connecting points of the 'Power of One' group of videos in their states of heterogeneity and multiplicities in their pre-YouTube avatars. On YouTube, these videos have their points of connections, heterogeneity, multiplicities and ruptures too. On the molar line, defined by the notion of the 'Power of One', the variants such as 'Power of One' by Bomshel (129,569 views) agree on the power of the segmentary line where the power of one individual can make a big difference in the world. The connections, heterogeneity and multiplicities are there for all to see in videos which have different molecular lines, but with similar molar lines. The molecular lines differ from one another in terms of their forms of content and expression, but as Deleuze and Guattari argued, do not threaten the segmentary lines. But as in the 'One World' group of videos, the line of flight eventually happens when the last frame invokes the power of one organization (One Earth Organization) as in the previous case of Italia Telecom. The emergence of this line of flight happens because of the impossibility of the coexistence of 'The Power of One' as individuals and 'Power of One' as organizations, commercial or otherwise. This is bound to happen in rhizomatic constructions mediated by the institutionalized forms of persuasive communication such as advertising. As Web 2.0 channels are largely driven by UGC, the possibility of television commercials entering the rhizomatic assemblage of YouTube through the mediating and non-mediating modes of user activities on YouTube is as high as other forms of content. On the other hand, the video of Donna Summers does not fail the segmentary line as it fails to give birth to the line of flight. This is also because of the very strong plane of the molecular line where the form of expression, as amplified by Donna Summers, coexists powerfully with the form of content, stressing and re-stressing 'The Power of One'.

* * *

To read the constructions of Mahatma Gandhi on Web 2.0 through the rhizomatic prism of Deleuze and Guattari is as instructive as it is interesting. The manner in which the words and ideals of Mahatma Gandhi are connected, contested and ruptured in multiplicitous and heterogeneous ways by Indians, Italians, Africans, Asians and others in the planes of Web 2.0 show that Gandhi remains a crowd-puller in its virtual *avatars* as well. This chapter also attests to the need to rethink Gandhi in antithetical locations and co-locations where Gandhi coexists with the likes of Hitler, encounters hate campaigns and yet conveys his message of love and truth to Italians and Indians alike through the plane of immanence that is Web 2.0.

10

Digital Civil Disobedience Movement
Revisiting Gandhian Thoughts in an International Commune

M. Shuaib Mohamed Haneef

Background

Based on the work and vision of Sri Aurobindo and The Mother, Auroville was founded on the principle of bringing together people from all over the world to realize human unity in diversity. The Universal Township project of Auroville, located in Tamil Nadu and some parts in Puducherry, started in 1968, and in 1966 UNESCO passed a resolution commending it as a project of importance to the future of humanity, thereby giving their full encouragement. Still considered to be an experiment, Auroville is practically researching into sustainable living and the future cultural, environmental, social and spiritual needs of mankind.

The present community of Auroville consists of over 100 settlements of varying sizes with close to 2,200 people inhabiting it. One-third of the population accounts for Indians, and the rest are mostly from European countries, such as France, Germany and Holland. The activities of the inhabitants are multifarious and mainly include educational research, health care, village development, applied technology, building construction, town planning, cultural activities, municipal services and a very large variety of small- and medium-scale businesses. The sustainability plan includes carrying out productive activities in the above-mentioned sectors, where each and every individual from the community, by virtue of the talents she or he possesses, contributes to the community.

The economic model of Auroville is dependent on contributions from members of the community and from outside, financial aid from the Government of India and UNESCO and the execution of self-sustainable projects for industries are some of the regular means through which the aid is obtained. The presence of people from various countries makes the community a multicultural site where different cultures, languages and people coexist governed by a common spiritual and human conscience. A few businessmen run industries outside and contribute to Auroville, notwithstanding that they draw flak for their measly contribution. The economic status of the members is not the same, and it is found to be low among people who hail from Russia. It is therefore a microcosm of a society with some beliefs that members are expected to adhere to.

There are several bodies governing Auroville and its various units. The Working Council is responsible for the entire gamut of activities taking place within the community, and many sub-level bodies are vested with the responsibility of addressing exclusive activities.

Auroville from the Gandhian Perspective

'Gandhi offers the ideal of the economically self-sufficient, politically self-governing and culturally non-violent village republic as the guarantee of genuine democracy, true humanism, civilising non-violence and lasting peace.' This principle of Gandhi, to all intents and purposes, has a very close similarity to the principles of the Mother and the Auroville she founded. In this context, it is essential to treat Auroville as a cultural space that amalgamates a pastiche of social activities practices through research inputs, media, architecture design, town planning, village actions, organic farming among others. Given that, this chapter seeks to investigate the coexistence or clash of (sometimes) cultural models and the power equations within the multicultural space of Auroville from the Gandhian perspective. In other words, the chapter seeks to relate the activities and the functioning of Auroville to Gandhian perspectives. Looking at the activities, one can gauge that Auroville engenders knowledge transcending spatial boundaries and flowing across the multicultural site of the community.

In this chapter, the Intranet of Auroville was used as a basis to situate the responses gathered through the interview schedule and extrapolate them to the activities in the virtual space. In particular, an issue over land becomes the centre of discussion, which I have tried to explain from Gandhian perspectives or point of view.

Auroville Media

Auroville has an established media unit that comprises Internet television, Internet radio, Auronet, the Intranet exclusively for the members of the community. In addition, it brings out a newsletter *Auroville News* and *News and Notes*. The *News and Notes* is multilingual and is printed in Tamil, English and French, catering to the local members of Auroville and the international audience.

In print editions (publications of Auroville), the gatekeeping is in the hands of the Working Council and members from other bodies which insinuate the Panopticon power structure of Foucault. Internet Television and Internet Radio feature events in English and rarely in French only to report about events in Auroville. Both print and television content is controlled by the institutions of Auroville. The Intranet, on the other hand, provides space to the members to participate and break down the power frontiers if any through blogs and discussion forums.

Decentralization of Power in the Context of Udumbu (Land Issue)

The residential zone of Auroville is divided into settlements, and 'Udumbu', one of the settlements in the community, is at the heart of the debate in this chapter to correlate the civil disobedience philosophy of Gandhi and digital activism facilitated through blogs and discussion forums of Auroville Intranet. The discussions on 'Udumbu' land have called into question the unified civic identity and the multicultural identity of Auroville following the Working Council issuing an order to an Indian Auroville member occupying the land in order to give stewardship to a French woman. Some members in the community were not happy with the decision taken by the Working Council, which resulted in polarized identities.

I know that you plan to ask Ramesh to move out of Udumbu; I will be really curious to read the reason why.

He is—once again—asked to leave what has been his house (albeit without toilet and kitchen ...) for a few years now, thus giving Udumbu in the hands of Ann who has started this problem, since she asked—from the beginning—that Ramesh be told to move out of Udumbu, and this is exactly what seems to be happening, and of course I find this NOT acceptable.

However, the social solidarity is not very far to seek with a group of people characterized by transnational identities supporting the Indian who allegedly was given the raw deal. The forum facilitated exchange of opinions for and against, and the depth of discourse in understanding the basic tenet of Auroville as a multicultural site fostering human love transcending religion, geography, colour, creed and cast was dominantly portrayed in the messages where a few members clarified the subject position taken by them.

anton
10 February 2011/10:15 am

My impression is that if a foreigner gets a FIR registrated against him/her, s/he can loose [sic] the visa or even get a quit notice. Quite a difference with an Indian, who can live in or around Auroville forever, I find.

bunty
10 February 2011/12:12 pm

So what's your point Anton? Are you trying to say Indians misuse this privilege? Please note that the above article is not about Indians vs Non Indians. Do not give it that colour...and digress from the core of the issue. Having said that – Indians are also very tolerant...if one is made to take such a step then it doesn't take much to figure out the kind of harassment the 'Indian' is facing.

anton
10 February 2011/01:32 pm

The only reason Aurovilians used to go to a police station was to registrate a (presumed) crime recognized by Indian law, like theft or robbery. The main thing the police could do was to registrate a FIR. Santo writes that he was planning to go there to complain about other Aurovilians about percieved [sic] unjustice. If that ends up with an FIR against a foreigner (even after having lived here for 20 years), that person could loose [sic] his/her visa, possibly forever. It is an issue of legal status.

santo
10 February 2011/03:22 pm

Dear Anton, you can see someone dying, drowning in a lake, and yet do nothing about it because of a sign saying 'Swimming not allowed'.

And your concern afterwards would probably be how will the authorities have him paying the fine for not respecting the law...

Me and you have different type of priorities, but that is normal, we Italians never really care about the law.... Look at our PM

Anyway, I do not want you to loose [sic] sleep over this one, do not worry I will not go to the police or whatever, but I will not accept either any decision which will make Ramesh pay for all sort of 'unsubstantiaited accusations' he has been the victim of, so that there is an excuse to tell him to vacate his place in Udumbu.

Take care enjoy wonderland,

santo

The community members did not agree with the arguments of the Working Council and posted their comments in the forum expressing their displeasure. The reports of the land issue that appeared in the *News and Notes*, a newsletter brought out by Auroville governing bodies, were reportedly filtered and did not address the concerns of those who opposed the governing body's decisions. However, the democratic deficit created by the newsletter was offset by the space and freedom given to the members in the virtual space. The Intranet with access privileges given exclusively to the members of Auroville encourages collective participation and sharing of views creating an anti-hierarchical networked platform for the users.

Gandhi believed in participatory democracy and advocated the decentralization of power to iron out differences and disparities. He said: 'Yours should not be a passive spirituality that spends itself in ideal meditation, but it should be an active thing which will carry war (*civil war such as protest*: *author's emphasis*) into the enemy's camp.' Decentralization of power gives subjects in a society the free will to exercise one's right to freedom of expression and dissent without being encumbered by domination of traditions, culture, societal norms and people. Decentralization of power when combined with altruistic perspectives can lead to production of discursive transnational identities that have a common agenda in an international community like Auroville.

Borrowing on the Civil Disobedience Movement led by Gandhi, the Electronic Civil Disobedience movement seeks to explain activism centred on the paradigms of discourse, dialogue, discussion, open access and grassroots protests sans vitriolic temper and spirit. The electronic disobedience movement is computerized activism that uses the Internet infrastructure as a means to communicate and express views freely across borders. The Internet, a site for communication and action, deterritorializes by bulldozing boundaries and facilitating networked interaction across multiple languages and cultures. In this chapter, Auroville sets up a striking contrast wherein the community is not an imagined space—physically and virtually—as it is a multicultural community housing people from many countries speaking different languages both face to face and in the electronic forum. Furthermore, the oxymoron of 'deterritorialization' is revealed in the study if one is to gauge the borderless communication taking place within defined spatial–temporal dimensions of Auroville with its members engaging in multicultural dialogue focusing on issues of common relevance in the Intranet. The protest over 'Udumbu' land issue and discussions on it produce the Habermassian Web that realizes the potential of the Internet as a tool for activism.

Drawing the cue from the Civil Disobedience Movement Gandhi led, the protest in the Auroville-run Intranet was characterized by civil dissent. The non-violent protests that Gandhi led were a method of fighting social and political injustice and dishonesty, and the forum's messages reflect the same spirit through computer-mediated communication. The messages bring out strong and trenchant criticisms, and the visibly perturbed and upset members of the community in their posts refer to the Working Council members saying 'they are not gods'.

Another respondent alluded to the Working Council condemning the complainant who reported the incident to the Auroville secretary. The steps taken by the Indian member living in 'Udumbu' to meet the secretary right away are questioned, and he has also been cautioned to abstain from going to the police as the community has always upheld the custom of dealing with issues within the territorial boundaries. The conflict does not align with the spirit of the Mother's ideologies.

The recent announcement by the AV Council regarding complaining to the AVF secretary or to any Govt. authority outside being against the spirit of Auroville rankled a little, because I see how issues, which are not getting the proper attention and response, fester in the minds of those who are at the receiving end, leaving them very few options for redressal or appeal.

Democratic Space and Non-violence in Auroville Intranet

In seeking to deconstruct Gandhian thought in constantly changing socio-economic and political conditions of Auroville, it can be found that his values, especially non-violence, can be used not only to achieve peace, as he states, but also to bring in transparency. His values, which he described in the context of British colonialism and the internal religious differences India witnessed, therefore, might change to suit the present practical context.

On the other hand, the Internet emerges as an alternative medium that allows the residents to participate in equal measure and resolve conflicts rather than allow a representative body to establish a hegemonic status. Aside from that, a new social organization is seen emerging in the virtual space of the Internet. Participation of Aurovilians in the virtual space is yet to grow into a phenomenon. Apart from the Internet, the members have now initiated a new venture in the virtual space to promote an organized site of democratic and dialogic practice. The launch of Auroleaks, a namesake of Wikileaks, was a celebrated announcement in Auroville media, and the discussion that occurred in the forum even before the site was launched reflects the members' need for having an open forum as an alternative to the Auronet. Initially, Auronet was considered to be an alternative space or media but later some of the members of Auroville realized that the moderators were unfair in filtering messages and therefore they decided to have in place Auroleaks that cannot be controlled by the governing bodies. They commented that moderations need to be relaxed while a few agreed with the degree of moderation exercised by the media and administrative team to display or not to display content. This explains the political power process and mode of governance in the Internet. Internet/Intranet opens up multipoint communication, short-circuits the filtering process (Wayne Rash Jr 1997). Seeing moderations as a big issue or standing in the way of free flow of information, Auroleaks has been initiated.

> We presume at times it might get flack [sic] from auronet editors and if it gets too hot we will transfer out of Auronet to the internet. here ▶ www.auroleaks.com

> Auroville working groups only listen to rumours and accept them as facts. Therefore it is imperative to start auroleaks so that when information is brought in it is truly checked out.

Gandhi propounded non-violence as a thesis to challenge and abolish imperialism in any form. He, on several occasions, reiterated non-violence as a necessary virtue of not only individuals but said that it could be used as a rule of conduct for the collective society. In this context, the rise of Auroleaks and the participation of the community members in expressing their views could be seen as an emerging social movement's political ideology to counter the unfair decisions of the Auroville authorities in handling the 'Udumbu' issue.

Auroleaks is welcomed as it does not reveal the source (who participates in the discussion) and rather the issue gets more salience and attention.

AV Net has avoided an anonymous section for a long time, and with the advent of auroleaks, it's a good time to reconsider. A lot of useful communication and discussion never takes place because things are not said, or if they're said, people react less to the ideas than to the source.

Post-modern condition in the 'Udumbu' issue reflects the confusion that arises from multiple views encouraged by a pluralistic society. A pluralistic and multicultural society at once, it is unacceptable to many members in Auroville to learn that the Working Council attempts to see truth in selective content and information. In other words, the Working Council rationalizes its decision based on filtered inputs and people see the decisions taken by them as biased.

Life in Auroville ... they are too many, the meanings are too many, views and opinions are too many, so communication is confounded. ...communication is so confoundedly confusing in a multi cultural society such as ours.

Gandhi rejects the domination of rationalism as the objective method to understand the world. Gandhi allowed his intuition and thoughts to evaluate truth in each incident he encountered and never applied a common framework to assess 'truth'. This assumes significance in a pluralistic community where knowledge cannot be said to originate from a central powerhouse as it is constructed by subjects, thereby making it a multi-perspectival concept. This again brings us back to the Udumbu issue and the participants in the forum wanting to acknowledge every individual's views negating the Working Council as a central source and decision-making authority.

Why are most meeting reports of our leading groups only published two months after they are discussed? Why when a decision is taken about a group or an individual, it is accepted as the final verdict.

Furthermore, a participant in the forum challenges the world of reason and rationalism discarding science and technology as givers of happiness. He also clarifies that Auroville was not established for its members to be led by technological progress that implies modernity and a self caught in a dilemma, absorbed in finding solutions for issues based on Cartesian divide or trying to place every argument in an epistemological framework. He affirms that Auroville has been constructed to experiment with the transcendental ethos of human life with spirituality as the base and contributing to community (communities such as villages in and around) development as its unstated responsibility—a mix of spirituality, controlled materialism and human development. A polarized view of rationalism and spiritual conscience comes through in the discussion when a comment made by a member is appreciated by an Auronet representative who sees the arguments reasonable as opposed to the other previous comments that she felt were filled with rage and opinions. Further to her comment, another member again took on her to convey that the decisions and the post by the Entry Service were biased besides agreeing to the fact that rational judgement and science and technology alone can provide happiness. Members even took objection to this totalized view predicating decisions on reason and science by emphasizing the human spiritual consciousness.

anu
12 February 2011/03:46 am

Dear Entry Group,

Surprised to see this note, already with condemnations.

I hope that after months of ignoring Ramesh's call for help and then slapping him down with a set of obviously biased rules, the Council and other groups will not think of asking him to leave Udumbu – that would be totally objectionable.

Ramesh could live there in harmony with another set of people as he did earlier and I hope you will consider it. This set of people has not worked together for some reason and is now toxic.

The other three who are new or relatively new, probably need to grow a little more in Auroville experience. They might benefit from change and of being in a new place, in the Greenbelt or elsewhere.

As the Entry Service you basically need take note of what happened in their newcomer's period.

Annemarie
12 February 2011/08:43 am

I 'like' this contribution by Anu not because I agree with the views she expressed (I still do not know enough about the situation at Udumbu to be able to judge), but because she brings forward reasonable arguments in a respectful way and sets a good example.

Auroprem
13 February 2011/04:45 pm

annemarie,

We also 'like' the contribution by Anu and your posting now. What we all didn't like about the Entry Service's posting was they had put forward false arguments not in respectful manner. And publishing something which is not theirs and setting a bad example for the future....

Below is a piece from Charlie's speech. I have just modified a little. Happy reading

We the people have the power to create happiness. We the people have the power to make life free and beautiful, to make this dream a wonderful adventure. Then in the name of Mother let's use that power – let us all unite. Let us fight for a better city, a decent city that will give men a chance to work, that will give you the future and old age and security. By the promise of these things, brutes have risen to power, but they lie. They do not fulfill their promise, they never will. Now let us fight to fulfill that promise. Let us fight to free the world, to do away with national barriers, do away with greed, with hate and intolerance. Let us fight for a world of reason, a world where science and progress will lead to all men's happiness.

Brothers & Sisters—in the name of Unity, let us all unite!

Wolfgang
14 February 2011/02:40 am

Do you really think Auroville is meant to 'fight for a world of reason, a world where science and progress will lead to all men's happiness'? This sounds like the past goal of the rational age. We are meant to go further, to go for the supramental consciousness.

It can also be inferred that the participants were unhappy and expressed their strong-felt need for building a tension-free Auroville which can be achieved through unfair, impartial and non-hegemonic discourses that the Mother quite adequately has expounded on. Citing a speech of another person, a member makes a fervent plea to unite and oppose forces that shirk their responsibilities by adopting reason that will help them establish justice. Thus, the Internet is seen as a potential and effective platform for the participants to share their views which did not get adequate representation through other means or in other media. The civil disobedience of Gandhi is what one witnesses in the electronic form where the members of Auroville express their concern for straightening the 'Udumbu' land issue that has been rankling the community for a while.

Discursive Frames of *Non-violence* in Auronet Discussion Forum

The discussion forums and the tonality of the postings convey the vehemence of some of the residents of Auroville—the views are polarized though—indicating their displeasure with the Working Council. Such an active resistance without involving ill will is what Gandhi, in his term, described as non-violence. It is a means of conflict resolution, political action and social movement to question injustice. In other words, non-violence can be used to bring in transparency as well as peace.

Although Auroville is deemed to be a community fostering goodwill and love for each other by helping the residents to attain a judicious balance between spirituality and materialism, the discussions demonstrate that the right to question unfair practices is in the domain of human conscience. In his Satyagraha, what is considered to be a truthful act to quell indiscretions, Gandhi advocates for a polite and a groundswell of protest to rise from within. Likewise, in an act of questioning the legitimacy of the Entry Service, which is in charge of recruiting new residents, a member categorically replies in the Auronet that the governing body does not have any role to interfere in the land issue. The discursive frame in which the messages are constructed evidences the potential of the Internet towards social movements at micro levels.

'The Internet has been about networking; not just networks of wires and hubs but networks of people. Protests, too, are always about networks.'[1] Network culture is not a freshly minted one

---

[1] Gurak, J. L., and J. Logie 2003. Internet Protests, from Text to Web. In *Cyberactivism: Online Activism in Theory and Practice*, edited by M. McCaughey and M. D. Ayers. New York: Routledge.

and has been a constituent of our social structure. With the advent of new media technologies, networks have become 'a key feature of social morphology'.[2]

Analysing the discourse of the messages in the Intranet reveals the deliberative communication the members engage in and their strong open opposition to the Entry Service who posted a message condemning the action of an individual involved in the Udumbu land issue. The democratic dissent was brought to the fore through the Intranet and the discussion generates a dialogic interaction with many of them who hardly have time to attend meetings, participating in it and expressing their opinions. The members of Auroville, the participants in the discussion, express their individual and collective interests through their networking practice technologically and politically.

Some of the frames in which the members opposed the decision of the Working Council and made snide remarks at the Entry Service include sarcastic criticism, offering suggestions and condemnation of their activities.

Dear community,

The Entry service, the Auroville Council and the Working Committee are currently drafting their decisions regarding the Udumbu situation. Interested parties will be called early next week to be communicated the final common decisions and related consequences.

Meanwhile, we wish to condemn the latests [sic] actions of an individual:

– to threaten to file a police complaint against another individual on unsubstantiated allegations, as well as his direct visit to the Secretary of the Auroville Foundation to complain against the same person.

---

[2] Castells, M. 1996. *The Rise of the Network Society.* Oxford. UK: Blackwell.

– to publish on Auronet allegations against the same person. This would be considered anywhere else in the world as defamation and could lead to legal action....

The Entry Service

Comments
<u>Auroprem</u>
10 February 2011/04:33 am

To the Entry Service,

Thank you for this update.

but i am just wondering if it was your duty to do this in your very very busy schedule. I think it is out of you mandate.

The dispute in udumbu should be dealt by the concerned working groups since it is in the Green Belt, then by the Council and finally by the the [sic] Residents Assembly, and your role would be to monitor the newcomer and give feedback and suggestions to the concerned working groups only when asked by them....

.

.

Coming back to Udumbu if this problem would have happend [sic] anywhere else I wonder what would have been the outcome?

thank you for understanding

<u>muni</u>
10 February 2011/08:24 am

Dear Aurovilians,

Reading the above note by the Entry Service it is crystal clear that even in this statement they are biased.

maybe its time that the entry group disband and Auroville ask the selection committee to start the process of looking for new members.

<u>bunty</u>
10 February 2011/09:29 am

Oh really? Entry Service...you condemn the actions of an individual whose claims are unsubstantiated? Especially when you read the comments of many individuals who have openly supported the very party you are condemning...it is ridiculous for you to come out with such a note. What have you done to find out the facts? If you have done nothing to find out, do not conclude on them as unsubstantiated. If one does not have a choice when all working groups cannot initiate action or are unable to do anything...what is the option left? Did you think of that or not?

How come you do not condemn the actions of the other party? Such biased views will only further erode the faith in working groups.

Please introspect your comments and try to judge the affect it will have on many in the community instead of condemning actions. If the allegations are unsubstantiated...how can you condemn an action.

Your posting stinks of bias. And please don't mislead the readers by calling it 'Udumbu update'. It is not an update.

<u>santo</u>
10 February 2011/09:26 am

Dear Entry service,

I myself was ready to find a way for the police to start an inquiry into how this problem in Udumbu has been tackled by the various AV working groups as I find the way Ramesh has been treated in violation of basic human rights of an individual who does not have any chance of a fair hearing other than going to the Secretary or the police.

.......By the way, are you sure that Patrick and co (or whoever on their behalf), have not visited the Secretary's office a few months ago BEFORE Ramesh did?...please check it out....

I doubt Patrick would sue Ramesh for what you consider defamatory statements as he knows very well that they are not so far from the truth as you would like people to believe, and an inquiry is more likely to damage him rather than Ramesh.

It is quite evident from the following comment posted by an Auronet representative who, after seeing the comments and seven members flagging a post (that of the Entry Service in the beginning), highlighted the rules of flagging a post to which erupts a slew of messages defending why the members flagged the post again undergirding the principle of disobedience or civil disobedience in a multicultural community through the Internet infrastructure. Despite the Auronet representative explaining that she did not find anything abusive in the content and hence it cannot be removed, the comments to this post evoked sniggering responses from the participants. A few gave diegetic replies instructing the Auronet to change the rules implicitly reproving the bias in the decision taken by the governing council and other bodies with regard to the Udumbu land issue.

Annemarie on behalf of Auronet
10 February 2011/04:04 pm

To the 7 people who flagged this posting, a few points for consideration.

1) *The option of flagging is provided in case any guideline as given in the Rules of the Game is violated. Now, there is no such objectionable content in this posting as far as we can see. We strongly discourage using the flagging option*

just to express strong disagreement with its content. This is a misuse.

2) *If anyone can show us where this posting does not respect the Rules of the Game, please assist us and put us in the picture. Also, if anyone finds a guideline missing in the established ones, and wishes to propose a new valid guideline, welcome. Failing this, we see no reason to remove this article.*

3) *Having said this, it is perfectly valid to question the content of the posting and come with sound arguments against it, in a respectful way. Calling for the dismissal of a group because one does not agree with its stance, is at this point counterproductive and justifies the reluctance of groups to publishing anything on Auronet.*

Annemarie & Manoj

<u>muni</u>
10 February 2011/04:22 pm

This is why i flagged this article.

RULES OF THE GAME see section bellow.

Please avoid publishing on Auronet:

1. *Any false, unsupported or deliberately partial information.*

muni
<u>Auroprem</u>
10 February 2011/04:26 pm

same here
<u>martanda</u>
10 February 2011/05:38 pm

I second that!
<u>Auroprem</u>
12 February 2011/05:08 am

Annemarie not 7 but 12 now more after.
Angad
11 February 2011/10:21 am

Flagged because I find the tone very offensive and completely unworthy of...the working group or the Entry Service. Besides, it isn't really their concern!

The economic model of Auroville suggests that funds are sourced from individuals as contributions, the Indian government, international agencies and NGOs. 'Auroville is no way poor', says Dr Albert, though it contrasts with a report and message posted in the Intranet and the newsletter—Auroville faces a budget deficit in 2010–2011.

Increase your Contribution—there is a budget deficit...the expected income of 10 per cent increase is not taking place and it is only 4 per cent.

One of the responses from the member of Auroville called for decreasing luxury and reducing the resources such as petrol, electricity and water. In addition, the participant said that selling of wood outside should be stopped and Aurovilians should use it as a natural source.

Another report describes the internal debate, a marker of democracy, in which a member from France received a payment from his country as compensation for the use of an Auroville housing asset. The estimated value of the asset was in fact half of that compensation. When he was asked to return the excess money to Auroville, he responded to it 'by starting a smear campaign to the extent of sending to a foreign embassy a letter full of false accusations and extremely serious defamation against the Housing Service and its coordinator who has been involved in trying to resolve this problem, as well as including disparaging remarks about Auroville'. The international agencies of Auroville questioned the Auroville here following the individual sending a detailed correspondence to many of our Auroville international centres.

Serving the Community/Environment: The Gandhian Model

Sustainable development seems to be one of the primary agendas of Auroville and the community is involved in a range of activities that are exclusively targeted at village women and kids. Though there are no specific programmes designed for men, they were recruited on a need basis in environment conservation and farming activities to name a few. The Village Action Group of Auroville offers training to women to make eco-friendly products. Auroville is also campaigning strongly against the use of pesticides for cashew crops. The members of the community are conducting training and camps to grow neem trees within the cashew field as well as prepare organic compost. However, only a very few subscribe to organic farming.

Therefore, knowledge is transmitted across community members and to people in the villages through research centres, educational institutions and other institutional bodies governing Auroville. Gandhi believed that rural development is the lynchpin of a country's overall development, and such an effort to contribute to the empowerment of women and villages by Auroville is a by-product of spirituality. As Gandhi rightly puts it, a spiritual being is one that discards material interests and crystallizes its energy on serving the human society. Auroville also uses natural resources such as solar energy for their basic needs.

Gandhiji was in favour of the development of cottage and small-scale industries, and he considered them to be a source of income for people in villages and wanted it to emerge as a political ideology. His ideology of development emphasizes energy production, empowering rural villages to grow self-reliant and produce indigenous products, all of which form part of the activities of Auroville. Men and women from nearby villages are involved in 23 small-scale units that produce bags, dress materials and a vast range of products.

According to Gandhi, economic power brings political power and democracy, and he particularly expressed it in the context of community or rural development. What is implicit in this argument is that Gandhi did not propose an individual trying to strengthen her/his economic resources. A contradiction, though, arises as a jarring note to learn that village women are trained to speak and communicate in English, which I admit is a necessity. However, one needs to explore if these women are literate in their native languages before they get a handholding on English. If not, a severe anomaly is setting in that deprives the local population of the traditional knowledge and an onslaught of cultural imperialism is taking place which Gandhi disapproved of.

However, the respondents expressed that in the last five years, the community has been experiencing new changes, some palatable and some not so palatable. The conflict needs to be understood in the context of how multiculturalism pans out in a community like Auroville and whether social cohesion gives way to fragmented identities. Are there fault lines that disturb the fabric of the community's lofty ideology?

First, Auroville that is 'a place of peace, concord, harmony' has its own conflicts to resolve if the Udumbu (Nature Camp and other issues) are anything to go by. If the use of conflicts is disparaging, one can say that Auroville is fraught with internal debates over land and financial issues. To consider that Auroville is an experiment and such debates will be part of a growing international community is an excuse to hide the spectre of disharmony that has begun to haunt the community.

Apart from the internal debates, one of the reasons that is presently occupying the domain of disharmony seems to reside in the land or space Auroville occupies; Aurovilians live in and Auroville wants to buy and sell. It is understood from the interview schedule that many Aurovilians from villages around Auroville continue to live in their own homes in the villages, which is considered to be counter-cultural to Auroville's ideology that demands members to leave behind assets and properties and live within the community.

That is, Auroville is rich, elitist and non-traditional compared to the villages it serves which are caught up in traditional social practices and financially poor. The discourse of the urban–rural continuum or a discourse revolving around Auroville and villages inheres in it a sense of divide. This divide further accentuates in the context of rich and elite Aurovilians within the community seeking to attain spirituality by serving the poor (spirituality can also be self-sustaining where an individual may seek to satiate his/her divine consciousness) and people from villages getting trained to make money and attracted to materialism. Another form of self-contradiction that disturbs some of the members is the opening of a new hospital exclusively for the members of Auroville called 'Kailash'. Dr Albert refuses to serve in the new hospital because it is against his professional ethics not to attend to a section of the community, especially those from the villages. He says it is very much unacceptable to the ethos of Auroville.

Rise in Crime Rate: Is Self in a Spot?

This is much closer to *ahimsa* postulated by Gandhi, but the recent reports of crimes and thefts as reported in the newsletter and as explained by the respondents point out that *ahimsa* is practically not possible due to the prevalence of social and economic disparities between the Auroville and the villages around.

As explained before, Auroville is a site of capitalist forces, and incidentally it houses mostly rich people who have come from far and wide. The spin-off is that such a set-up is bound to change the social and economic conditions and expectations of the members within the community and the villages nearby. It is a capitalist, pluralistic community that has gathered here to serve others and attain spirituality.

Tempering spirituality, self-discipline and serving the community under the growing materialistic demands in a multicultural setting is a challenge the community is embroiled in. Most of them, especially those who came long back and settled down in Auroville, do not manifest materialistic desires like the newcomers who are rich and own cars and motorbikes. The use of cars and motorbikes has increased, and the recent news in the newsletter point to the rise in the purchase of vehicles and guidance offered to the members not to buy vehicles registered with PY (Pondicherry) and news tips on what to look for when foreigners buy vehicles/cars from local residents.

The self apparently goes through the turmoil of 'ontological security' and gets lured by liquid modernity (liquid cash in hands) and the community's essentialism right now is to make money and enjoy the comforts of life. Dr Albert, one of the respondents, confesses: 'Everyone in the community wants to make money and build a big house or buy a car. I also need to make money. Yes, money is important.' A few had to leave the community as they found that the economic compensation given by the community was not sufficient for survival.

Gandhi argues that social cause should be placed above individual desires. Auroville, in that sense, today is staged in a polemical plane with some members, especially those who have been living here for close to 20 years and more, devoting life to development and social concerns while some of them are happy being the members of Auroville making little contributions to Auroville in their own way.

What are the changes that accompany such a multitude of forces? As a by-product of these changes, crimes in the fringes of Auroville, such as murders and thefts in addition to protest within, have increased. The crimes reported cannot be seen in isolation, but they need to be viewed by drawing on the perspectives of culture and economy. In this context, Gandhi's maxim of 'Simple living and high thinking' may not be practically followed in other parts of the society but given the philosophical pedigree of Auroville, life needs to be simple and thoughts lofty to attain spiritual conscience.

Clash of Cultural Models

A report in the *News and Notes* informing the community members to drive their vehicles slowly and another report telling the Tamil audience (members of Auroville) to adopt a socially acceptable dressing style indicate cultural imperialism and the hegemonic takeover within the multicultural setting. The news highlights the difference between foreign and Indian culture and the Tamil Aurovilians were advised to wear proper outfits when they go to government offices. This was in response to the complaint received by the Working Council from Tindivanam RTO office in Tamil Nadu.

Another cultural vacuum that needs immediate attention would be to have the student community from Auroville to reach out the villages. Students mostly are cut off from activities, and they do not participate in organic farming or other activities Auroville has designed. This leaves a gap in the social practices of the elders and the youth. The youth are more interested in attending functions, events and participating in workshops organized to enhance their intellectual skills. However, there is no transfer of knowledge from them, and this is another paradox that asks whether the younger generation will use Auroville as an urbanized colony for material and empirical achievements. Further, there is not much interaction taking place between the Auroville students and the village students who study in different Auroville schools meant for them, stated a respondent as well as a guest who visited the community. This dilutes Gandhi's philosophy of involving everyone in the community work. It also raises serious questions of when the students of Auroville would be shaped up to become 'servitors' as stated in the Chapter of the community.

Further, the freedom to be what they want to be has thrown up convoluted practices, one of which reportedly was drugging and partying. Gandhi, while stressing on the spiritual development, emphasized self-discipline as a component of restraint, fearlessness and self-sacrifice. He further eulogizes that voluntary self-discipline is a fusion of freedom and internal control. Although Auroville has banned New Year bash for fear of anonymous members entering and creating problems, Dr Albert says that one cannot keep an eye on every individual to know what he/she is doing. Auroville is synonymous with freedom as the inhabitants can choose to perform any activity that contributes to humanity. But freedom in Auroville is a no-holds-barred phenomenon, and when freedom is not interlaced with internal control, it only causes trouble to others than helping the society. In the absence of internal control, one cannot control cultural degradation and moral decadence that are essentially spin-offs of multiplying desires effectuated by modernization. In fact, at one point of time, students of Ashram school were not allowed to visit Auroville, according to an old Ashram student, as they feared they could get influenced by the drugs and other foreign cultures. Gobi says: 'It's said that hippies were the first to come to Auroville as they could hang out in a calm environment.'

The Future of Auroville

Rapid urbanization with outstanding infrastructure will soon surround Auroville that includes extension of the airport to the outer boundaries of the community, four-lane highway abutting it, proposed (not on paper) ECR railway track connecting Pondicherry and Chennai, port and IT industries. If villagers are turning to Auroville because they are benefitting from it by way of acquiring knowledge, it would not be a surprise if the same villagers get attracted to the employment demands of the industrialization. In this context, the economy may shift to different geographical locations, and villages around Auroville might be influenced by 'the fantasy of wanting to move' that may become irresistible. One has to wait and watch how Auroville will tackle such a looming danger to the fabric of multiculturalism and Gandhi's *Swaraj*. What activities will the Aurovilians engage themselves in if men and women are required to move to work in a new landscape? If a migration to other geographical location ever happens, Aurovilians will end up looking after themselves with no social cause attached. This might create a spiritual vacuum. What gives pleasure to many is the social service. But when opportunities decline, will they continue to stay here or leave as the present youth from Auroville go out to explore the world after their school education?

***

The efforts of Auroville to function as a multicultural entity in realizing the goals of the Mother are no less intense, and the various institutions contributing to health, education and village development are in consonance with what Gandhi encapsulated in his ideology of rural development. A democratic space will have conflicts and resolving them through participation and enfranchising every member of the community to express views is what Gandhi solely believed in. The political power of a community emerges from the freedom enjoyed by the members of a community in sharing their views and participating in a deliberative communication. A few members express the absence of democratic currency and the Internet emerges as a popular space for the people to express and rise against the Working Council and question its decisions. On the other hand, it cannot be completely dismissed that cultural imperialism is not taking place, which at times can prove to be destructive such as drugs. According to some of the respondents, a community from a certain part of Europe trying to have an upper hand is not completely ruled out. In the same vein, elite settlements remain inaccessible to most of the Aurovilians, which again creates a power structure. In all, it is caught in two streams of being able to engage in sustainable projects, knowledge production and transformation versus internal debates and unrest within the community and outside. The other paradox Auroville creates within itself is the social distance between the Auroville students of transnational origin/identities and the villages. On the contrary, parents are interacting with villagers and training them on acquiring various skills. In other words, the construction of local identities of students in a cultural place of belonging excludes local communities.

About the Editor and Contributors

Editor

Biswajit Das is Professor and Founding Director of the Centre for Culture, Media and Governance, Jamia Millia Islamia, New Delhi. He has over three decades of teaching and research experiences in the field of theory, method and history of communication in India. Professor Das has been a Visiting Professor at York University; Fellow at the University of Windsor, Canada; Fellow at MSH, Paris; INALCO, Paris; Charles Wallace Trust, London; and the Indian Institute of Advanced Studies, Shimla, India.

Contributors

Alok Bajpai is an independent research scholar who has been doing research for over two decades. His specialized areas are Mahatma Gandhi and Indian National Movement. He was awarded PhD in History under the title 'A Holistic View of Mahatma Gandhi's Politics in Theoretical Realms'. He is a prominent member of Bipan Chandra School in Modern Indian History. Some of the themes of his research papers include Satyagraha, Gandhian Non-violence, Gandhi and Untouchability, Nehru as Gandhi's Political heir, Gandhi and Congress, and Colonial Science and Technology. He has been a Fellow at Nehru Memorial Museum & Library, Teen Murti House, New Delhi, in 2009–2019. His research papers and articles have been published in various journals, newspapers, magazines and in edited books. He was awarded Professor P. S. Gupta Memorial Prize and J. C. Jha Prize in Indian History Congress 2011.

Arunabha Ghosh is a retired officer of the High Court of Kolkata. An occasional writer and translator, he has published in *The Telegraph*, *Economic and Political Weekly* and *Sahitya Akademi* journal. He has contributed to and co-edited *Culture, Society and Development in India* (2009), and edited *Withered Leaves*, a fiction by Jayanta Ray (2011).

M. Shuaib Mohamed Haneef is an assistant professor at the Department of Electronic Media and Mass Communication, School of Media and Communication, Pondicherry University.

Sadan Jha is an Associate Professor at Centre for Social Studies, Surat. With a formal training in history, he has two broad research interests: history of visuality and contemporary urban experiences. He has worked on history of symbols (Indian National Flag, Spinning Wheel and Bharat Mata) and history of colours with an interdisciplinary approach. His second research interest focuses upon the urban transformation of Surat in the last six decades. His publications include *Reverence, Resistance and the Politics of Seeing the Indian National Flag* (2016), *Devnagari Jagat ki Drishya Sanskriti* (Hindi, 2018), *Half Set Chaay Aur Kuchh Youn He* (creative writing in Hindi, 2018) and a number of academic as well as non-academic articles in *Indian Economic and Social History Review*, *Economic and Political Weekly*, *History and Sociology of South Asia* (SAGE), *Indian Express*, *Manushi*, *The Conversation* and *Huffington Post*.

Prafulla C. Kar, currently the Director of Forum on Contemporary Theory, was formerly the Head of the Department of English, The Maharaja Sayajirao University of Baroda. He received his PhD from the University of Utah, USA, in 1973. A former Deputy Director and Academic Associate at the American Studies Research Center, Hyderabad, he was the recipient of both pre-doctoral and postdoctoral Fulbright Fellowships to study in the United States. He was also a Fellow of the School of Criticism and Theory, Dartmouth College, in 1986. Professor Kar is the

Editor of the *Journal of Contemporary Thought* and has published several books and papers on American literature, literary theory, Indian English literature and cultural studies.

Keval J. Kumar is Adjunct Professor at MICA, Ahmedabad, and Visiting Faculty at IIM Indore, and FLAME University, Pune. He is a former Director, Symbiosis Institute of Mass Communication, and a former Reader and Head, Department of Communication and Journalism, University of Pune. He has also taught in Ohio State University, Siegen University, Jacobs University Bremen and Bahrain Training Institute. He is the Founder Director of the Centre for Media Education and Research, Pune. He was Chair of the Media Education Research Section, International Association for Media and Communication Research, from 1998 to 2006, and since 2003 has been an Associate Member of ORBICOM, the Association of UNESCO Chairs in Communication. He was Chief Adviser to NCERT's Committee on Media Studies. Dr Kumar is the author of *Mass Communication in India, Media Education, Communication and Public Policy* and co-author of *Environmentalism and the Mass Media: The North–South Divide.* He has contributed 'entries' to three international encyclopaedias and chapters to over a dozen edited books. He has participated in four international research projects and published/presented around 50 research papers. His research interests include critical communication theory, journalism studies, media literacy, religious communication, political communication and new media studies.

Dev Nath Pathak teaches sociology and anthropology at South Asian University, New Delhi, India. Some of his recent publications include *Living and Dying: Meanings in Maithili Folklore* (2019); *Sociology and Social Anthropology in South Asia: Histories and Practices* (2018); *Culture and Politics in South Asia: Performative Communication* (2017); *Another South Asia!* (2017) and *Intersections of Art, Sociology and Art History* (2016). He is a Reviews Editor with the journal *Society and Culture in South Asia* and editorial member with *Journal* *of Human Values*. He was a Charles Wallace Fellow at Queen's University, Belfast, UK, in 2015, and a scholar in residence at the Indian Institute of Management Calcutta in 2019.

Gopalan Ravindran has been working as a Professor and Head, Department of Journalism and Communication, University of Madras, since 2008. His previous positions include Visiting Fellow, Graduate School of International Development, Nagoya University, Japan; Lecturer, School of Communication, Universiti Sains Malaysia, Penang; and Reader and Head, Department of Communication, Manonmaniam Sundaranar University, Tirunelveli, India. His teaching/research areas include critical theories and philosophies, political economy of journalism and communication, spatiality and materiality of communication, film cultures, digital cultures and diasporic cultures.

Partha Ray is currently Professor of economics at the Indian Institute of Management Calcutta. From 2007 to 2011, he was Adviser to Executive Director (India) at the International Monetary Fund, Washington, DC.

Ratnakar Tripathy did an MA (1980) and PhD in Philosophy (1987) specializing in the Philosophy of social sciences. He spent a number of years in the print and television media working on research-based stories and projects. He has done a series of academic research projects around the themes of Hindi cinema, Bhojpuri cinema and Music industry, internal and transnational migration funded by a number of Indian and international agencies. He has written a number of academic papers as outcomes of these projects. He has already done work on Bihar, parts of Eastern Uttar Pradesh, and Haryana. Between 2016 and 2018, he was a Fellow at the Indian Institute of Advanced Study, Shimla, where he studied the regional cultures and languages of Himachal Pradesh. Many of these projects are a part of his larger plan to investigate and map the growth of the regional languages in the Hindi-speaking parts of India, wherein he traces and maps their ever-increasing presence in recent times in the digital media and the Internet. He has been attached to the Asian Development Research Institute as a Senior Research Fellow since 2007 and is based in Patna, Bihar.

Shashi Bhushan Upadhyay is Professor with the Faculty of History in Indira Gandhi National Open University. His research interests are mainly in the fields of historiography, labour history, Dalit studies and literary studies. His publications include books titled *Historiography in the Modern World* (2016), *Existence, Identity and Mobilization: The Cotton Millworkers of Bombay, 1890–1919* (2004), two co-edited volumes, *Dalit Assertion in Society, Literature and History* (2010) and *School Education, Pluralism and Marginality* (2012), and about 20 articles on labour, Dalits and Premchand.

Index